D0011957

A Concise Public Speaking Handbook

Second Edition

Steven A. Beebe
Texas State University–San Marcos

Susan J. Beebe
Texas State University–San Marcos

Boston   New York   San Francisco
Mexico City   Montreal   Toronto   London   Madrid   Munich   Paris
Hong Kong   Singapore   Tokyo   Cape Town   Sydney

Editor in Chief: Karon Bowers
Series Editorial Assistant: Jessica Cabana
Marketing Manager: Suzan Czajkowski
Production Editor: Patrick Cash-Peterson
Editorial Production Service: Lifland et al., Bookmakers
Composition Buyer: Linda Cox
Manufacturing Buyer: JoAnne Sweeney
Electronic Composition: Modern Graphics
Interior Design: Joyce Weston; Modern Graphics
Cover Administrator: Joel Gendron

For related titles and support materials, visit our online catalog at www.ablongman.com.

Between the time website information is gathered and then published, it is not unusual for some sites to have closed. Also, the transcription of URLs can result in typographical errors. The publisher would appreciate notification where these errors occur so that they may be corrected in subsequent editions.

Library of Congress Cataloging-in-Publication Data

Beebe, Steven A., 1950–
  A concise public speaking handbook / Steven A. Beebe, Susan J. Beebe.
    p. cm.
  Includes bibliographical references and index.
  ISBN-13: 978-0-205-50244-8
  1. Public speaking—Handbooks, manuals, etc. I. Beebe, Susan J. II. Title.
  PN4129.15.B42 2009
  808.5′1—dc22

                                                    2007048779

Printed in the United States of America
10 9 8 7 6 5 4 3 2   Q-L   11 10 09 08

Contents

Preface

This second edition of *A Concise Public Speaking Handbook* integrates the steps in preparing and delivering a speech with the ongoing process of considering the audience. Although developed and delivered by the speaker, a good speech is centered on the needs, values, and hopes of the audience. Therefore, the audience should be kept in mind during every step of the speech crafting and delivery process. Being audience-centered means that, as a speaker, you are constantly aware of and striving to adapt to the cultural, gender, and experiential diversity of the people to whom you are speaking. Adapting to diverse audiences is incorporated into every step of the audience-centered approach.

A Concise Public Speaking Handbook, Second Edition, also emphasizes that an effective speaker is an ethical speaker. Ethical speakers articulate truthful messages, formulated so as to give the audience free choice in responding to the message, while also using effective means of ensuring message clarity and credibility.

Every chapter contains "Quick Checks," lists of items that can be checked off as each step in the process of preparing a speech is completed. Each also contains a feature called "A Question of Ethics," which focuses on the need for ethical conduct while preparing and delivering a speech. The role of technology in enhancing a speaker's message is also covered.

New to the Second Edition

- New examples and sample speech outlines throughout the text ensure that the examples are contemporary and useful for students.

■ More emphasis on rhetorical analysis helps students better analyze their own speeches and the speeches of others (Chapter 5).

■ A new section on understanding your listening style encourages students to become better audience members (Chapter 5).

■ An expanded discussion of how to analyze an audience provides students with additional information on this critical step in the process (Chapter 6).

■ New tips and strategies are included to help students achieve their speaking goals by editing out the superfluous and the unnecessary (Chapter 14).

■ A breakdown of nonverbal communication and verbal communication into two separate chapters increases the emphasis on these core topics (Chapters 17 and 18).

■ A new section on how to respond to questions offers students key information about a common element in many "public" speeches (Chapter 18).

■ Theoretical information about listening style (Chapter 5), emotions (Chapter 19), and persuasion theory, including the use of fear appeals (Chapter 25), provides students with additional background on these important topics.

■ A section on the elaboration likelihood model of persuasion has been added (Chapter 25).

■ An expanded discussion of using humor wisely helps students connect with listeners (Chapter 27).

Strategies to Improve Speaker Confidence

A big obstacle to success is the anxiety people experience when they think about speaking in front of an audience. An entire chapter is devoted to improving speaker confidence, to help readers manage this fear. Techniques for managing speaker apprehension, such as how to look for positive listener support when delivering a message, are also included.

Critical Listening Skills

Besides learning how to speak in public, one of the most valued benefits of studying public speaking is becoming a more discriminating listener. A section on listening, critical thinking, and analyzing and evaluating speeches helps students better understand their roles as speakers and listeners.

Instructors' Supplements

To support the teaching of public speaking and supplement instructors' skill and experience, we offer an abundance of resources.

Print Materials

Instructor's Manual and Test Bank. This detailed Instructor's Manual and Test Bank contains learning objectives for each chapter, chapter outlines, discussion questions, and skills development activities to illustrate the concepts, principles, and skills of human communication. In addition, the Test Bank portion of the manual contains numerous multiple-choice, true/false, fill-in-the-blank, and essay questions.

Great Ideas for Teaching Speech (GIFTS), 3/e by Raymond Zeuschner. This instructional booklet provides descriptions of and guidelines for assignments successfully used by experienced public speaking instructors in their classrooms.

New Teachers Guide to Public Speaking, 3/e by Calvin Troup, Duquesne University. This guide helps new teachers teach the public speaking course effectively. It covers such topics as preparing for the term, planning and structuring your course, evaluating speeches, utilizing the textbook, integrating technology into the classroom, and much more.

Public Speaking Transparency Package, Version II. One hundred full-color transparencies created with PowerPoint™ software provide visual support for classroom lectures and discussions.

Electronic Materials

TestGen EQ: Computerized Test Bank. The user-friendly interface enables instructors to view, edit, and add questions; transfer questions into tests; and print tests in a variety of fonts. Search and sort features allow instructors to locate questions quickly and arrange them in preferred order. It is available through our Instructor's Resource Center at www.ablongman.com/irc.

Communication Digital Media Archive, Version 3.0. The Digital Media Archive CD-ROM contains electronic images of charts, graphs, maps, tables, and figures, along with media elements such as video, audio clips, and related Web links. These media assets are fully customizable to use with our pre-formatted PowerPoint™ outlines or to import into the instructor's own lectures. The CD-ROM is available in Windows and Mac formats.

Lecture Questions for Clickers by William Keith, University of Wisconsin–Milwaukee. An assortment of questions and activities covering a multitude of topics in public speaking and speech delivery are presented in PowerPoint. These slides will help liven up your lectures and can be used along with the Personal Response System to get students more involved in the material.

MySpeechKit (www.myspeechkit.com). MySpeechKit is an interactive and instructive online solution for introductory public speaking. Designed to be used as a supplement to a traditional lecture course, MySpeechKit includes book-specific learning objectives, chapter summaries, flashcards, and practice tests, as well as Web links, an outlining wizard, media clips, and interactive activities to aid student learning and comprehension. Also included in MySpeechKit is Research Navigator, a valuable tool to help students conduct online research (see more information under "Print Materials" in Student Supplements). An access code is required. Visit www.myspeechkit.com or contact your Allyn & Bacon representative for additional information.

VideoWorkshop for Public Speaking Version 2.0
by Tasha Van Horn of Citrus College and Marilyn Reineck of Concordia University, St. Paul. VideoWorkshop for Public Speaking is more than just video footage you can watch. It's a total learning system. Our complete program includes quality video footage on an easy-to-use dual platform CD-ROM, plus a Student Learning Guide with textbook-specific Correlation Grids. The result? A program that brings textbook concepts to life with ease, helping your students understand, analyze, and apply the objectives of the course. VideoWorkshop is available for your students as a value-pack option with this textbook.

Allyn & Bacon PowerPoint Presentation Package for Public Speaking. Available at www.ablongman.com/ppt, this package includes 125 slides and a brief User's Guide.

Video Materials

A&B Contemporary Classic Speeches DVD.
This exciting supplement includes over 120 minutes of video footage in an easy-to-use DVD format. Each speech is accompanied by a biographical and historical summary that helps students understand the context and motivation behind the speech. Speakers featured include Martin Luther King Jr., John F. Kennedy, Richard Nixon, the Dalai Lama, and Christopher Reeve.

A&B Public Speaking Video Library. Allyn & Bacon's Public Speaking Video Library contains a range of videos from which adopters can choose. The videos feature different types of speeches delivered on a multitude of topics. Please contact your Allyn & Bacon representative for details and a complete list of videos and their contents, to choose which would be most useful in your class. Each video has its own ISBN and must be ordered separately.

Students' Supplements

To support student learning, we provide a selection of study and enrichment materials.

Print Materials

Study Cards for Public Speaking. Colorful, affordable, and packed with useful information, Allyn & Bacon's Study Cards make studying easier, more efficient, and more enjoyable. Course information is distilled down to the basics, helping students quickly master the fundamentals, review a subject for understanding, or prepare for an exam. Because they're laminated for durability, students can keep these Study Cards for years to come and pull them out whenever they need a quick review.

Preparing Visual Aids for Presentations, 4/e by Dan Cavanaugh. This brief booklet provides a host of ideas for using today's multimedia tools to improve presentations, including suggestions for how to plan a presentation, guidelines for designing visual aids and storyboarding, and a walkthrough that shows how to prepare a visual display using PowerPoint.

Multicultural Activities Workbook by Marlene C. Cohen and Susan L. Richardson, both of Prince George's Community College, Maryland. This workbook is filled with hands-on activities that help broaden the content of speech classes to reflect the diverse cultural backgrounds of the class and society. The book includes checklists, surveys, and writing assignments that all help students succeed in speech communication by offering experiences that address a variety of learning styles.

Public Speaking in the Multicultural Environment, 2/e by Devorah Lieberman of Portland State University. This two-chapter essay focuses on speaking and listening to a culturally diverse audience and emphasizes preparation, delivery, and how speeches are perceived.

The Speech Preparation Workbook by Suzanne Osborn of the University of Memphis. This workbook contains forms to help students prepare a self-introductory speech, analyze the audience, select a topic, conduct research, organize supporting materials, and outline the speech.

Speech Preparation Workbook by Jennifer Dreyer and Gregory H. Patton of San Diego State University. This workbook takes students through the stages of speech creation—from audience analysis to writing the speech—and includes guidelines, tips, and easy-to-fill-in pages.

The Speech Outline: Outlining to Plan, Organize, and Deliver a Speech: Activities and Exercises by Reeze L. Hanson and Sharon Condon of Haskell Indian Nations University. This brief workbook includes activities, exercises, and answers to help students develop and master the critical skill of outlining.

ResearchNavigator.com Guide: Speech Communication by Steven L. Epstein of Suffolk County Community College. This guide includes tips, resources, and URLs to aid students conducting research on Pearson Education's research Web site, www.researchnavigator.com. The guide contains a student access code for the Research Navigator database, offering students unlimited access to a collection of more than 25,000 discipline-specific articles from top-tier academic publications and peer-reviewed journals, as well as the *New York Times* and popular news publications. The guide introduces students to the basics of the Internet and the World Wide Web and includes tips for searching for articles on the site, plus a list of journals useful for research in their discipline. Also included are hundreds of Web resources for the discipline, as well as information on how to correctly cite research. The guide is available packaged with new copies of the text.

Electronic Materials

MySpeechKit (www.myspeechkit.com).
MySpeechKit is an interactive and instructive
online solution for introductory public speaking. Designed to be used as a supplement to a
traditional lecture course, MySpeechKit includes
book-specific learning objectives, chapter summaries, flashcards, and practice tests, as well
as Web links, an outlining wizard, media
clips, and interactive activities to aid student
learning and comprehension. Also included in
MySpeechKit is Research Navigator, a valuable
tool to help students conduct online research
(see more information under "Print Materials").
An access code is required. Visit
www.myspeechkit.com or contact your Allyn &
Bacon representative for additional information.

Public Speaking Web Site (www.ablongman
.com/pubspeak). This open access Web site contains six modules students can use along with
their public speaking text to learn about the
process of public speaking and help them prepare for speeches. The Web site focuses on the
five steps of speech preparation: assess your
speechmaking situation, analyze your audience,
research your topic, organize and write your
speech, deliver your presentation, and discern
other talks. Interactive activities aid in speech
preparation. "Notes from the Instructor" provide additional details on selected topics.

Public Speaking Study Site (http://www
.abpublicspeaking.com). This course-specific
Web site features public speaking study materials for students, including flashcards and a
complete set of practice tests for all major topics. Students also will find Web links to sites
with speeches in text, audio, and video formats,
as well as links to other valuable sites.

**News Resources for Speech Communication
Access Code Card.** Highlighted by an hourly
feed of the latest news in the discipline from the
New York Times, News Resources for Speech
Communication with Research Navigator pro-

vides one-stop access to the latest news events, allowing students to stay on the forefront of currency throughout the semester. In addition, using Pearson's Research Navigator™ is the easiest way for students to start a research assignment or research paper. Complete with extensive help on the research process and four exclusive databases of credible and reliable source material, including the EBSCO Academic Journal and Abstract Database, New York Times Search by Subject Archive, and Financial Times Article Archive and Company Financials, Research Navigator helps students quickly and efficiently make the most of their research time.

Speech Writer's Workshop CD-ROM, Version 2.0. This speechwriting software includes a Speech Handbook, with tips for researching and preparing speeches; a Speech Workshop, which guides students step by step through the speech writing process; a Topics Dictionary, which gives students hundreds of ideas for speeches; and the Documentor citation database, which helps them to format bibliographic entries in either MLA or APA style.

VideoLab CD-ROM. This interactive study tool for students can be used independently or in class. It provides digital video of student speeches, which can be viewed in conjunction with corresponding outlines, manuscripts, note cards, and instructor critiques. A series of drills to help students analyze content and delivery follows each speech.

VideoWorkshop for Public Speaking Version 2.0 by Tasha Van Horn of Citrus College and Marilyn Reineck of Concordia University, St. Paul. VideoWorkshop for Public Speaking is more than just video footage you can watch. It's a total learning system. Our complete program includes quality video footage on an easy-to-use dual platform CD-ROM, plus a Student Learning Guide with textbook-specific Correlation Grids. The result? A program that brings textbook concepts to life with ease, which helps

students understand, analyze, and apply the objectives of the course. VideoWorkshop is available for students as a value-pack option with
this textbook.

Part 1

Introduction

Chapter 1

Speaking in Public

As you study public speaking, you will learn and practice strategies for effective delivery and critical listening. You will discover new applications for skills you may already have, such as focusing and organizing ideas and gathering information from print and electronic sources. In addition to learning and applying these fundamental skills, you will gain long-term advantages related to *empowerment* and *employment*.

The ability to speak with competence and confidence will provide **empowerment**. It will give you an edge that other, less skilled communicators lack—even those who may have superior ideas, training, or experience.

Perhaps an even more compelling reason to study public speaking is that the skills you develop may someday help you get a job. In a nationwide survey, prospective employers of college graduates said they seek candidates with "public speaking and presentation ability."[1] Surveys of personnel managers, both in the United States and internationally, have confirmed that they consider communication skills the top factor in helping graduating college students obtain employment.[2] (See Table 1.1.)

Public Speaking and Conversation

Public speaking has much in common with conversation. Like conversation, public speaking requires you to focus and verbalize your thoughts. When you have a conversation, you have to make decisions "on your feet." If your friends look puzzled or interrupt with questions, you re-explain the idea you have been talking about. If they look bored, you insert a funny story or talk more animatedly. As

Table 1.1 ■ Top Factors Employers Seek in Job Candidates

Rank/Order	Factors/Skills Evaluated
1	Oral (spoken) communication
2	Written communication skills
3	Listening ability
4	Enthusiasm
5	Technical competence
6	Work experience
7	Appearance
8	Poise
9	Résumé
10	Part-time or summer employment

Source: Jerry L. Winsor, Dan B. Curtis, and Ronald D. Stephens, "National Preferences in Business and Communication Education: A Survey Update," *Journal of the Association for Communication Administration* 3 (September 1997): 174.

a public speaker, you will learn to make similar adaptations based on your knowledge of who your listeners are, their expectations for your speech, and their reactions to what you are saying.

Public Speaking Is Planned

Public speaking is more planned than conversation. A public speaker may spend hours or even days planning and practicing his or her speech.

Public Speaking Is Formal

Public speaking is also more formal than conversation. The slang or casual language you often use in conversation is not appropriate for most public speaking. Audiences expect speakers to use standard English grammar and vocabulary.

The nonverbal communication of public speakers is also more formal than nonverbal behavior in ordinary conversation. People engaged in conversation often sit or stand close together, gesture spontaneously, and move about restlessly. The physical distance between public speakers and their audiences is usually greater than that between people in conversation. And although public speakers may certainly use extemporaneous gestures while speaking, they also plan and rehearse some gestures and

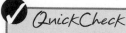

QuickCheck
Become an Effective Public Speaker

■ Plan your speech.
■ Focus and vocalize your thoughts.
■ Adapt your speaking to your listeners.
■ Use standard English vocabulary and grammar.
■ Use more formal nonverbal communication.

movements to emphasize especially important parts of their speeches.

The Roles of Speakers and Audiences Are Clearly Defined

Public speaking is less fluid and interactive than conversation. People in conversation may alternately talk and listen, and perhaps even interrupt one another; but in public speaking the roles of speaker and audience are more clearly defined and remain stable. Rarely do audience members interrupt or even talk to speakers.

The Communication Process

Even the earliest communication theorists recognized that communication is a process. The models they formulated were linear, suggesting a simple transfer of meaning from a sender to a receiver.

Communication as Action

■ A public speaker is a **source** of information and ideas for an audience.
■ The job of the source or speaker is to **encode**, or translate, the ideas and images in his or her mind into verbal or nonverbal symbols (a **code**) that an audience can recognize. The speaker may encode into words (for example, "The fabric should be two inches square") or into gestures (showing the size with his or her hands).
■ The **message** in public speaking is the speech itself—both what is said and how it is said.

- If a speaker has trouble finding words to convey his or her ideas or sends contradictory nonverbal symbols, listeners may not be able to **decode** the speaker's verbal and nonverbal symbols back into a message.

- A message is usually transmitted from sender to receiver via two **channels:** *visual* and *auditory.* Audience members see the speaker and decode his or her nonverbal symbols—eye contact (or lack of it), facial expressions, posture, gestures, and dress. If the speaker uses any visual aids, such as graphs or models, these too are transmitted along the visual channel. The auditory channel opens as the speaker speaks. Then the audience members hear words and such vocal cues as inflection, rate, and voice quality.

- The **receiver** of the message is the individual audience member whose decoding of the message will depend on his or her own particular blend of past experiences, attitudes, beliefs, and values. An effective public speaker should be receiver- or audience-centered.

- Anything that interferes with the communication of a message is called noise. **External noise** is physical, such as the roar of a lawn mower or a noisy air-conditioner. **Internal noise** may stem from either physiological or psychological causes and may directly affect either the source or the receiver. A bad cold (physiological noise) may cloud a speaker's memory or subdue his or her delivery. An audience member who is worried about an upcoming exam (psychological noise) is unlikely to remember much of what the speaker says. Noise interferes with the transmission of a message.

Communication as Interaction

One way in which public speaking differs from casual conversation is that the public speaker does most or all of the talking. But public speaking is still interactive. Without an audience to hear and provide **feedback,** public speaking serves little purpose. Skillful public speakers are audience-centered. They depend on the nods, facial expressions, and murmurings of the audience to adjust their rate of speaking, volume, vocabulary, type and amount of supporting material, and other variables to communicate their message successfully.

The **context** of a public-speaking experience is the environment or situation in which the speech occurs. It includes such elements as the time, the place, and the speaker's and audience's cultural traditions and expectations.

The person whose job it is to deliver an identical message to a number of different audiences at different times and in different places can attest to the uniqueness of each speaking context. If the room is hot, crowded, or poorly lit, these conditions affect both speaker and audience. The audience that hears a speaker at 10 a.m. is likely to be fresher and more receptive than a 4:30 p.m. audience. A speaker who fought rush-hour traffic for 90 minutes to arrive at his or her destination may find it difficult to muster much enthusiasm for delivering the speech.

We send and receive messages concurrently, adapting to the context and interpreting the verbal and nonverbal feedback of others as we speak. (See Figure 1.1 for an interactive model of communication.)

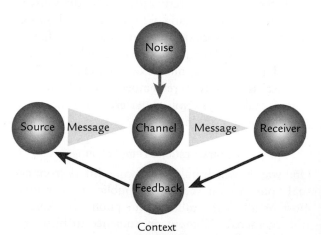

Context

Figure 1.1 ■ An interactive model of communication.

The Rich Heritage of Public Speaking

Long before many people could read, they listened to public speakers:

Fourth century B.C.	Golden age for rhetoric in the Greek Republic, where the philosopher Aristotle formulated guidelines for speakers that we still follow today.
Nineteenth century	Students of public speaking practiced the arts of **declamation**—the delivery of an already famous address—and of **elocution**—the expression of emotion through posture, movement, gestures, facial expression, and voice.
Twenty-first century	A new era of speechmaking that draws on age-old public-speaking traditions and expands the parameters of public speaking, summoning public speakers to meet some of the most difficult challenges in history.

Public Speaking and Diversity

During the last half of the twentieth century, attention focused on the rhetorical implications of diversity. People are just beginning to understand that such factors as the gender, ethnicity, and culture of both the speaker and the audience are crucial components of the context of a speaking event.

Different audiences have different expectations for appropriate and effective speech topics, argument structure, language style, and delivery. To be effective, public speakers need to understand, affirm, and adapt to diverse audiences. This focus on and consideration of an audience can guide a speaker effectively through each stage of speech preparation and delivery.

A Question of Ethics

Declamation is defined as "the delivery of an already famous address." Is it ethical to deliver a speech that was written and/or already delivered by someone else? Explain your answer.

Chapter 2

The Audience-Centered Speechmaking Process

In this chapter, we preview the preparation and presentation skills that you will learn in this course.

An Audience-Centered Speechmaking Model

Talking to people has seemed such a natural part of your life that you may never have stopped to analyze the process. But as you think about preparing your first speech, you may wonder, "What do I do first?" You need some idea of how to begin.

Figure 2.1 diagrams the various tasks involved in the speechmaking process, emphasizing the audience as the central concern at every step of the process.

Consider Your Audience

The needs, attitudes, beliefs, values, and other characteristics of your audience influence the topic you choose and every later step of the speechmaking process. Your selection of topic, purpose, and even major ideas should be based on a thorough understanding of your listeners.

After you select your topic, consider how the audience will respond to your examples, organization, and delivery. If you learn new information about your audience at any point during the process, you may need to revise your thinking or your material.

Being audience-centered involves making decisions about the content and style of your speech *before* you speak, based on knowledge of your audience's values and beliefs. It also means being sensitive to your audience's responses *during* the speech so that you can make appropriate adjustments.

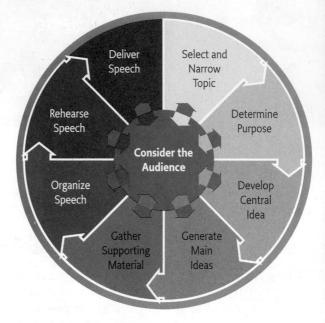

Figure 2.1 ■ This model of the speechmaking process emphasizes the importance of considering your audience as you work on each task in the process of designing and presenting a speech.

Different cultures have radically different conventions for public speaking. It is important to adapt your speech to the cultural expectations of different audiences:

- Adjust your topic and pattern of organization.
- Adjust your delivery style.
- Adjust your dress.

If you learn to analyze your audience and adapt to their expectations, you can apply these skills in numerous settings.

Select and Narrow Your Topic

While keeping your audience foremost in mind, determine what you will talk about and how to limit your topic to fit the constraints of your speaking assignment.

It is not uncommon to be asked to speak on a specific subject. Often, though, the task of selecting and narrowing a topic will be yours. You may discover a topic by asking three standard questions:

1. Who is the audience?
2. What is the occasion?
3. What are my interests, talents, and experiences?

Once you choose your topic, narrow it to fit the time limits for your talk.

Determine Your Purpose

Decide on both a general and a specific purpose before you start the research process. There are three **general purposes** for giving speeches:

1. **To inform.** The primary objective of class lectures, seminars, and workshops is to inform. When you inform, you teach, define, illustrate, clarify, or elaborate on a topic.
2. **To persuade.** Ads on TV and radio, sermons, political speeches, and sales presentations are examples of speeches designed to persuade. When you persuade, you seek to change or reinforce attitudes, beliefs, values, or behavior.
3. **To entertain.** After-dinner speeches and comic monologues are intended mainly for entertainment. The key to an effective, entertaining speech lies in your choice of stories, examples, and illustrations, as well as in your delivery.

After you are sure you understand your general purpose, formulate a **specific purpose**: a concise statement indicating what you want your listeners to be able to do when you finish your speech. *A statement of your specific purpose identifies the audience response you desire.*

- It is important to focus on the audience as you develop your specific purpose.
- Phrase your purpose in terms of what you would like the audience to be able to do by the end of the speech.
- Your specific purpose should be a fine-tuned, audience-centered goal.
- Once you formulate your specific purpose, write it down and keep it before you as you read and gather ideas for your talk.
- Your specific purpose should guide your research and help you choose supporting materials that are related to your audience.

■ As you continue to work on your speech, you may even decide to modify your purpose.

Develop Your Central Idea

You should now be able to write the **central idea** of your speech. Your central idea identifies the essence of your message. Think of it as a one-sentence summary of your speech. Here is an example:

Topic:	Kachina dolls
General Purpose:	To inform
Specific Purpose:	At the end of my speech, the audience will be able to describe the significance of kachina dolls to the Hopi Indians.
Central Idea:	Kachina dolls, carved wooden figures used in Hopi Indian ceremonies, are believed to represent spirits of the dead that will help produce a good harvest.

Generate the Main Ideas

Effective speakers are good thinkers; they say something. They know how to play with words and thoughts to develop their **main ideas**. The ancient Romans called this skill **invention**—the ability to develop or discover ideas that result in new insights or new approaches to old problems.

Once you have an appropriate topic, a specific purpose, and a well-worded central idea, identify the major divisions of your speech, or key points that you wish to develop. To determine how to subdivide your central idea into key points, ask these three questions:

1. Does the central idea have logical divisions? Looking for logical divisions in your speech topic is the simplest way to determine key points.
2. Are there several reasons why the central idea is true? If your central idea is a statement that

something is good or bad, you should focus on the reasons your central idea is true. Use these reasons as the main ideas of the speech.

3. Can the central idea be supported with a series of steps? Your time limit, topic, and information gleaned from your research will determine how many major ideas will be in your speech. A 3- to 5-minute speech might have only two major ideas. In a very short speech, you may develop only one major idea with examples, illustrations, and other forms of support. Don't spend time trying to divide a topic that does not need dividing.

Gather Verbal and Visual Supporting Material

With your main ideas in mind, gather material to support them—facts, examples, definitions, and quotations from others that illustrate, amplify, clarify, and provide evidence. It is important to be an audience-centered speaker. Don't just give people data; connect facts to their lives. Here are some criteria for choosing verbal supporting material:

■ Tell stories based on your own experiences and provide vivid descriptions of things that are tangible so that your audience can visualize what you are talking about.

■ Besides sight, supporting material can appeal to touch, hearing, smell, and taste. The more senses you trigger with words, the more interesting your talk will be.

■ Relating abstract statistics to something tangible can help communicate your ideas more clearly.

You can find interesting and relevant supporting material by developing good research skills. Although it is important to have good ideas, it is equally important to know how to build on existing knowledge. In order to speak intelligently about a topic to an audience, you will probably need to do some research.

■ Learn to use the library's computerized card catalog, the *Social Sciences Index*, the *Directory of American Scholars, Bartlett's Familiar Quotations*, government document holdings, your library's periodical indexes, and an assortment of CD-ROM indexes.

■ Learn to use electronic databases such as LEXIS-NEXIS and directories and search engines such as Excite, Google, and Yahoo!. Learn to use browsers such as Netscape and Internet Explorer to navigate the Web. There are also any number of Web sites that will help you both design and deliver your speeches.

■ Be on the lookout as you read, watch TV, and listen to the radio for ideas, examples, illustrations, and quotations that you could use in a speech.

■ Learn how to gather information through interviews and written requests for information on various topics.

■ Seek visual supporting material. For many people, seeing is believing. You can enhance almost any presentation by reinforcing key ideas with visual aids. Often the most effective visual aids are the simplest: an object, a chart, a graph, a poster, a model, a map, or a person—perhaps you—to demonstrate a process or skill.

Organize Your Speech

A clearly and logically structured speech helps your audience remember what you say. A logical structure also helps you feel more in control of your speech, and greater control helps you feel more comfortable while delivering your message.

You need to present ideas, information, examples, illustrations, stories, and statistics in an orderly sequence so that listeners can easily follow what you are saying.

Divide Your Speech

Every well-prepared speech has three major divisions:

1. The introduction helps capture attention, serves as an overview of the speech, and provides the audience with reasons to listen to you.

2. The body presents the main content of your speech.
3. The conclusion summarizes your key ideas.

You may have heard this advice on how to organize a speech: "Tell them what you're going to tell them (the introduction), tell them (the body of the speech), and tell them what you told them (the conclusion)."

Because your introduction previews your speech and your conclusion summarizes it, prepare your introduction and conclusion after you have carefully organized the body of your talk.

Outline Your Speech

If you have already generated your major ideas on the basis of logical divisions, reasons, or steps, you are well on your way to developing an outline.

Indicate your major ideas by Roman numerals. Use capital letters for your supporting points. Use Arabic numerals if you need to subdivide your ideas further. Do not write your speech word for word. If you do, you will sound stilted and unnatural. It may be useful, however, to use brief notes—written cues on note cards—instead of a complete manuscript.

Consider Presentation Aids

In addition to developing a written outline to use as you speak, consider using presentation aids to add structure and clarity to your major ideas. Simple visual reinforcers of your key ideas can help your audience retain essential points. Once you are comfortable with the structure of your talk and you have developed your visual aids, you are ready to rehearse.

Rehearse Your Speech

A speech is a performance. As with any stage performance, you need to rehearse. The best way to practice is to rehearse your speech aloud, standing just as you will when you deliver it to your audience. As you rehearse, try to find a comfortable way to phrase your ideas, but don't try to memorize your talk. In fact, if you have rehearsed your speech so many times that you are using exactly the same words every time, you have rehearsed long enough. Rehearse just enough so that you can discuss your ideas and supporting material without leaving out major parts of your speech. It is all right to use notes, but limit the number of notes you use.

Here are a few points to remember as you rehearse:

- Practice making eye contact with your imaginary audience as often as you can.
- Be aware of the volume of your voice; you will need to practice speaking loudly enough for all in the room to hear.
- If you are not sure what to do with your hands when you rehearse, just keep them at your side. Focus on your message, rather than worrying about how to gesture.
- Avoid jingling change with your hand in your pocket or using other gestures that could distract your audience.
- If you practice your speech as if you were actually delivering it, you will be a more effective speaker when you talk to the audience.

The words you choose and your arrangement of those words make up the style of your speech. Some audiences respond to a style that is simple and informal. Others prefer a grand and highly poetic style. To be a good speaker, you must become familiar with the language your listeners are used to hearing and must know how to select the right word or phrase to communicate an idea. Work to develop an ear for how words will sound to your audience.

Deliver Your Speech

Delivery is the final step in the preparation process. Before you walk to the front of the room, look at your listeners to see whether the audience assembled is what you were expecting. Are the people out there of the age, race, and gender that you had predicted? Or do you need to make last-minute changes in your message to adjust to a different mix of audience members?

- When you are introduced, walk calmly and confidently to the front of the room.
- Establish eye contact with your audience.
- Smile naturally.
- Deliver your attention-catching opening sentence.
- Concentrate on your message and your audience.
- Deliver your speech in a conversational style.
- Try to establish rapport with your listeners.
- Deliver your speech just as you rehearsed it before your imaginary audience:
  - Maintain eye contact.
  - Speak loudly enough to be heard.
  - Use some natural variation in pitch.
- Remember the advice of columnist Ann Landers: "Be sincere, be brief, and be seated."

Quick Check
Prepare for a Speech

- Consider your audience before and during your speech.
- Consider the type of occasion, and decide what you will talk about.
- Choose a topic based on your interests, talents, or experiences, and limit your topic to fit the constraints of your speaking assignment.
- Determine your general purpose (to inform, to persuade, to entertain).
- Determine the specific audience response you desire.
- Develop your central idea; then generate the main ideas.
- Gather verbal and visual supporting material.
- Organize, rehearse, and deliver your speech.

A Question of Ethics

One of your friends took public speaking last year and still has a file of speech outlines. Since you will give the speech yourself, is it ethical to use one of your friend's outlines as the basis for your speech? Explain your answer.

Chapter 3

Ethics and Free Speech

Ethics

Ethics are the beliefs, values, and moral principles by which people determine what is right or wrong. Ethics serve as criteria for many of the decisions we make in our personal and professional lives and also for our judgments of others' behavior. The student who refuses to cheat on a test, the employee who will not call in sick to gain an extra day of vacation, and the property owner who does not claim more storm damage than actually occurred have all made choices based on ethics.

Free Speech

Although you are probably familiar with ethical issues, you may have given less thought to those that arise in public speaking. These issues center around one main concern: In a country in which **free speech** is protected by law, the right to speak freely must be balanced by the responsibility to speak ethically. In 1999, the National Communication Association developed a Credo for Communication Ethics, which emphasizes the fundamental nature and far-reaching impact of ethical communication:

> Ethical communication is fundamental to responsible thinking, decision making, and the development of relationships and communities within and across contexts, cultures, channels, and media. Moreover, ethical communication enhances human worth and dignity by fostering truthfulness, fairness, responsibility, personal integrity, and respect for self and others.[1]

Aristotle used the term *ethos* to refer to a speaker's credibility. He thought that to be credible, a public speaker should be ethical, possess good character, have common sense, and be concerned for the well-being of the audience.

Ethical considerations should guide every step of the public-speaking process. As you determine the goal of your speech, outline your arguments, and select your evidence, think about the beliefs, values, and morals of your audience, as well as your own. Ethical public speaking is inherently audience-centered, always taking into account the needs and rights of the listeners.

Any discussion of ethical public speaking is complicated by the fact that ethics are not hard-and-fast objective rules. Each person's ethical decisions reflect his or her individual values and religious beliefs, as well as cultural norms.

Speaking Freely

1791   **First Amendment** to the U.S. Constitution guaranteed that "Congress shall make no law abridging the freedom of speech." Since then, many have sought to define, through both law and public policy, the phrase "freedom of speech."

1919   U.S. Supreme Court ruled that it was lawful to restrict speech that presented "a clear and present danger" to the nation. This led to the founding of the American Civil Liberties Union, the first organization formed to protect free speech.

1940   Congress declared it illegal to urge the violent overthrow of the federal government. However, for most of the last half of the twentieth century, the U.S. Supreme Court continued to protect rather than limit free speech, upholding it as "the core aspect of democracy."[2]

1964   Supreme Court narrowed the definition of slander and ruled that before a public official can recover damages for slander, he or she must prove that the slanderous statement was made with "actual malice."[3]

1989   Supreme Court defended the burning of the U.S. flag as a **"speech act"** protected by the First Amendment.

1997   Supreme Court struck down the federal Communications Decency Act of 1996 and ruled that "the interest in encouraging freedom of expression in a democratic society outweighs any theoretical but unproven benefit of censorship."[4]

In the aftermath of the terrorist attacks on September 11, 2001, free speech faces new challenges as the United States engages in what has been called "a new, more difficult debate over the balance among national security, free speech, and patriotism."[5]

Speaking Ethically

As the boundaries of free speech expand, the importance of **ethical speech** increases. There is no definitive ethical creed for a public speaker, but many agree that an ethical speaker is one who has a clear, responsible goal; uses sound evidence and reasoning; is sensitive to and tolerant of differences; is honest; and avoids plagiarism.

Have a Clear, Responsible Goal

The goal of a public speech should be clear to the audience. If you keep your true agenda hidden, you violate your listeners' rights. In addition, an ethical goal should be socially responsible. A socially responsible goal is one that gives the listener choices, whereas an irresponsible, unethical goal is psychologically coercive.

If your overall objective is to inform or persuade, it is probably ethical; if your goal is to coerce or corrupt, it is unethical.

Use Sound Evidence and Reasoning

Ethical speakers use critical-thinking skills such as analysis and evaluation to draw conclusions and formulate arguments. Unethical speakers manipulate emotion and substitute false claims for evidence and logical arguments. It is sometimes tempting to resort to false claims to gain power over others, but it is always unethical to do so.

One important requirement for the ethical use of evidence and reasoning is to share with an audience all information that might help them reach a sound decision, including information that may be potentially damaging to your case. Even if you proceed to refute the opposing evidence and arguments, you have fulfilled your ethical responsibility by presenting the perspective of the other side.

Be Sensitive to and Tolerant of Differences

Being audience-centered requires that you become as aware as possible of others' feelings, needs, interests, and backgrounds. Sometimes called **accommodation**, sensitivity to differences does not mean that you must abandon your own convictions. It does mean that you should demonstrate a willingness to listen to opposing viewpoints and learn about different beliefs and values. Such willingness not only communicates respect; it can also help you to select a topic, formulate a purpose, and design strategies to motivate an audience.

A speaker who is sensitive to differences also avoids language that might be interpreted as biased or offensive. Although it may seem fairly simple and a matter of common sense to avoid overtly abusive language, it is not easy to avoid language that discriminates more subtly.

Be Honest

Knowingly offering false or misleading information to an audience is an ethical violation. A seeming exception to the dictum to avoid false information is the use of hypothetical illustrations—illustrations that never actually occurred but that might happen. Many speakers rely on such illustrations to clarify or enhance their speeches. As long as you make clear to the audience that the illustration is indeed hypothetical—for example, prefacing the illustration with a phrase such as "Imagine that"—such use is ethical.

Avoid Plagiarism

Honesty also requires that you give credit for ideas and information that are not your own. Presenting the words and ideas of others without crediting them is called **plagiarism**.

Even those who would never think of stealing money or shoplifting may be tempted to plagiarize—to steal ideas. Perhaps you can remember copying a grade-school report directly from the encyclopedia, or maybe you've even purchased or "borrowed" a paper to submit for an assignment. These are obvious forms of plagiarism. A less obvious form is **patchwork plagiarism**—lacing a speech with compelling phrases you find in a source that you do not credit. Whether your lapse is intentional or due merely to careless or hasty note taking, it is a serious offense.

Do Your Own Work   The most flagrant cases of plagiarism result from not doing your own work. You will be doing yourself a disservice if you do not learn how to compose a speech on your own.

Another way speakers sometimes attempt to shortcut the speech preparation task is to ask another person to edit a speech so extensively that it becomes more the other person's work than their own. This is another form of plagiarism.

Acknowledge Your Sources   An ethical speaker is responsible for doing his or her own research and then sharing the results of that research with audience members. Some information is so widely known that you do not have to acknowledge a source for it. For example, you need not credit a source if you say that a person must be infected with the HIV virus in order to develop AIDS. This information is widely available in a variety of reference sources. However, if you decide to use any of the following in your speech, then you must give credit to the source:

- direct quotations, even if they are only brief phrases
- opinions, assertions, or ideas of others, even if you paraphrase them rather than quote them verbatim
- statistics
- any non-original visual materials, including graphs, tables, and pictures

Take Careful Notes   To be able to acknowledge your sources, you must first practice careful and systematic note taking. Indicate with quotation marks any phrases or sentences that you photocopy or copy by hand verbatim from a source, and be sure to record the author, title, publisher or Web site, publication date, and page numbers for all sources from which you take quotations, ideas, statistics, or visual materials.

Cite Sources Correctly   In addition to keeping careful records of your sources, you must also know how to cite your sources for your audience, both orally and in writing.

An **oral citation** can be integrated smoothly into a speech. For example, you might say, "In a March 2001 online fact sheet entitled 'Facts about Mold,' the New York City Department of Health describes *Stachybotrys chartarum* as"—then pause briefly to signal that you are about to begin quoting—" 'a greenish-black mold that can grow on materials with a high cellulose content—such as drywall sheetrock, dropped ceiling tiles, and wood—that become chronically moist or water-damaged.' "[6] This example provides the author, the title, the year, and the fact that the information is available online, which is sufficient for oral documentation of an online source.

You can also provide a **written citation** for a source. You can use a style guide such as those published by the MLA (Modern Language Association) or the APA (American Psychological Association), both of which are now available online as well as in traditional print format.

What about those times when you are not certain whether information or ideas are common knowledge? A good rule is this: When in doubt, document. You will never be guilty of plagiarism if you document something you didn't need to, but you could be committing plagiarism if you do not document something you really should have.

QuickCheck

Deliver an Ethical Speech

- Have a clear, responsible goal.
- Provide your listeners with choices, and use sound evidence and reasoning.
- Share all evidence that will help your audience reach a sound decision.
- Be sensitive to and tolerant of differences, and avoid language that is biased or offensive.
- Be honest and do your own work.
- Avoid plagiarism, and give credit for any ideas and information that are not your own.
- Acknowledge your sources accurately and completely.

A Question of Ethics

It has been openly acknowledged that George Bush's speech to Congress and the nation on Thursday, September 20, 2001, "was a collaboration by administration wordsmiths." Is the use of such "ghostwriters" unethical? Why or why not?

Chapter 4

Improving Your Confidence

Many people are nervous about giving a speech. As one anonymous sage observed, "The mind is a wonderful thing. It starts working the minute you're born and never stops until you get up to speak in public." It's normal to be nervous.

Understand Your Nervousness

Public speaking ranks as the most anxiety-producing experience most people face. It is unrealistic to try to eliminate speech anxiety. Your goal is to manage your nervousness so that it does not create so much internal noise that it keeps you from speaking effectively.

The reasons people feel nervous when they speak in public include

- fear of humiliation
- concern about not being prepared
- worry about how they look
- pressure to perform
- personal insecurity
- concern that the audience won't be interested in them or the speech
- inexperience
- fear of making mistakes
- overall fear of failure

Realize that your audience cannot see evidence of everything you feel. If you worry that you are going to appear nervous to others, you may, in fact, increase your anxiety. Your body will exhibit more physical changes to deal with your self-induced state of anxiety:

- extra adrenaline
- increased blood flow
- pupil dilation
- increased endorphins to block pain
- increased heart rate

Physical changes caused by anxiety improve your energy level and help you function better than you might otherwise. Your heightened state of readiness can actually help you speak better, especially if you view the public-speaking event positively instead of negatively.

Speakers who label their feelings of physiological arousal as "nervousness" are more likely to feel anxious and fearful, but the same physiological feelings are experienced as enthusiasm or excitement by speakers who don't label the increased arousal as fear, anxiety, or nervousness. You are more likely to gain the benefits of the extra help your brain is trying to give you if you think positively rather than negatively about speaking in public. Don't let your initial anxiety convince you that you cannot speak effectively.

Build Your Confidence

There are several things you can do to help manage your nervousness and anxiety.

Don't Procrastinate in Preparing Your Speech

Fear of speaking often leads speakers to delay preparing their speeches until the last minute. The lack of thorough preparation often results in a poorer speech performance, which reinforces a speaker's perception that public speaking is difficult.

Know Your Audience

Know to whom you will be speaking, and learn as much about your audience as you can. The more you can anticipate the kind of reaction your listeners will have to your speech, the more comfortable you will be in delivering your message. Make an effort to be audience-centered rather than speaker-centered. Focus on connecting to listeners rather than on your fear.

Select an Appropriate Topic

You will feel less nervous if you talk about something with which you are familiar or have had some personal experience. Your comfort with the subject of your speech will be reflected in your delivery.

Be Prepared

Being prepared means that you have

■ researched your topic
■ developed a logically coherent outline
■ practiced your speech several times before you deliver it

Develop and Deliver a Well-Organized Speech

Most speeches should have a beginning, a middle, and an end and should follow a logical outline pattern. Anxiety about a speech assignment decreases and confidence increases when you closely follow the directions and rules for developing a speech.

Know Your Introduction and Conclusion

You are likely to feel the most anxious during the opening moments of your speech. Therefore, have a clear plan for how you will start your speech. Being familiar with your introduction will help you feel more comfortable about the entire speech.

If you know how you will end your speech, you will have a safe harbor in case you lose your place. If you need to end your speech prematurely, a well-delivered conclusion can permit you to make a graceful exit.

Re-Create the Speech Environment When You Practice

When you practice your speech, stand up. Imagine what the room looks like and the audience you will actually address. Consider rehearsing in the room in which you will deliver your speech. Practice aloud, rather than just saying the speech to yourself.

Use Deep-Breathing Techniques

Nervous speakers tend to take short, shallow breaths. To help break the anxiety-induced breathing pattern, take a few slow deep breaths before you rise to speak. No one will be able to detect that you are taking deep breaths if you just slowly inhale and exhale. Besides breathing deeply, try to relax your entire body.

Channel Your Nervous Energy

As you are waiting to be introduced, focus on remaining calm. Give yourself a pep talk; tense and release your muscles to help you relax. Then, when your name is called, walk to the front of the room in a calm and collected manner. Before you present your opening, attention-catching sentence, take a moment to look for a friendly supportive face. Think calm and act calm to feel calm.

Visualize Your Success

Imagine yourself giving your speech. Picture yourself walking confidently to the front and delivering your well-prepared opening remarks. Visualize yourself giving the entire speech as a controlled, confident speaker. Imagine yourself calm and in command.

Give Yourself a Mental Pep Talk

When you feel yourself getting nervous, use positive messages to replace negative thoughts that may creep into your consciousness. Examples include the following:

Negative Thought	Positive Self-Talk
I'm going to forget what I'm supposed to say.	I've practiced this speech many times. I've got notes to prompt me. If I lose my place, no one will know I'm not following my outline.

So many people
are looking at me.

I can do this! My listeners
want me to do a good
job. I'll seek out friendly
faces when I feel nervous.

Focus on Your Message Rather Than Your Fear

The more you think about being anxious about
speaking, the more you will increase your level of
anxiety. Instead, think about what you are going to
say. In the few minutes before you address your listeners, mentally review your major ideas, your introduction, and your conclusion. Focus on your
ideas rather than on your fear.

Look for Positive Listener Support

When you are aware of positive audience support,
you will feel more confident and less nervous.
Although there may be some audiences that won't
respond positively to you or your message,
the overwhelming majority of listeners will be positive. Looking for positive, reinforcing feedback and
finding it can help you feel more confident as a
speaker.

Seek Speaking Opportunities

The more experience you gain as a public speaker,
the less nervous you will feel. Consider joining organizations and clubs that provide opportunities for
you to participate in public presentations. Consider
joining a local chapter of Toastmasters, an organization dedicated to improving public-speaking
skills by providing a supportive group of people to
help you polish your speaking and overcome your
anxiety.

After Your Speech, Focus on Your Accomplishment, Not Your Anxiety

When you finish your speech, tell yourself something positive to celebrate your accomplishment.
Say to yourself, "I did it! I spoke and people

QuickCheck
Build Your Confidence

- Prepare your speech early.
- Know your audience and select an appropriate topic.
- Be prepared and well organized. Know your introduction and conclusion.
- Re-create the speech environment when you practice.
- Use deep-breathing techniques.
- Channel your nervous energy.
- Visualize your success.
- Give yourself a mental pep talk.
- Focus on your message, not on your fear.
- Look for positive listener support.
- Seek additional speaking opportunities.
- After your speech, focus on your accomplishment, not your anxiety.

listened." Don't replay your mental image of yourself as nervous and fearful. Instead, mentally replay your success in communicating with your listeners.

A Question of Ethics

As a listener, you are ethically responsible for what you accept from others. What can you do to be less distracted by the delivery and emotional elements of a speaker's message and be more focused on the substance or content of the message? Explain your answer.

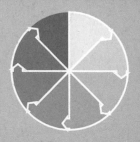

Part 2

Analyzing an Audience

Chapter 5

Listening

You hear more than one billion words each year. Yet how much information do you retain? Improving your listening skills will make you not only a better listener but also a better speaker. In addition, improving your listening skills will strengthen your ability to think critically and evaluate what you hear.

Barriers to Effective Listening

Listening barriers are created when you fail to select, attend to, or understand a message or remember what was said.

- To **select** a sound is to single out a message from several competing messages. A listener has many competing messages to sort through. Your job as a speaker is to motivate listeners to select *your* message.
- To **attend** to a sound is to focus on it. One of your key challenges as a speaker is to capture and hold the attention of your listeners. Your choice of supporting material is often the key.
- To **understand** is to assign meaning to the stimuli that come your way. As a speaker, it is your job to facilitate listener understanding by making sure you clearly explain your ideas in terms and images to which your listeners can relate.
- To **remember** is to recall ideas and information. The main way to determine whether audience members have been listening is to determine what they remember.

Information Overload

As a public speaker, you can keep your audience from tuning out by

- delivering a message that is clear and easy to understand
- using interesting and vivid supporting material to keep your listeners listening
- building redundancy into your message so that if listeners miss an idea the first time you present it, perhaps they will catch it during your concluding remarks

Personal Concerns

As a speaker, focus on maintaining your audience's attention and use occasional "wake-up" messages such as "Now listen carefully, because. . . ." As a listener, recognize when your own agenda keeps you from listening, then force yourself to focus on the speaker's message.

Outside Distractions

When you are the speaker, try to control the physical arrangements of the speaking situation before you begin your speech and try to empathize with your listeners.

- Check out the room ahead of time, sit where your audience will be seated, and look for possible distractions.
- Do the best you can to reduce or eliminate distractions.

As a listener, do your best to control the listening situation.

- Move to another seat.
- Close the blinds.
- Turn up the heat.
- Turn off the lights.
- Close the door.
- Do whatever is necessary to minimize distractions.

Prejudice

To counteract **prejudice**, use your opening statements to grab the audience's attention. Focus on your listeners' interests, needs, hopes, and wishes. Use arguments and evidence that your listeners will find credible. If you think audience members are likely to disagree with you, use careful language, sound reasoning, and convincing evidence. As a listener, guard against becoming so critical of a message that you don't listen to it or so impressed that you decide too quickly that the speaker is trustworthy.

Differences between Speech Rate and Thought Rate

Most people talk at a rate of 125 words a minute but are able to listen to up to 700 words a minute. The difference gives you time to ignore a speaker periodically. Eventually, you stop listening. Listen more effectively by mentally summarizing what the speaker is saying from time to time.

As a speaker, be aware of your listeners' tendency to stop paying attention. Build in message redundancy, be well organized, and make your major ideas clear.

Receiver Apprehension

Receiver apprehension is fear of misunderstanding, misinterpreting, or not being able to adjust psychologically to messages spoken by others.[1] If this describes you, use a tape recorder, summarize mentally what you hear a speaker saying, or take accurate notes.

As a speaker, be more redundant. Offer clear preview statements that give an overview of your main ideas. Include appropriate internal summaries. Summarize major ideas at the end of your talk. To help increase comprehension and decrease receiver

QuickCheck
Minimize Distractions

- Decide what is important in a speech and focus on that.
- Force yourself to focus on the speaker's message.
- Try to minimize outside distractions.
- Don't prejudge a message or speaker.
- Use the time lag created by the difference between speech rate and thought rate to summarize what the speaker is saying.
- Minimize receiver apprehension by recording a speech, summarizing the speech mentally, or taking notes.

apprehension, use presentation aids to summarize key ideas.

Become a Better Listener

Good listeners focus on a speaker's message, not on his or her delivery style. To be a good listener, you must adapt to the particular idiosyncrasies some speakers have. Poor speakers are not the only challenge to good listening. You also need to guard against glib, well-polished speakers.

Listen with Your Eyes as Well as Your Ears

Don't ignore a speaker's body language. Nonverbal clues play a major role in communicating a message. Emotion is communicated primarily by unspoken messages.

If you have trouble understanding a speaker, get close enough so that you can see the speaker's mouth. A good view can increase your level of attention and improve your understanding.

Monitor Your Emotional Reaction to a Message

Heightened emotions can affect your ability to understand a message. If you become angry at a word or phrase a speaker uses, your listening comprehension decreases. Don't let a speaker's language close down your mind.

Avoid Jumping to Conclusions

Give a speaker time to develop and support his or her main point before you decide whether you agree or disagree or whether the message has any value. If you mentally criticize a speaker's style or message, your listening efficiency will decline.

Be a Selfish Listener

If you find your attention waning, ask yourself questions such as "What's in this for me?" Find ways to benefit from the information you are listening to, and try to connect it with your own experiences and needs.

Listen for Major Ideas

Listen for major ideas and principles. Facts are useful only when you can connect them to a principle or concept. In speeches, facts as well as examples are used primarily to support major ideas. Try to mentally summarize the major idea that the specific facts support.

Identify Your Listening Goal

There are at least four major listening goals. Being conscious of your listening goal can help you listen more effectively.

- **Listen for pleasure.** When listening for pleasure, just enjoy what you hear. You can, however, observe how effective speakers gain and maintain your attention and keep you interested in their messages.
- **Listen to empathize.** Listening to empathize requires these essential steps:
  - **Stop.** Stop what you are doing and give your complete attention to the speaker.
  - **Look.** Make eye contact and pay attention to nonverbal cues that reveal emotions.
  - **Listen.** Pay attention to both the details of the message and the major ideas.
  - **Imagine.** Visualize how you would feel if you had experienced what the speaker experienced.
  - **Check.** Check your understanding by asking questions to clarify what you heard and by summarizing what you think you heard.
- **Listen to evaluate.** When you evaluate a message, you make a judgment about its content. You are interested in whether the information is reliable, true, and useful. The challenge is to not become so critical of the message that you miss a key point the speaker is making.
- **Listen for information.** Listen for the details of a message, and make certain you link the details to major ideas. Concentrate on both facts and major ideas, and mentally summarize the information you hear to increase your ability to remember messages. Also, compare unfamiliar information to ideas and concepts with which you are familiar.

As a speaker, know your audience's objectives. Audience-centered speakers consider the listening goals of their audiences.

Practice Listening

Listening skills do not develop automatically. Skill develops as you practice listening to speeches, music, and programs with demanding content.

Understand Your Listening Style

There are at least four different listening styles. Understanding your listening style can help you become a better and more flexible listener.[2]

- **People-oriented listeners** are comfortable listening to others express feelings and emotions.
- **Action-oriented listeners** listen for actions that need to be taken. Action-oriented listeners tend to be skeptical and prefer being given evidence to support recommendations for action.
- **Content-oriented listeners** prefer to listen to complex information laced with facts and details. They reject messages that don't have adequate support.
- **Time-oriented listeners** like messages to be delivered succinctly. Time is important to them, so they want the speaker to get to the point. They don't like long-winded messages with lots of fillers.

Become an Active Listener

An active listener is one who remains alert and mentally re-sorts, rephrases, and repeats key information when listening to a speech. To be a more active speaker:

- Re-sort disorganized or disjointed ideas. Seek ways to rearrange them into a new, more logical pattern.
- Rephrase or summarize what the speaker is saying. Listen for main ideas, and then put them into your own words.
- Repeat key points you want to remember. Go back to essential ideas and restate them to yourself.
- Look for "information handles" provided by the speaker. Listen for the overall structure of the message conveyed through an overview, transitions, signposts, and summary statements.

QuickCheck
Become a Better Listener

- Adapt to the speaker's delivery.
- Listen with your eyes as well as your ears.
- Monitor your emotional reaction to a message, and avoid jumping to conclusions.
- Be a selfish listener.
- Listen for major ideas.
- Identify your listening goal, practice listening, and become an active listener.

Listen Ethically

Audience members share responsibility with speakers for ethical communication. The following guidelines for ethical listening incorporate what Harold Barrett calls "attributes of the good audience."[3]

Communicate Your Expectations and Feedback

As an audience member, you have the right—even the responsibility—to enter a communication situation with expectations about both the message and how the speaker will deliver it.

- Know what information and ideas you want to get out of the communication transaction.
- Expect a coherent, organized, and competently delivered presentation.
- Communicate your objectives, and react to the speaker's message and delivery through appropriate nonverbal and verbal feedback.
- If a question-and-answer period follows the speech, ask any questions you still have about the speaker's topic or point of view.

Demonstrate Sensitivity to and Tolerance of Differences

As a member of an audience, it is important for you to exercise social and cultural awareness and tolerance.

- Be attentive and courteous.
- Consider diverse cultural norms and audience expectations as part of the context within which you listen to and evaluate the speaker.

- Make an effort to understand the needs, goals, and interests of both the speaker and other audience members so that you can judge how to react appropriately and ethically as a listener.

Hold the Speaker Responsible

The following questions will help you decide whether the speaker is living up to his or her ethical responsibilities.

- Is the speaker presenting both sides of the issue?
- Is the speaker disclosing all the information to which he or she has access, or is the speaker trying to hide something?
- Is the speaker being honest about the purpose of the speech?

Although you can and should refuse to sanction unethical messages and tactics, seek ways to question and refute ideas and arguments without being discourteous or resorting to unethical tactics yourself.

- You can communicate to the speaker through nonverbal feedback during a speech. Frowning, shaking your head, or looking away can signal to the speaker that you do not approve of his or her message.
- If there is a chance that you may have misunderstood the speaker, take advantage of opportunities after the speech to question him or her.
- Read more about the topic to check the speaker's facts.
- Discuss your opinion with others, and seek out or create a forum through which you can express your dissent.

Improve Your Note-Taking Skills

It is difficult to recall the details of a lengthy speech unless you have taken notes. Coupling improved listening skills with better note-taking skills can greatly enhance your ability to retrieve information.

Come Prepared

Come prepared to take notes, even if you're not sure you need to. Bring a pencil or pen and paper to every lecture or meeting.

Determine Whether You Need to Take Notes

After the presentation has started, decide whether you need to take notes. If notes seem necessary, decide whether you need to outline the speech, identify facts and principles, jot down key words, or just record major ideas. The type of notes you take will depend on how you intend to use the information you get from the speech.

Make Your Notes Meaningful

Beware of taking too many notes; the goal is to remember the message, not to transcribe it. Instead, use the re-sorting and rephrasing techniques you learned earlier and write down only what will be meaningful to you later.

Listen and Think Critically

Critical listening is the process of listening to evaluate the quality, appropriateness, value, and importance of the information you hear. Related to being a critical listener is being a critical thinker. **Critical thinking** is a mental process of making judgments about the conclusions presented in what you see, hear, and read. Your goal as a critical listener is to assess the quality of the information and the validity of the conclusions presented.

Separate Facts from Inferences

Facts are based on something that has been proven true by direct observation. An **inference** is a conclusion based on partial information or an evaluation that has not been directly observed. Facts are in the realm of certainty; inferences are in the realm of probability and opinion.

Evaluate the Quality of Evidence

Evidence consists of the facts, examples, opinions, and statistics that a speaker uses to support a conclusion. Without credible supporting evidence, it would not be wise to agree with a speaker's conclusion.

Some speakers support a conclusion with **examples**. But if the examples aren't typical, or only one or two examples are offered, or other known examples differ from the one the speaker is using, then you should question the conclusion.

An **opinion** is a quoted comment from someone. A credible source is someone who has the credentials, experience, and skill to make an observation about the topic at hand.

A **statistic** is a number that summarizes a collection of examples. Are the statistics reliable, unbiased, recent, representative, and valid?

Evaluate the Underlying Logic and Reasoning

Logic is a formal system of rules applied to reach a conclusion. A speaker is logical if he or she offers appropriate evidence to reach a valid, well-reasoned conclusion.

Reasoning is the process of drawing a conclusion from evidence within the logical framework of the arguments. As a critical listener, review the logic and reasoning used to reach a conclusion. If a speaker wants to change your behavior, listen especially carefully to the logic or structure of the arguments presented.

Analyze and Evaluate Speeches

When you evaluate something, you judge its value and appropriateness. In making a judgment about the value of something, it's important to use criteria for what is and is not effective or appropriate. **Rhetorical criticism** is the process of using a method or standards to evaluate the effectiveness and appropriateness of messages.

Understand Criteria for Evaluating Speeches

What makes a speech good? Underlying any list of what a good speaker does are two fundamental goals: creating a speech that is both effective and ethical. The mission of the National Communication Association—to promote effective and ethical communication—mirrors these two goals.

The Message Should Be Effective   To be effective, the message should be understandable to listeners and should achieve its intended purpose.[4] A goal of any communication effort is to create a common understanding of the message on the part of both the sender and the receiver. If listeners fail to comprehend the speaker's ideas, the speech fails.

Another way to evaluate the effectiveness of a message is to assess whether it achieved its intended goal. Typical general goals of public speaking are to inform, to persuade, and to entertain. The challenge in using this criterion in evaluating the speeches of others is that you may not know what the speaker's true intent is. Often the best you can do is try to determine the purpose by being a careful listener.

The Message Should Be Ethical   A good speaker is an ethical speaker. An ethical public speaker tells the truth, gives credit for ideas and words where credit is due, and doesn't plagiarize. If the audience clearly understands the message and the speaker gets the reaction he or she desires but uses unethical means to do so, the message may be *effective*, but it is not *appropriate*.

Identify and Analyze Rhetorical Strategies

Rhetoric is the use of symbols to achieve goals. **Symbols** are words, images (a flag, a cross, a six-pointed star), and behaviors that create meaning for others.

One way to enhance your listening skills and become more mindful of how messages influence your behavior is to analyze the rhetorical strategies a speaker uses. **Rhetorical strategies** are methods and techniques that speakers employ to achieve their speaking goals. Speakers sometimes use unethical rhetorical strategies to achieve their goals, such as misusing evidence, relying too heavily on emotion to persuade, or fabricating information.

Rhetorician Robert Rowland offers a simple but comprehensive framework for describing and analyzing rhetorical messages: Be conscious of the goal of the message, its organization, the speaker's role, the overall tone of the message, the intended audience, and the techniques the speaker uses to achieve the goal.[5] The more clearly you can identify and analyze the speaker's methods, the more effectively you can assess whether the message and the messenger are worthy of your support.

Give Feedback to Others

When you have an opportunity to critique a speech, provide the following kinds of feedback.

1. **Be descriptive.** In a neutral way, describe what you saw the speaker doing. Act as a mirror for the speaker to help him or her become aware of gestures and other nonverbal signals.
2. **Be specific.** Make sure your descriptions are precise enough to give the speaker a clear image of your perceptions.
3. **Be positive.** Begin and end your feedback with positive comments. Beginning with negative comments immediately puts the speaker on the defensive and can create so much internal noise that she or he stops listening.
4. **Be constructive.** Give the speaker some suggestions or alternatives for improvement.
5. **Be sensitive.** Use *I-statements* as a way of phrasing your feedback so that your comments reflect your personal point of view ("I found my attention drifting during your speech"). A *you-statement* is less sensitive because it implies that the other person did something wrong ("You didn't summarize very well").
6. **Be realistic.** Provide usable information. Provide feedback about things over which the speaker has control.

Give Feedback to Yourself

Consider the following suggestions for enhancing your own self-critiquing skills.

1. **Look for and reinforce your skills and speaking abilities.** Take mental note of how your audience analysis, organization, and delivery were effective in achieving your objectives.
2. **Evaluate your effectiveness based on your specific speaking situation and audience.** Give yourself permission to adapt principles and practices to specific speech situations.

3. **Identify one or two areas for improvement.**
   Identify what you did right; then give yourself a suggestion or two for ways to improve. Concentrate on one or two key skills you would like to develop.

A Question of Ethics

Marianne strongly believes that the drinking age should be raised to 22 in her state. When she surveyed her classmates, the overwhelming majority thought the drinking age should be lowered to 18. Should Marianne change the topic and purpose of her speech to avoid facing a hostile audience? Why or why not?

Chapter 6

Analyzing Your Audience

Audience analysis is the process of examining information about the listeners who will hear your speech. That analysis helps you understand your audience and adapt your message so that your listeners will respond as you wish.

Demographic Audience Analysis

Demographics are statistics on audience characteristics such as age, race, gender, educational level, and religious views. Demographic information can help you develop a clear and effective message by providing clues about your listeners.

Age

Know the age of your audience when you choose your topic and approach. The audience's age can suggest the kinds of examples, humor, illustrations, and other types of supporting material you use in your speech. Use caution, however, in generalizing from only one factor.

Gender

Gender is the perception of one's self as feminine or masculine. As an audience-centered speaker, avoid sexist language or remarks. Take time to educate yourself about what words, phrases, or perspectives are likely to offend or create psychological noise for your listeners. Make your language, and your message, as inclusive as possible. If you are speaking to a mixed audience, make sure your speech relates to all your listeners, not just to one gender.

Sexual Orientation

Your attitudes and beliefs should not interfere with your goal of being an effective, audience-centered public speaker. An audience-centered speaker is sensitive to issues and attitudes about sexual orientation; the speaker's goal should be to enhance understanding rather than create noise that may distract an audience from listening.

Culture, Ethnicity, and Race

Culture is a learned system of knowledge, behavior, attitudes, beliefs, values, and norms shared by a group of people. **Ethnicity** is that portion of a person's cultural background that relates to a national or religious heritage. A person's **race** is his or her biological heritage—for example, Caucasian or Asian. To be an effective speaker, adapt to differences in culture, race, and ethnicity.

Ethnocentrism is an assumption that your own cultural approaches are superior to those of other cultures. Be sensitive to cultural differences and avoid saying things that disparage the cultural background of the audience.

Group Membership

Know what groups your listeners belong to so that you can make inferences about their likes, dislikes, beliefs, and values. When touching on religious beliefs or an audience's values, use great care in what you say and how you say it. Remember that some members of your audience will not share your beliefs. Find out which political, social, service, or professional organizations they have joined. Making specific references to the activities that your audience members may participate in can help you tailor your speech to your specific audience.

Socioeconomic Status

Socioeconomic status is a person's perceived importance and influence based on such factors as income, occupation, and educational level. The amount of disposable income of your listeners can influence your topic and your approach to the topic. Knowing what people do for a living can give you useful information about how to adapt your message to them. Knowing the educational background of your audience can also help you make decisions about your choice of vocabulary, your

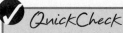

QuickCheck
Become an Audience-Centered Speaker

- Know the age of your audience.
- Avoid making sweeping judgments based on gender stereotypes.
- Consider your audience's sexual orientation.
- Avoid an ethnocentric mind-set, and use great care when touching on religious beliefs.
- Learn what groups, clubs, or organizations your audience belongs to. Consider your audience's socioeconomic status.
- Remember that your audience will be made up of a diversity of individuals.

language style, and your use of examples and illustrations.

Psychological Audience Analysis

A **psychological audience analysis** explores an audience's attitudes toward a topic, purpose, and speaker, while probing the underlying beliefs and values that might affect these attitudes.

- An **attitude** reflects likes or dislikes.
- A **belief** is what you hold to be true or false. Beliefs underlie attitudes. If you can understand why audience members feel as they do about a topic, you may be able to address that underlying belief, whether trying to change an attitude or reinforce one.
- A **value** is an enduring concept of good and bad, right and wrong. More deeply ingrained than either attitudes or beliefs, values are more resistant to change. Values support both attitudes and beliefs.

Analyze Attitudes toward Your Topic

Know how members of an audience feel about your topic. Are they interested or apathetic? How much do they already know about the topic? If the topic is controversial, are they for or against it? Knowing the answers to these questions from the outset lets you adjust your message accordingly.

With an interested audience, your task is simply to hold and amplify interest throughout the speech. If your audience is uninterested, you need to find ways to "hook" the members. Given our visually oriented culture, consider using visual aids to gain and maintain the attention of apathetic listeners.

You may also want to gauge how favorable or unfavorable your audience may feel toward you and your message before you begin to speak. Some audiences, of course, are neutral, apathetic, or simply uninformed about what you plan to say. But even if your objective is just to inform, it is useful to know whether your audience is predisposed to respond positively or negatively toward you or your message.

A captive audience has externally imposed reasons for being there (such as a requirement to attend class). Your goal with a captive audience is to make your speech just as interesting and effective as one designed for a voluntary audience. You still have an obligation to address your listeners' needs and interests and to keep them engaged in what you have to say. To be effective, a speech designed for a captive audience should not seem as if you are presenting it only because you must.

Analyze Attitudes toward You, the Speaker

Your **credibility**—the degree to which you are perceived as trustworthy, knowledgeable, and interesting—is one of the main factors that will shape your audience's attitude toward you. If you establish your credibility before you begin, your listeners will be more likely to believe what you say and to think that you are knowledgeable, interesting, and dynamic.

An audience's positive attitude toward you as a speaker can overcome negative or apathetic attitudes they may have toward your topic or purpose. If your analysis reveals that your audience does not recognize you as an authority on your subject, you will need to build your credibility into the speech. If you have had personal experience with your topic, be sure to let the audience know. You will gain credibility instantly.

Situational Audience Analysis

Situational audience analysis includes a consideration of the time and place of your speech, the size of your audience, and the speaking occasion. Although these are not technically elements of audience analysis, they can have a major effect on how listeners respond to you.

Time

Consider the time of day, as well as audience expectations about the length of the speech. Be mindful of your time limits. If your audience expects you to speak for 20 minutes, it is good to end either right at 20 minutes or even a little earlier.

Location

If possible, visit the place where you will speak. Physical conditions can affect your performance, the audience's response, and the overall success of the speech. The arrangement of chairs, placement of audiovisual materials, and opening or closing of drapes should all be in your control.

Size of Audience

As a general rule, the larger the audience, the more likely they are to expect a more formal style. With an audience of 10 or fewer, you can punctuate a conversational style by taking questions from your listeners. If you and your listeners are so few that you can be seated around a table, they may expect you to stay seated for your presentation.

Occasion

Knowing the occasion helps you predict both demographic characteristics of the audience and the members' psychological state of mind.

QuickCheck
Analyze the Situation

- How many people are expected to attend?
- How will the audience seating be arranged?
- How close will you be to the audience?
- Will you speak from a lectern?
- Will you be expected to use a microphone?
- Will you be on a stage or raised platform?
- What is the room lighting like?
- Will you have the appropriate equipment for your visual aids?
- Where will you appear on the program?
- Will there be noise or distractions outside the room?
- What is the occasion that brings the audience together?

Gather Information about Your Audience

As an audience-centered speaker, try to find out as much as you can about the audience before planning the speech. There are two approaches you can take: informal and formal.

Informal Analysis

Observe your audience informally and ask questions before you speak. Informal observations can be especially important in helping you assess obvious demographic characteristics.

Also talk with people who know something about the audience you will be addressing. What is their average age? What are their political affiliations? What are their attitudes toward your topic? Try to get as much information as possible about your audience before you give your speech.

Formal Analysis: Surveys and Questionnaires

If time and resources permit, you may want to conduct a more formal survey of your listeners.

- Decide what you want to know about your audience that you don't already know.
- Let your topic and the speaking occasion help you determine the kinds of questions you should pose.

■ Once you have found out what you specifically want to know, ask your potential audience straightforward questions about such demographic information as age, sex, occupation, and memberships in professional organizations.

Although knowing your audience's demographics can be helpful, use caution in making inferences based on general information, as they may lead to faulty conclusions. Whenever possible, ask specific questions about audience members' attitudes.

You can ask two basic types of questions:

1. **Open-ended questions** allow for unrestricted answers, rather than limiting answers to choices or alternatives. Use open-ended questions when you want more detailed information from your audience.
2. **Closed-ended questions** offer several alternatives from which to choose. Multiple-choice, true/false, and agree/disagree questions are examples of closed-ended questions.

After you develop questions, test them on a small group of people to make sure they are clear and will encourage meaningful answers.

Analyze Your Audience after You Speak

After you have given your speech, it is important to evaluate your audience's positive or negative response to your message. Why? Because this evaluation can help you prepare your next speech. From that analysis you can learn whether your examples were clear and your message was accepted by your listeners.

Nonverbal Responses

Nonverbal responses at the end of the speech may express some general feeling of the audience, but they are not much help in identifying which strategies were the most effective.

The most obvious nonverbal response is applause. Is the audience simply clapping politely, or is the applause robust and enthusiastic, indicating pleasure and acceptance? Responsive facial expressions, smiles, and nods are other nonverbal signs that the speech has been well received.

Realize, however, that audience members from different cultures respond to speeches in different ways. Japanese audience members, for example, are likely to be restrained in their response to a speech and to show little expression. Some Eastern European listeners may not maintain eye contact with you; they may look down at the floor when listening. In some contexts, African American listeners may enthusiastically voice their agreement or disagreement with something you say during your presentation.[1]

Verbal Responses

Also consider what the members of the audience say, both to you and to others, after your speech. General comments, such as "I enjoyed your talk" or "Great speech," are good for the ego—which is important—but are not of much analytic help. Specific comments can indicate where you succeeded and where you failed. If you have the chance, try to ask audience members how they responded to the speech in general, as well as to points you are particularly interested in.

Survey Responses

You may want to survey your audience after you speak. You can then assess how well you accomplished your objective. Use the same survey techniques discussed earlier. Develop survey questions that will help you determine the general reactions to you and your speech, as well as specific responses to your ideas and supporting materials.

Behavioral Responses

If the purpose of your speech was to persuade your listeners to do something, you will want to learn whether they ultimately behave as you intended. Your listeners' actions are the best indicators of your speaking success.

A Question of Ethics

Steven has decided to develop a speech about socialized medicine, a topic with which he is unfamiliar. He reasons that he has several friends who are knowledgeable and feel strongly about the topic and he will learn more about the topic as he does research to support his speech. Is it ethical for Steven to adopt his friends' opinions about the topic and then find material to support their opinions? Why or why not?

Chapter 7

Adapting to Your Audience

Adapt to Your Audience as You Speak

Prespeech analyses help with each step of the public-speaking process, but audience analysis and adaptation do not end when you have crafted your speech. They continue as you deliver your speech.

Read Nonverbal Cues

Once you begin speaking, you must rely on nonverbal cues from the audience to judge how people are responding to the message.

To develop this skill, be aware of the often unspoken clues that your audience either is hanging on every word or is bored. After learning to "read" your audience, you then need to consider developing a repertoire of behaviors to help you connect with your listeners.

Eye Contact Note the amount of eye contact your audience has with you. The more contact they have, the more likely it is that they are listening to your message. If you find them looking down at the program (or, worse yet, closing their eyes), you can reasonably guess that they have lost interest.

Facial Expression Members of an attentive audience not only make direct eye contact but also have attentive facial expressions. Beware of a frozen, unresponsive face. The classic in-a-stupor expression consists of a slightly tilted head; a faint, frozen smile; and a hand holding up the chin. This expression may give the appearance of interest, but it more often means that the person is daydreaming.

Movement An attentive audience doesn't move much. Squirming, feet shuffling, and general body movement often indicate that members of the audience have lost interest in your message.

Nonverbal Responses   An interested audience responds when encouraged or invited to do so by the speaker. When you ask for a show of hands and audience members sheepishly look at one another and eventually raise a finger or two, you can reasonably infer lack of interest and enthusiasm. Frequent applause and nods of agreement with your message are indicators of interest and support.

Verbal Responses   Audience members may shout out a response or more quietly express agreement or disagreement to people seated next to them. A sensitive public speaker constantly listens for verbal reinforcement or disagreement.

Respond to Nonverbal Cues

If your audience seems interested, supportive, and attentive, your prespeech analysis has clearly guided you to make proper choices in preparing and delivering your speech.

If you think audience members are drifting off into their own thoughts or disagreeing with what you say, or if you suspect that they don't understand what you are saying, then a few spontaneous changes may help.

If your audience seems inattentive or bored:
- Tell a story.
- Use an example to which the audience can relate, or use a personal example.
- Remind your listeners why your message should be of interest to them.
- Eliminate some abstract facts and statistics.
- Use appropriate humor.
- Make direct references to the audience.
- Invite the audience to participate by asking questions or asking them for an example.
- Ask for a direct response, such as a show of hands, to see whether your listeners agree or disagree with you.
- Pick up the pace of your delivery, or pause for dramatic effect.

If your audience seems confused or doesn't seem to understand your point:

- Be more redundant.
- Try phrasing your information in another way, or think of an example you can use to illustrate your point.
- Use a visual aid such as a chalkboard or flipchart to clarify your point.
- If you have been speaking rapidly, slow your speaking rate.
- Ask for feedback from an audience member to help you discover what is unclear.
- Ask someone in the audience to summarize the key point you are making.

If your audience seems to be disagreeing with your message:

- Provide additional data and evidence to support your point.
- Remind your listeners of your credibility, credentials, or background.
- Rely less on anecdotes and more on facts to present your case. Write facts and data on a chalkboard, overhead transparency, or flipchart if one is handy.
- If you don't have the answers and data you need, tell listeners you will provide more information by mail, telephone, or e-mail (and make sure you get back in touch with them).

Remember, it is not enough to note your listeners' characteristics and attitudes. You must also respond to the information you gather by adapting your speech to retain their interest and attention. Moreover, you have a responsibility to ensure that your audience understands your message. If your approach to the content of your speech is not working, alter it and note whether your audience's responses change. If all else fails, you may need to abandon a formal speaker-listener relationship with your audience and open up your topic for discussion.

Customize Your Message to Your Audience

Audiences prefer messages that are adapted just to them. What are some ways to communicate to your listeners that your message is designed specifically for them? Here are a few suggestions.

■ Appropriately use audience members' names to relate information to specific people. Before you speak, ask the people for permission to use their names in your talk.

■ Refer to the town, city, or community. Make a specific reference to the place where you are speaking.

■ Refer to a significant event that happened on the date of your speech. Most libraries have books (such as the *Speaker's Lifetime Library*) that identify significant events in world or national history. Relating your talk to a historical event that occurred on the same day can give your message a feeling of immediacy. It tells your audience that you have thought about this specific speaking event.

■ Refer to a recent news event. Always read the local paper to see whether there is a local news story that you can connect to the central idea of your talk.

■ Refer to a group or organization. If you're speaking to an audience of service, religious, political, or work group members, make specific positive references to that group. But be honest.

■ Relate information directly to your listeners. Find ways to apply facts, statistics, and examples to the people in your audience. For example, if you know that four out of ten women are likely to experience gender discrimination, customize that statistic by saying "Forty percent of women listening to me now are likely to experience gender discrimination. That means of the 20 women in this audience, 8 of you are likely to be discriminated against."

Adapt to Diverse Listeners

Audience diversity involves more factors than just ethnic and cultural differences. *Diversity* simply means differences. Audiences are diverse.

A **target audience** is a specific segment of your audience that you most want to address or influence. As a speaker, you may want to customize your message to influence a certain portion of your audience, especially if your audience is diverse.

You can also use a variety of strategies to reflect the diversity of your audience. Because of your efforts to gather information about your audience, you should know the various constituencies that will likely be present for your talk.

Use a variety of supporting materials to appeal to people with different backgrounds. Most listeners, regardless of culture and language, can comprehend visual expressions of pain, joy, sorrow, and happiness. The more varied your listeners' cultural experiences, the more effective it can be to use visual materials to illustrate your ideas.

QuickCheck
Adapt to a Culturally Diverse Audience

- Assess your listeners' cultural backgrounds and expectations about the speaking process.
- Assess your own cultural background, expectations, and biases about the speaking process.
- Assess the level of formality your listeners expect.
- Assess whether your listeners will respond to a linear, step-by-step structure.
- Beware of developing a message that would be effective only with people just like you; be audience-centered.
- Avoid making sweeping generalizations about your audience's culture or ethnicity.
- Use a mix of supporting materials to make your points clear and memorable.
- Use visual aids that have universal appeal.
- Present stories, illustrations, and narratives with messages that span cultural backgrounds.
- Tailor your speech to a set of target or primary listeners in your audience.
- Identify common values and assumptions held by your listeners.

A Question of Ethics

While in the library gathering material for a speech, you find a great magazine article from which you plan to quote extensively, and you take copious notes. In your excitement about finding the article, you neglect to record the bibliographic information on your note cards. As you compose your speech the night before you will deliver it, you discover your omission and have no time to return to the library. How can you solve your problem in an ethical way?

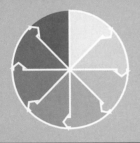

Part 3

Preparing a Speech

Chapter 8

Developing Your Speech

Early steps in developing a speech include the following:

1. Select and narrow your topic.
2. Determine your purpose.
3. Develop your central idea.
4. Generate your main ideas.

Select Your Topic

Your first task is to choose a topic to speak about. You will then need to narrow this topic to fit your time limits. But how do you go about choosing an appropriate, interesting topic?

Consider the Audience

As you search for potential speech topics, keep in mind each audience's interests and expectations. Not only should your topic be relevant to the *interests* and *expectations* of your listeners; it should also take into account the *knowledge* listeners already have about the subject.

Choose Important, Appropriate Topics

Choose topics that are important—topics that matter to your listeners, as well as to yourself. Table 8.1 offers examples of topics appropriate for the interests, expectations, knowledge, and concerns of given audiences. To be successful, a topic must be appropriate to both audience and occasion.

Table 8.1 ■ Sample Audience-Centered Topics

Audience	Topic
Retirees	Preserving Social Security benefits
Civic organizations	The Special Olympics
Church members	Starting a community food bank
First graders	What to do in case of a fire at home
Teachers	Building children's self-esteem
College fraternity	Campus service opportunities

Consider Yourself   The best public-speaking topics are those that reflect your personal experience or that especially interest you. An alternative to selecting a topic with which you are already familiar is to select one you would like to know more about. Your interest will motivate both your research and your eventual delivery of the speech.

Brainstorm   Use **brainstorming** to generate ideas for speech topics. To brainstorm a list of potential topics, write down the first topic that comes to mind. Do not allow yourself to evaluate it. Just write it down in a word or a phrase.

Now jot down a second idea—again, anything that comes to mind. The first topic may remind you of a second possibility. "Piggybacking" of ideas is okay. Continue without restraint. At this stage, anything goes. Your goal is quantity—as long a list as you can think up in the time you have.

Listen and Read   Very often, something you see, hear, or read triggers an idea for a speech. A current story on the evening news or in your local paper may suggest a topic. In addition to discovering topics in news stories, you might find them in an interesting segment of *60 Minutes*, *20/20*, *Dateline*, or *Oprah*. Chances are that a topic covered in one medium has been covered in another as well, allowing extended research on the topic.

Just as you jotted down possible topics generated by brainstorming sessions, remember to write down topic ideas you get from media, class lectures, or informal conversations.

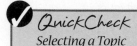

QuickCheck
Selecting a Topic

- Is the topic relevant and important to your audience?
- How much does your audience know about the topic?
- Is the topic important to your audience?
- Is the topic appropriate to the occasion?
- Is the topic of interest and importance to you?

Scan Web Directories   Access a Web directory such as Yahoo! (www.yahoo.com). Select a category at random. Click on it, and look through the subcategories that come up. Click on one of them. Continue to follow the chain of categories until you see a topic that piques your interest—or until you reach a dead end, in which case you can return to the Yahoo! homepage and try again.

Don't Procrastinate!

For most brief speeches (under 10 minutes), you should allow at least one week from topic selection to speech delivery. A week gives you enough time to develop and research your speech. The whole process will be far easier than if you delay work until the night before you are supposed to deliver your speech.

Narrow the Topic

Now that you have a topic, you need to narrow it so that it fits within the time limits of your speech. Write your general topic at the top of a list, and make each succeeding word in the list a more specific or concrete topic. Be careful not to narrow your topic so much that you cannot find enough information for even a 3-minute talk. If you do, just go back a step.

Determine Your General Purpose

The **general purpose** of virtually any speech is either to inform, to persuade, or to entertain. It is important that you fully understand what constitutes each type of speech so that you do not confuse them.

Speaking to Inform

Informative speakers give listeners information.

- Informative speakers define, describe, or explain a thing, person, place, concept, process, or function.
- Informative speakers try to increase the knowledge of their listeners.
- Although informative speakers may use an occasional bit of humor in their presentations, their main objective is not to entertain.
- Although informative speakers may provoke an audience's interest in the topic, their main objective is not to persuade.

Speaking to Persuade

Persuasive speakers may offer information, but they use the information to try to change or reinforce an audience's convictions and often to urge some sort of action. They try to get you to believe or do something.

Speaking to Entertain

The entertaining speaker tries to get the members of an audience to relax, smile, perhaps laugh, and generally enjoy themselves. Like persuasive speakers, entertaining speakers may inform their listeners, but providing knowledge is not their main goal. Their objective is to produce at least a smile and at best a belly laugh.

Determine Your Specific Purpose

Now that you have a topic and you know generally whether your speech should inform, persuade, or entertain, it is time for you to decide on its **specific purpose**. Unlike the general purpose, the specific purpose of your speech must be decided on by you alone, because it depends directly on the topic you choose.

Identify a Behavioral Objective

To arrive at a specific purpose for your speech, you must think in precise terms about what you want your audience to be able to do at the end of your speech. This kind of goal or purpose is called a **behavioral objective**, because you specify the behavior you seek from the audience.

Formulate the Specific Purpose

Specific-purpose statements begin with the same 12 words: "At the end of my speech, the audience will be able to. . . . ." The next word should be a verb that names an observable, measurable action that the audience should be able to take by the end of the speech.

Use verbs such as *list, explain, describe,* or *write.* Do not use words such as *know, understand,* or *believe.* You can discover what your listeners know, understand, or believe only by having them show their increased capability in some measurable way.

Focus on the Audience

A statement of purpose does not say what you, the *speaker,* will do. The techniques of public speaking help you achieve your goals, but they are not themselves goals. The following guidelines will help you prepare your statement of purpose.

■ In wording your specific purpose, use verbs that refer to observable or measurable behavior.

■ Limit the specific purpose to a single idea. If your statement of purpose has more than one idea, you will have trouble covering the extra ideas in your speech. You will also run the risk of having your speech "come apart at the seams." Both unity of ideas and coherence of expression will suffer.

■ Make sure your specific purpose reflects the interests, expectations, and knowledge level of your audience. Also, be sure that your specific purpose is important.

Behavioral statements of purpose help remind you that the aim of public speaking is to win a response from the audience. In addition, using a specific purpose to guide the development of your speech helps you focus on the audience during the entire preparation process.

Use the Specific Purpose

Everything you do while preparing and delivering the speech should contribute to your specific purpose.

The specific purpose can help you assess the information you are gathering for your speech. For example, you may find that an interesting statistic, although related to your topic, does not help achieve your specific purpose. In that case, you can substitute material that directly advances your purpose.

As soon as you have decided on it, write the specific purpose on a 3-by-5-inch note card. That way you can refer to it as often as necessary while developing your speech.

Develop Your Central Idea

The central idea is a one-sentence summary of your speech. The central idea (sometimes called the *thesis*), like the purpose statement, restates the speech topic. But whereas a purpose statement focuses on audience behavior, the central idea focuses on the content of the speech.

- The central idea should be a complete declarative sentence—not a phrase or clause, and not a question. Use direct, specific language rather than qualifiers and vague generalities.
- The central idea should be a single idea. More than one central idea, like more than one idea in a purpose statement, only leads to confusion and lack of coherence in a speech.
- The central idea should reflect consideration of the audience. You considered your audience when selecting and narrowing your topic and when composing your purpose statement. In the same way, you should consider your audience's needs, interests, expectations, and knowledge when stating your central idea. If you do not consider your listeners, you run the risk of losing their attention before you even begin developing the speech.

QuickCheck
Developing Your Central Idea

- Is your central idea a complete, declarative statement?
- Does it use direct, specific language?
- Is it a single idea?
- Does it reflect consideration of your audience?

Generate and Preview Your Main Ideas

Write the central idea at the top of a clean sheet of paper. Then ask these three questions:

1. Does the central idea have *logical divisions*? (These may be indicated by such phrases as "three types" or "four means.")
2. Can you think of several *reasons* why the central idea is true?
3. Can you support your central idea with a series of *steps* or a chronological progression?

You should be able to answer yes to one or more of these questions. With your answer in mind, write down the divisions, reasons, or steps you thought of.

Consult your purpose statement as you generate your main ideas. If these main ideas do not help achieve your purpose, you need to rethink your speech. You may finally change either your purpose or your main ideas; but whichever you do, be sure to synchronize these two elements. Remember, it is much easier to make changes at this point than after you have done your research and produced a detailed outline.

Once you have generated your main ideas, you can add a preview of those main ideas to your central idea to produce a **blueprint** for your speech. Preview the ideas in the same order you plan to discuss them in the speech.

A Question of Ethics

You have decided on a topic for your speech and have been conducting a great deal of research. However, you have not been able to find enough material to support your speech. Is it ethical to create supporting material or distort facts to make your point if you have been unable to find what you need? Explain your answer.

Chapter 9

Gathering Supporting Material

Creating a successful speech requires knowledge of both the sources and the types of supporting material that speechmakers typically use. In this chapter, we identify various sources of information and discuss ways to access them.

Personal Knowledge and Experience

Your speech may be on a skill or hobby in which you are expert. Or you may talk on a subject with which you have had some personal experience. You may be able to provide an effective illustration, explanation, definition, or other type of support from your own knowledge and experience. As an audience-centered speaker, you should realize that personal knowledge often has the additional advantage of heightening your credibility in the minds of your listeners.

The Internet

The Internet is a vast collection of computers accessible to millions of people all over the world. The **World Wide Web** is the information-delivery system most often used today by those searching for supporting material for a speech. Understanding the World Wide Web, the tools for accessing it, and some of the amazing types of information available can make research easier, more productive, and even more fun.

The World Wide Web

Web sites and **Web pages** may include the following:

- personal and company pages
- periodicals

- newspapers
- reference material
- government documents
- indexes and catalogs of these resources

Each Web site and Web page has its own address, or uniform resource locator (**URL**), which you can use in your browser to access the site.

As well as being accessible by address, Web pages are hyperlinked. Clicking on a **hyperlink** automatically calls up the linked page. Hyperlinks are usually colored and underlined text, but they may be images. You can also set an electronic **bookmark** on any interesting page so that you can return to it directly.

Directories and Search Engines

When you are just beginning to research a topic, you may not know the address of a relevant Web site. Even if you do, you may not find the hyperlinks there particularly useful. You need a **Web directory** or **search engine,** such as those listed below.

Alta Vista	www.altavista.com
Ask.com	www.ask.com
Google	www.google.com
Lycos	www.lycos.com
Yahoo!	www.yahoo.com

Regardless of whether you have spent countless hours surfing the Web or are a relative newcomer to its remarkable array of resources, today's directories and search engines make the Web easy to use.

Browsing Broad Categories of Information   At times, you might want to browse broad categories of information on the Web, just as you would browse a section of library shelves for books all on the same subject. Directories work by setting up broad categories that are subdivided into ever-more-specific categories.

Using Keywords   At other times, you might prefer to access Web sites and Web pages by keywords or subjects, much as you would search a traditional library card catalog. Search engines index the World Wide Web in this manner.

Doing an Advanced Search   One strategy that can help you narrow your search is an advanced, or Boolean, search. With a **Boolean search**, you can enclose phrases in quotation marks or parentheses so that the results include only those sites on which all words of the phrase appear in that order, rather than sites that contain the words at random. You can also insert "AND" or "+" between words and phrases to indicate that you wish to see only results that contain both phrases.

Conversely, you can exclude certain words and phrases from Boolean searches. And you can restrict the dates of your hits so that you see only documents posted within a specified time frame. These relatively simple strategies can help you to narrow a list of hits from, in some cases, millions of sites to a more workable number.

Evaluating Web Resources

No search strategy can ensure the quality of the sites you discover. As you begin to explore sites, you need to evaluate them according to a consistent standard. The following six criteria can serve as such a standard.[1]

Accountability   Find out what individual or organization is responsible for the Web site.

- Look to see whether the page is signed. If you find the name of the author but not his or her qualifications, you need to seek further information in order to assess the author's expertise and authority. You may be able to get such information by following hyperlinks from the page you found to other documents.
- Another way to get information is to enter the author's name, enclosed in quotation marks, in a search engine.[2] You may find information about or other pages by this author.
- If the Web site is unsigned, you may still be able to find out what organization sponsors it. Look for a header or footer that indicates affiliation.

- You may be able to follow a hyperlink at the top or bottom of the page to the homepage of which this document is a part.
- If you can identify an organization but still do not know anything about its reputation, the domain, indicated by the last three letters of a site's URL, can give you additional information. The following domains are used by the types of organizations indicated:[3]
  - **.com** or **.net**—commercial sites
  - **.org**—nonprofit groups
  - **.edu**—educational institutions
  - **.gov**—government agencies
  - **.mil**—military groups
- You can also try entering the name of the organization, enclosed in quotation marks, in a search engine.

If you have tried these strategies and still cannot identify or verify the author or sponsor of a Web site, be extremely wary of the site. If no one is willing to be accountable for the information it contains, you cannot be accountable to your audience for using the information in a speech. Continue your search elsewhere.

Accuracy   It may be difficult to determine whether the information a site contains is accurate unless you are an expert in the area the site addresses. However, two considerations can help you assess accuracy.

1. Accuracy is closely related to accountability. If the author or sponsor of a Web site is a credible authority on the subject, the information posted on the site is more likely to be accurate than information on an anonymous or less thoroughly documented site.
2. References or hyperlinks should be provided for any information that comes from a secondary source. The site should also be relatively free of common errors in usage and mechanics. A site laden with such errors may contain content errors as well.

If you find yourself still feeling somewhat uncertain about the accuracy of information you find on a Web site, conduct further research. You may be able to verify or refute the information by consulting another site or a print resource.

Objectivity   Objectivity is related to accountability. Once you know who is accountable for a site, consider the interests, philosophical or political biases, and sources of financial support of that individual or organization. Are these interests or biases likely to slant the information presented? The more objective the author, the more credible the facts and information presented.

Recency   Look for evidence that the site was posted recently or is kept current. At the bottom of many sites you will find a statement specifying when the site was posted and when it was last updated. When you are concerned with factual data, the more recent, the better.

Usability   The layout and design of the site should facilitate its use. Some sites offer a "text-only" or "non-tables" option. Also consider whether there is a fee to gain access to any of the information on the site.

Diversity   A diversity-sensitive Web site will be free of material that communicates bias against either gender; against any ethnic, racial, or sexual preference subgroup; and against people with disabilities.[4]

✔ *QuickCheck*
Evaluate Web Resources

■ I know who is accountable for the Web site.
■ I can verify the accuracy of the information.
■ The site is objective.
■ The site is current.
■ The site is easy to use and provides links to other sites.
■ The site is culturally diverse and free of bias.

Library Resources

Spend some time becoming familiar with your library's layout and services. Learn what electronic resources are available and where they are located. In addition, learn where and how to access the following resources and services.

Books

Libraries' collections of books are called the **stacks**. In an open-stack library, collections are on open shelves and available to anyone who wishes to browse through them. The closed-stack library is one in which only people granted certain privileges are allowed in the stacks. There, you fill out a retrieval card with the title, author, and call number of the book and present the slip to the appropriate person, who will find the book and send it to circulation. Then you can either check it out or use it in the study area of the library.

You probably have used a **card catalog** in a smaller public or school library. To access a computerized catalog, go to a computer screen or monitor and follow the directions. Many libraries' card catalogs are available online, enabling you to build preliminary bibliographies of books and call numbers before you ever enter the library.

Periodicals

The term *periodicals* refers to both general-interest magazines, such as *Newsweek* and *Consumer Reports*, and trade and professional journals, such as *Communication Monographs* and *American Psychologist*.

To decide what periodicals might be useful, refer to any of the **periodical indexes**. Many of these indexes are available online or on CD-ROM. Some of the best-known indexes include the following:

- *The Reader's Guide to Periodical Literature* lists both popular magazines and a few trade and professional journals.
- *InfoTrac* is a collection of indexes available from a single company. Examples of specific InfoTrac indexes include the *Health Reference*

Center, Expanded Academic Index, General BusinessFile, and *Business Index Backfile.*

■ The *Social Sciences Index* and the *Humanities Index* list professional, trade, and specialty publications dealing with the social sciences and the humanities.

■ The *Education Index* lists articles about education and various subjects that are taught.

■ The *Public Affairs Information Service (PAIS) Bulletin* indexes both periodicals and books in such fields as sociology, political science, and economics.

■ The *Business Periodicals Index,* the *Psychology Index,* the *Music Index,* the *Art Index,* and the *Applied Science and Technology Index* are a few specialized publications that you may wish to explore.

Full-Text Databases

Full-text databases combine an index and text, enabling you to locate not only bibliographic information but also the resources themselves through a keyword or subject search. Periodicals are the most common resource available in this format, although newspapers and government documents may also be included.

■ *LEXIS-NEXIS* is an extensive database that includes periodicals, newspapers, government documents, and law journals.

■ *Academic Search Premier* is billed as the world's largest multidisciplinary academic database. Updated daily, it provides the full text of more than 4,700 scholarly publications in virtually every academic field.

A number of other databases provide some combination of index, abstracts, and full-text documents. Popular resources in this category include *ERIC,* which focuses on education; *ABI/ Inform,* which indexes more than 1,000 business and trade periodicals; and *Periodical Abstracts,* which covers more than 600 general and academic periodicals.

Newspapers

Newspapers are more current than periodicals and may offer more detailed coverage of events and special stories than do periodicals. Newspapers also usually cover stories of local significance that most often would not appear in national news magazines.

To find relevant information on your subject, consult a **newspaper index**, such as the electronic *National Newspaper Index* and *Newspaper Source*. A number of medium-sized and large newspapers publish their own indexes.

When doing newspaper research, keep this tip in mind: If you need information about a specific event and you know the date when it occurred, you can simply locate a newspaper from that or the following day and probably find a news story on the event.

Generally, libraries have only the latest newspapers in their racks. Back issues are either transferred to microfilm for storage or available online.

Reference Resources

Reference resources include encyclopedias, dictionaries, directories, atlases, almanacs, yearbooks, books of quotations, and biographical dictionaries.

- Encyclopedias can be general, or they can specialize in a particular field (such as medicine, philosophy, or law). There are also encyclopedias that cover a wide variety of topics from a particular cultural, ethnic, or national perspective.
- The *Oxford English Dictionary*, or *OED*, provides definitions, pronunciations, etymologies, and usage histories for every word in the dictionary. Specialty dictionaries also exist. *Black's Law Dictionary*, which provides legal definitions, is one example.
- Directories, such as the *Encyclopedia of Associations*, the *Directory of Nonprofit Organizations*, and telephone directories, are usually available in the reference section.
- An atlas is a geographical tool that provides maps, tables, pictures, and facts about the people and resources of various regions. Frequently

used atlases include *Goode's World Atlas*, the *Rand McNally College World Atlas*, and the *Township Atlas of the United States*. There are also specialized atlases of history and politics.

■ Almanacs and yearbooks are compilations of facts. The *Statistical Abstract of the United States* is published annually by the Census Bureau and contains statistics on nearly every facet of life in the United States, including birth and mortality rates, income, education, and religion. The *World Almanac* contains factual information about almost every subject imaginable.

■ Books of quotations are compilations of quotes on almost every conceivable subject. The *Oxford Dictionary of Quotations* and *Bartlett's Familiar Quotations* are two widely consulted works. An early edition of Bartlett's is now available online at www.bartleby.com/100/.

■ Biographical dictionaries are reference works that contain biographical articles on people who have achieved recognition. The *Who's Who* series include brief biographies of international, national, and regional figures of note. The *Dictionary of National Biography* provides biographies of famous British citizens who are no longer living; the *Dictionary of American Biography* does the same for deceased Americans of note. The *Directory of American Scholars* provides information about American academicians.

Government Documents

The federal government researches and publishes information on almost every conceivable subject and keeps exhaustive records of almost all official federal proceedings.

The most important index of government documents is the *Catalog of U.S. Government Publications*, available online in recent years and soon to be integrated into the even more comprehensive online *National Bibliography of U.S. Government Publications*. Also useful is the *American Statistics Index*, which indexes government statistical publications exclusively and is now available through some libraries online.

Interviews

Consider interviewing a person who might know the answers to some of the important questions raised by your speech topic. Before you decide on an interview, be sure that your questions cannot be answered easily by doing some preliminary research. If you decide that only an interview can give you the material you need, you should prepare for it in advance.

Determine the Purpose of the Interview

Establish a purpose or objective for the interview. What do you need to find out? Do you need hard facts that you cannot obtain from other sources? Do you need the interviewee's expert testimony on your subject?

Plan the Interview

Once you have a specific purpose for the interview, decide whom you need to speak with and arrange a meeting. Telephone the person in advance, explain briefly who you are and why you are calling, and ask for an appointment. Most people are flattered to have their authority and knowledge recognized and willingly grant interviews if their schedule permits.

To ensure the results you want, plan your questions.

- **Gather background information.** Find out as much as you can about both your subject and the person you are interviewing. Build your line of questioning on facts, statements the interviewee has made, or positions he or she has taken publicly.
- **Plan specific questions.** Think about how you can combine closed-ended and open-ended questions.
- **Plan a sequence of questions.** You may want to organize questions according to subject categories or arrange them according to complexity of information, with the easiest questions first.

Or you may want to order them by the sensitivity of the content.

■ **Plan a recording strategy.** Audio and video recorders can free you from having to take copious notes. You can concentrate instead on processing and analyzing the ideas and information being presented. Another advantage is that your record of the interview is complete. Be prepared to turn off the device and switch to manual note taking if you sense at any time that the interviewee is distracted by the recorder.

Conduct the Interview

■ **Dress appropriately.** Conservative, businesslike clothes show that you are serious about the interview and that you respect the norms of your interviewee's world.

■ **Bring note-taking supplies.** Even if you plan to use a tape recorder, you may want to turn it off at some point during the interview, so you'll need an alternative.

■ **Arrive a few minutes ahead of schedule.** Be prepared, however, to wait patiently, if necessary.

■ **Remind the interviewee of your purpose.** If you have decided to use a recorder, set it up. You may keep it out of sight once the interviewee has seen it, but never try to hide a recorder at the outset—such a ploy is unethical. If you are going to take written notes, get your supplies ready.

■ **Conduct the interview.** Use the questions you have prepared as a guide. If the person you are interviewing mentions something you did not think of, don't be afraid to pursue the point. Listen carefully to the person's answers, and ask for clarification of any ideas you don't understand.

■ **End the interview on time.** Thank your interviewee for his or her contribution, and leave.

Follow Up the Interview

As soon as possible after the interview, read through your notes carefully and rewrite any portions that

QuickCheck

Guidelines for a Successful Interview

- Determine your purpose.
- Choose an appropriate person to interview.
- Arrange a meeting.
- Get permission to record.
- Gather appropriate background material.
- Plan specific open-ended and closed-ended questions.
- Develop a sequence for questions.
- Plan and implement a recording strategy.
- Dress appropriately.
- Arrive a few minutes ahead of time.
- Use the questions you prepared.
- Stay within the time limits.
- Follow up.

may be illegible. If you recorded the interview, label the tape with the date and the interviewee's name. You will soon want to transfer any significant facts, opinions, or anecdotes from notes or tape to either index cards or a word-processing file.

Resources from Special-Interest Groups and Organizations

Business and industrial groups, nonprofit organizations, and professional societies produce pamphlets, books, fact sheets, and other information about an extraordinarily wide variety of subjects. To find such resources, you may want to do a Web search or consult some of the reference works already discussed. Although reference works may not indicate specific publications, they provide the names, addresses, and telephone numbers of businesses and organizations that may have a special interest in, and produce resources related to, your topic.

Research Strategies

Well-organized research strategies can make your efforts easier and more efficient. You need to develop a preliminary bibliography, evaluate the usefulness of resources, take notes, and identify possible presentation aids.

Develop a Preliminary Bibliography

Create a **preliminary bibliography,** or list of promising resources. Include electronic resources as well as print materials. You will probably discover more resources than you actually look at or refer to in your speech; at this stage, the bibliography simply serves as a menu of possibilities.

■ **Keep track of resources.** Web browsers let you bookmark pages for future reference and ready access. If you are using a CD-ROM index, you may be able to print out references. If you are using more traditional catalogs and indexes, you will need to copy the necessary bibliographical information. Using 3-by-5-inch note cards will give you the greatest flexibility. Later you can omit some of the cards, add others, write comments on them, or alphabetize them much more easily than if you had made a list on a sheet of paper.

■ **Use a consistent format.** That way you can easily find and cite the page number, title, publisher, or some other vital fact about a publication. The two most common formats, or documentation styles, are those developed by the MLA (Modern Language Association) and the APA (American Psychological Association).

For a book, record the author's name, title of the book, place of publication, publisher, date of publication, and the library's call number (see Figure 9.1). For an article in a periodical or newspaper, document the author's name, title of the article, title of the periodical, date of publication, and inclusive page numbers of the article.

For government publications, pamphlets, newsletters, fact sheets, or other specialized information formats, record the title, author, publisher, date, and page number. For a government document, also record the Superintendent of Documents classification number, available in the *Catalog of U.S. Government Publications*.

Electronic resource formats are still evolving, although they are similar to the formats for other kinds of material.

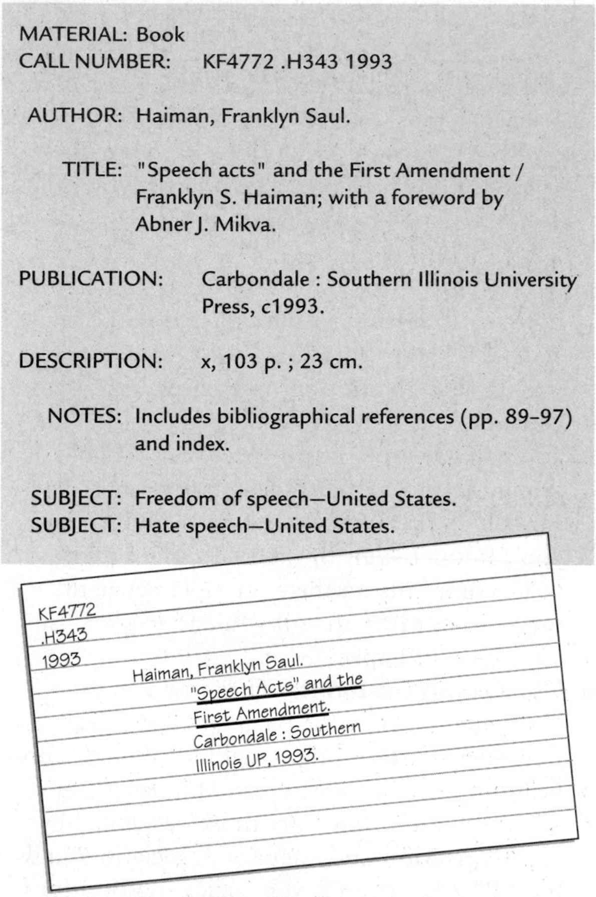

MATERIAL: Book
CALL NUMBER: KF4772 .H343 1993

AUTHOR: Haiman, Franklyn Saul.

   TITLE: "Speech acts" and the First Amendment /
           Franklyn S. Haiman; with a foreword by
           Abner J. Mikva.

PUBLICATION: Carbondale : Southern Illinois University
               Press, c1993.

DESCRIPTION: x, 103 p. ; 23 cm.

   NOTES: Includes bibliographical references (pp. 89–97)
           and index.

SUBJECT: Freedom of speech—United States.
SUBJECT: Hate speech—United States.

KF4772
.H343
1993
        Haiman, Franklyn Saul.
            "Speech Acts" and the
            First Amendment.
            Carbondale : Southern
            Illinois UP, 1993.

Figure 9.1 ■ Information transferred from an electronic catalog entry to a bibliography card.

Following is the basic MLA format:

Author's name (last name first). **"Title of article"** (if any, enclosed in quotation marks). <u>**Title of Web site**</u> (underlined) or a **description such as Homepage** (not underlined). **Date of Internet publication or the latest update. Name of sponsoring organization. Date of your access <URL>.** (The URL should be enclosed in angle brackets, as shown here. Break a URL from one line to the next only after a slash, period, or hyphen.)

If you cannot find one element of this information (such as the author or the date of Internet publication or latest update), simply skip it and go directly to the next item. The most distinctive features of

Web documentation are, of course, the address of the Web page and the date you accessed the page.

How many resources should you list in a preliminary bibliography for, say, a 10-minute speech? A reasonable number might be 10 or 12 that look promising. If you have many more than that, you may feel overwhelmed. If you have fewer, you may have too little information.

Evaluate the Usefulness of Resources

It makes sense to gauge the potential usefulness of your resources before you begin to read more closely and take notes. Think critically about how the various resources you have found are likely to help you achieve your purpose and about how effective they are likely to be with your audience. Glance over the tables of contents of books, and flip quickly through the texts to note any charts, graphs, or other visual materials that might be used as visual aids. Skim a key chapter or two. Skim shorter articles, pamphlets, and fact sheets as well.

Take Notes

Once you have located, previewed, and ranked your resources, you are ready to begin more careful reading and note taking.

- Start with the resources that you think have the greatest potential. If you are looking at a Web page, an article, a pamphlet, an encyclopedia entry, or another kind of short document, you can read the whole text fairly quickly. But you probably do not have time to read entire books, so read only those chapters or sections that seem particularly relevant and potentially useful to your speech.
- When you find an example, a statistic, an opinion, or other material that might be useful to your speech, write it down, photocopy it, download it into a computer file, or print it. Be sure to identify the source.
- Even if you plan to photocopy or enter most of your notes into a word-processing file, it is a good idea to carry a few note cards with you

whenever you are working on a speech. You can use one to jot down an idea that comes to mind while you are sipping coffee or to record a fact you discover in a magazine article. Another advantage of using note cards is that you can later arrange them in the order of your speech outline, simplifying the integration of your ideas and supporting material into the speech.

■ Put only one item of supporting material or one idea on each card or on each page of your notebook or word-processing file. The amount of useful supporting material you find will vary widely from one source to another.

■ If you copy a phrase, sentence, or paragraph verbatim from a source, be sure to put quotation marks around it when you write it down or enter it. You may need to know later in the preparation process whether it was a direct quote or a paraphrase.

■ In addition to copying the information, indicate its source. If you consistently record your sources when you take notes, you will avoid the possibility of committing unintentional plagiarism later.

■ Finally, leave enough space at the top of each note card or page to summarize the idea expressed in the note. Such headings make it easier to find a particular bit of material quickly when you are ready to assemble the speech.

Identify Possible Presentation Aids

In addition to discovering verbal supporting material in your sources, you may also find charts, graphs, photographs, and other potentially valuable visual material.

Even if you are not certain that you will use presentation aids in your speech, it can't hurt to print out, photocopy, or sketch on a note card any good possibilities, recording sources of information just as you did for your written materials. Then, when the time comes to consider if and where presentation aids might enhance the speech, you will have some at hand.

QuickCheck
Research Strategies

- Develop a preliminary bibliography.
- Locate sources.
- Consider the potential usefulness of sources.
- Take notes.
- Identify possible presentation aids.

A Question of Ethics

You plan to give a speech about nuclear energy. Though the process of producing energy this way is extremely complex, you will need to make your presentation very simple. How can you prevent your audience from assuming your topic is simple rather than complex? Should you let the audience know that you are oversimplifying the process? Explain your answer.

Chapter 10

Supporting Your Speech

Gathering appropriate supporting material is an essential step in the speech-preparation process. And once you have gathered a variety of material, you will need to make decisions about how to use your information to best advantage.

Use Illustrations

Everybody likes to hear a story. An **illustration**—a story or anecdote that provides an example of an idea, issue, or problem you are discussing—almost always ensures audience interest.

- **Brief illustrations** are often no longer than a sentence or two. A series of brief illustrations can sometimes have more impact than either a single brief illustration or a more detailed extended illustration. In addition, although an audience could dismiss a single illustration as an exception, two or more strongly suggest a trend or norm.
- **Extended illustrations** are longer and more detailed than brief illustrations; they resemble a story. They are more vividly descriptive, and they have a plot—which includes an opening, complications, a climax, and a resolution. To use an extended illustration takes more time than to cite a brief example, but longer stories can be more dramatic and emotionally compelling. Extended illustrations can work well as speech introductions.
- **Hypothetical illustrations** may be either brief or extended. They describe situations or events that have not actually occurred but that *might* happen. Plausible hypothetical illustrations may

serve your purpose better than real examples by enabling your audience to imagine themselves in a particular situation.

Illustrations are almost guaranteed attention getters, as well as a way to support your statements. Use illustrations that are typical and audience-centered—ones your audience can relate to. Be certain that your illustrations are directly relevant to the idea or point they are supposed to support.

- Choose illustrations that represent a trend.
- Make your illustrations vivid and specific.
- Use illustrations with which your listeners can identify. The best illustrations are the ones that your listeners can imagine experiencing themselves.
- Remember that the best illustrations are personal ones.

Use Descriptions and Explanations

A **description** tells you what something is like. Descriptions provide the details that allow audience members to develop mental pictures of what speakers are talking about. Good descriptions are vivid, accurate, and specific; they make people, places, and events come alive for the audience. A description may be used in a brief example, in an extended illustration, in a hypothetical instance, or by itself.

An **explanation** is a statement that makes clear how something is done or why it exists in its present form or existed in its past form. Speakers who discuss or demonstrate processes of any kind rely at least in part on explanations of *how* those processes work. Explaining *why* involves giving causes or reasons for a policy, principle, or event. Often, having explained causes or reasons, a speaker can then tailor a solution to those specific causes. Explaining why some condition or event exists provides an analysis that often leads to better solutions.

Keep Descriptions and Explanations Brief

An explanation should supply only as many details as necessary for an audience to understand how or why something works or exists. You can hold your audience's attention more effectively if you alternate explanations and descriptions with other types of supporting material, such as brief examples or statistics.

Use Specific, Concrete Language

Vivid and specific language brings your explanations alive. Liveliness helps you hold the audience's attention and paint in your listeners' minds the image you are trying to communicate.

Provide Definitions

Define any and all specialized, technical, or little-known terms in your speech. Such **definitions** are usually the kind you would find in a dictionary. A dictionary definition has authority. If you quote a reputable dictionary, the audience usually accepts without question the definition you are using.

You can also define a term by showing how it works or how it is applied in a specific instance. These definitions are usually original; they are not found in dictionaries. Although they may lack the credibility of dictionary definitions, they can be specifically tailored to a speech by explaining how something works or what it does.

The following suggestions can help you use definitions more effectively in your speeches.

■ Use a definition only when needed. Unnecessary definitions are boring and, more serious still, insulting to the listeners' intelligence.
■ Make certain you give your audience definitions that are immediately and easily understandable—or you will have wasted your time and perhaps even lost your audience.
■ Be certain that your definition and your use of a term are consistent throughout a speech.

Use Analogies

An **analogy** is a comparison. Like a definition, it increases understanding; unlike a definition, it deals with relationships and comparisons—between the new and the old, the unknown and the known, or any other pair of ideas or things.

Analogies can help your listeners understand unfamiliar ideas, things, and situations by showing how these are similar to something they already know. The more alike the two things being compared, the more likely it is that an analogy will stand up under attack.

Literal Analogies

A **literal analogy** is a comparison between two similar things. But because it is creative, it is inherently interesting and should help grab an audience's attention. Be sure that the two things you compare in a literal analogy are very similar. In an informative speech, a literal analogy that doesn't quite work may hamper rather than help an audience's understanding of the thing or idea you are trying to explain. If you present a persuasive speech, few things will give those who disagree with you as much joy as being able to point out a major dissimilarity in a literal analogy.

Figurative Analogies

A **figurative analogy** is not considered "hard" evidence because it relies on imaginative insights, not on facts or statistics. Be sure that the essential similarity between the two objects in a figurative analogy is readily apparent. If you do not, your audience will end up wondering what in the world you are talking about. And you will only confuse your listeners further if you try to draw on that same analogy later in your speech.

Use Statistics as Support

Just as three or four brief examples may be more effective than just one, a statistic that represents hundreds or thousands of individuals may be more persuasive still. Statistics can help a speaker express the magnitude or seriousness of a situation. Or, statistics can express the relationship of a part to the whole.

Use Reliable Sources

Statistics can be produced to support almost any conclusion desired. Your goal is to cite *reputable*, *authoritative*, and *unbiased* sources.

As you evaluate your sources, try to find out how the statistics were gathered. For example, if a statistic relies on a sample, how was the sample taken? Sample sizes and survey methods do vary widely, but most legitimate polls involve samples of 500 to 2,000 people, selected at random from a larger population. Of course, finding out about the statistical methodology may be more difficult than discovering the source of the statistic, but if you can find it, the information will help you to analyze the value of the statistic.

Interpret Statistics Accurately

People are often swayed by statistics that sound good but have in fact been wrongly calculated or misinterpreted. A speaker's skillful analysis can help listeners understand the true situation. Unfortunately, in other cases, the speaker may be the culprit in misinterpreting the statistics. Both as a user of statistics in your own speeches and as a consumer of statistics in articles, books, and speeches, be constantly alert to what the statistics actually mean.

Make Your Statistics Understandable and Memorable

You can make your statistics easier to understand and more memorable in several ways.

■ Compact statistics or express them in limits that are more meaningful or more easily understandable to your audience.

■ Explode statistics. Exploded statistics are created by adding or multiplying related numbers—for example, cost per unit times number of units. Because it is larger, the exploded statistic seems more significant than the original figures from which it was derived.

■ Compare statistics. Comparing your statistic with another heightens its impact.

■ Round off numbers, but do so without distorting or falsifying the statistic.

✓ *QuickCheck*
Select Effective Statistics

- Are the data from primary sources?
- Are the sources reputable, unbiased, and authoritative?
- Did you interpret the statistics accurately?
- Are the statistics easy to understand?
- Are they memorable?
- Can you convert the statistics into visual aids?

■ Use visual aids to present your statistics. Displaying numbers in a table or graph in front of your listeners enables them to more easily grasp the statistics.

Use Opinions

Expert testimony, the testimony of a recognized authority, can add a great deal of weight to your arguments. You may quote experts directly or paraphrase their words, as long as you are careful not to alter the intent of their remarks.

Like illustrations, **lay testimony** can stir an audience's emotions. And, although neither as authoritative nor as unbiased as expert testimony, lay testimony is often more memorable.

To make a point memorable, include a **literary quotation** in your speech. Brief, pointed quotations usually have greater audience impact than longer ones. Literary quotations have the advantage of being easily accessible. You'll find any number of quotation dictionaries on the Web and in the reference sections of most libraries. Even though a relevant literary quote may be just right for a speech, use it with caution. Be sure that you have a valid reason for citing a literary quotation, and then use only one or two at most in a speech.

Here are a few suggestions for using opinions effectively in your speeches.

■ Be certain that any authority you cite is an expert on the subject you are discussing.
■ Identify your sources. Unless the audience is aware of the qualifications of your authority, they may not grant him or her any credibility.

■ Quote your sources accurately.
■ Cite unbiased authorities.
■ Cite opinions that are representative of prevailing opinion.

Select the Best Supporting Material

You should consider accountability, accuracy, objectivity, recency, usability, and diversity in evaluating any supporting material you hope to use. How do you decide what to use and what to eliminate?

■ **Magnitude.** Bigger is better. The larger the numbers, the more convincing your statistics. The more experts who support your point of view, the more your expert testimony will command your audience's attention.

■ **Proximity.** The best supporting material is whatever is the most relevant to your listeners, or "closest to home." If you can demonstrate how an incident could affect audience members themselves, that illustration will have far greater impact than a more remote one.

■ **Concreteness.** If you need to discuss principles and theories, explain them with concrete examples and specific statistics.

■ **Variety.** A mix of illustrations, opinions, definitions, and statistics is much more interesting and convincing than the exclusive use of any one type of supporting material.

■ **Humor.** Audiences usually appreciate a touch of humor in an example or opinion. Only if your audience is unlikely to understand the humor or if your speech is on a very somber and serious topic is humor not appropriate.

■ **Suitability.** Your final decision about whether to use a certain piece of supporting material will depend on its suitability to you, your speech, the occasion, and your audience.

Question of Ethics

An aide assigned to work with speakers and speeches during both the 1996 and the 2000 Republican National Conventions compared the relative freedom allowed speakers at the 2000 convention with the censorship imposed on the 1996 convention speeches. Speeches at the 1996 convention "were diligently reviewed and monitored by convention organizers, who insisted that speakers promise to stick to their script before allowing them to go on." Is such censorship a violation of the speakers' freedom of speech?

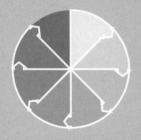

Part 4

Crafting a Speech

Chapter 11

Organizing Your Speech

No matter how knowledgeable a speaker you may be, you must organize your ideas in logical patterns to ensure that your audience can follow, understand, and remember what you say.

Organize Your Main Ideas

Previously, you learned how to generate a preliminary plan for your speech by determining whether your central idea had logical divisions, could be supported by several reasons, or could be explained by identifying specific steps.

Now you are ready to decide which of your main ideas to discuss first, which one second, and so on. You can choose from among five organizational patterns or you can combine several of these patterns:

- chronological
- topical
- spatial
- cause and effect
- problem-solution

Order Ideas Chronologically

Chronological organization is organization by time; that is, your steps are ordered according to when each occurred or should occur. You can choose to organize your main points either from earliest to most recent (forward in time) or from recent events back into history (backward in time). The progression you choose depends on your personal preference and on whether you want to emphasize the beginning or the end of the sequence. According to the principle of **recency**, the event discussed last is usually the one the audience will remember best.

How-to explanations usually follow a sequence or series of steps arranged from beginning to end, from the first step to the last—forward in time.

Organize Ideas Topically

If your central idea has natural divisions, you can often organize your speech topically. Speeches on such diverse topics as factors to consider when selecting a mountain bike, types of infertility treatments, and the various classes of ham-radio licenses all could reflect **topical organization**.

Natural divisions are often basically equal in importance. It may not matter which point you discuss first, second, or third. You can simply arrange your main points as a matter of personal preference.

Recency   At other times, you may wish to emphasize one point more than the others. If so, you will again need to consider the principle of recency. Audiences tend to remember best what they hear last.

Primacy   By contrast, if your topic is controversial and you know or suspect that your audience will be skeptical of or hostile to your ideas, you may want to organize your main ideas according to the principle of **primacy**, or putting the most important or convincing idea first. This way you do not risk losing or alienating your audience before you can reach your most significant idea. Further, your strongest idea may so influence your listeners' attitudes that they will be more receptive to the rest of your speech.

Complexity   One other set of circumstances may dictate a particular order of the main points in your speech. If your main points range from simple to complicated, it makes sense to arrange them in order of **complexity**, progressing from the simple to the more complex.

Arrange Ideas Spatially

A speaker who relies on **spatial organization** arranges items according to their location and direction. It does not usually matter whether the speaker chooses to progress up or down, east or west, forward or back, as long as ideas are developed in a logical order. If the speaker skips up, down, over, and back, he or she will only confuse the audience rather than paint a distinct word picture.

Organize Ideas to Show Cause and Effect

A speech organized to show **cause and effect** may first identify a situation and then discuss the effects that result from it (cause→effect). Or, the speech may present a situation and then seek its causes (effect→cause). As the recency principle would suggest, the cause-effect pattern emphasizes the effects; the effect-cause pattern emphasizes the causes.

Organize Ideas by Problem and Solution

If you want to emphasize how best to *solve* a problem, you will probably use a **problem-solution pattern** of organization.

Like causes and effects, problems and solutions can be discussed in either order. If you are speaking to an audience that is already fairly aware of a problem but uncertain how to solve it, you will probably discuss the problem first and then the solution(s).

If your audience knows about an action or program that has been implemented but does not know the reasons for its implementation, you might select instead a solution-problem pattern of organization.

✔ *QuickCheck*
Organize Main Ideas
- ■ Chronologically
- ■ Topically
- ■ Spatially
- ■ To show cause and effect
- ■ To present problems and solutions

Acknowledge Cultural Differences in Organization

Although the five patterns just discussed are typical of the way speakers in the United States are expected to organize and process information, they are not necessarily typical of all cultures.[1] In fact, each culture teaches its members patterns of thought and organization that are considered appropriate for various occasions and audiences.

On the whole, U.S. speakers tend to be more linear and direct than speakers from Semitic, Asian, Romance, or Russian cultures. Semitic speakers support their main points by pursuing tangents that might seem "off topic" to many U.S. speakers. Asians may only allude to a main point through a circuitous route of illustration and parable. And speakers from Romance and Russian cultures tend to begin with a basic principle and then move to facts and illustrations that they only gradually connect to a main point. The models in Figure 11.1 illustrate these culturally diverse patterns of organization.

Of course, these are very broad generalizations. But as an audience member, recognizing the existence of cultural differences when you are listening to a speech can help you appreciate and understand the organizational pattern of a speaker from a culture other than your own. He or she may not be disorganized, but simply using organizational strategies different from the ones presented earlier in this chapter.

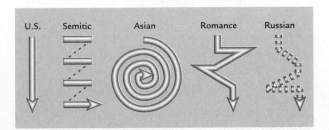

Figure 11.1 ■ Organizational patterns by culture.

Source: D. A. Lieberman, *Public Speaking in the Multicultural Environment.* Copyright © 2000. All rights reserved. Reprinted by permission of Allyn and Bacon.

Subdivide Your Main Ideas

After you have decided how to organize your main ideas, you may need to subdivide at least some of them.

You can arrange your main ideas according to one pattern and your subpoints according to another. For example, the organization of the main ideas of a speech may be chronological, but the subpoints of the first main idea may be arranged topically. Any of the five organizational patterns that apply to main ideas can apply to subpoints as well.

Right now, don't worry about such outlining details as Roman numerals, letters, and margins. Your goal at this point is to get your ideas and information on paper. Keep in mind, too, that until you've delivered your speech, none of your decisions is etched in stone. You may add, regroup, or eliminate main ideas or subpoints at any stage in the preparation process, as you consider the needs, interests, and expectations of your audience.

The Nobel Prize–winning author Isaac Bashevis Singer observed, "The wastebasket is a writer's best friend." He could just as accurately have said "speaker" instead of "writer." Multiple drafts indicate that you are working and reworking ideas to improve your product and make it the best you can. They do not mean that you are a poor writer or speaker.

Integrate Your Supporting Material

Once you have organized your main ideas and subpoints, you are ready to flesh out the speech with your supporting material.

Word-Processing Files

If you have entered your supporting material into a word-processing file, you may want to print out a hard copy of this file so that you can have it in front of you while you work on your speech plan. When you determine where in the speech you need supporting material, find what you need on the hard copy and then go back into the word-processing file to cut and paste that supporting material electronically into your speech plan.

Note Cards

If you have written or pasted supporting material on note cards, write each main idea and subpoint on a separate note card of the same size as the ones on which you recorded your supporting material. Arrange these note cards in the order in which you have organized your speech. Then go through your supporting-material note cards, one by one, and decide where in the speech you will use each one. The heading you wrote at the top of each card should help in this process. Place each supporting-material card behind the appropriate main-idea or subpoint card. You now have a complete plan for your speech on note cards.

Photocopies

If most of your supporting material is photocopied, search these copies for what you need and then write or type this supporting material into your speech plan.

Regardless of which strategy you use to integrate your supporting material, take care not to lose track of the source of the supporting material.

Smoothly Incorporating Supporting Material

Once your supporting material is logically placed into your plan, your next goal is to incorporate it smoothly into your speech so as not to interrupt the flow of ideas. Notice how skillfully this goal is met by a speaker delivering a speech on media literacy:

> While schools provide our children with a formal education, the media is one of the most predominant informal ways that children learn about the world around them. In fact, according to Stephen Kline's 1993 book *Out of the Garden*, by high school graduation, the average child will spend about 11,000 hours in the classroom. Yet nearly double that time, more than 20,000 hours, will be spent in front of the television. The key, then, is that the media is a teacher that kids find extremely attractive.[2]

In this example, the speaker has followed four steps to integrate the supporting material into the speech:

1. **State the point.** This statement should be concise and clear so that the audience can grasp it immediately. In our example, the speaker's point is "While schools provide our children with a formal education, the media is one of the most predominant informal ways that children learn about the world around them."

2. **Cite the source of the supporting material.** This does not mean that you have to give complete bibliographic information. It is unlikely that your listeners will either remember or copy down a Web site address. Use oral citations to prevent suspicion of plagiarism, providing the author's name (if available) and the title and date of the publication. The speaker in our example mentions all three. He might also have offered an additional bit of information: the qualifications of the author. Chances are that none of his audience will recognize as an authority the name Stephen Kline.

3. **Present the supporting material.** State the statistic, opinion, illustration, or other form of supporting material you have chosen to substantiate your idea. In the example, the speaker uses the statistic from Kline's book to make his point.

4. **Explain how the supporting material substantiates or develops the point.** Do not assume that audience members will automatically understand the connection. The speaker in our exam-

---

✓ **QuickCheck**
Integrate Supporting Material

■ State the point.
■ Cite the source.
■ Present the supporting material.
■ Explain how the supporting material substantiates or develops the point.

ple draws the conclusion that "the media is a teacher that kids find extremely attractive."

Your listeners may not remember many specific facts and statistics after a speech, but they should remember the important points. Connecting ideas and supporting material make it more likely that they will.

Organize Your Supporting Material

Suppose you have decided what supporting material to use and identified the ideas in your speech that require support. Now you realize that in support of your second main idea you have an illustration, two statistics, and an opinion. In what order should you present these items?

You can sometimes use the five standard organizational patterns to arrange your supporting material, as well as your main ideas and subpoints. Illustrations, for instance, may be organized chronologically.

At other times, however, none of the five patterns may seem suited to the supporting materials you have. In those instances, you may need to turn to an organizational strategy more specifically adapted to your supporting materials. These strategies include (1) primacy or recency, (2) specificity, (3) complexity, and (4) "soft" to "hard" evidence.

Primacy or Recency

The principles of primacy and recency can determine whether you put material at the beginning or the end of your speech. Suppose that you have several statistics to support a main point. All are relevant and significant, but one is especially gripping. In your speech, then, you might opt to arrange the statistics according to recency, saving the most dramatic one for last. The principles of primacy and recency can also be applied to groups of examples or opinions or to any combination of supporting materials.

Specificity

Sometimes your supporting material will range from very specific examples to more general overviews of a situation. You may either offer your specific information first and end with your general statement or make the general statement first and support it with specific evidence.

Complexity

Moving from the simple to the complex is a way to organize subtopics. The same method of organization may also be applied to supporting material. In many situations, it makes sense to start with the simplest ideas, which are easy to understand, and work up to more complex ones.

Soft to Hard Evidence

Supporting material can also be arranged from "soft" to "hard."

■ **Soft evidence** rests on opinion or inference. Hypothetical illustrations, descriptions, explanations, definitions, analogies, and opinions are usually considered soft.
■ **Hard evidence** includes factual examples and statistics.

Actually, it is more accurate to think of soft and hard as two ends of a continuum, with most supporting material falling somewhere in between. The U.S. Surgeon General's analysis of the AIDS crisis, for example, would be placed nearer the hard end of the continuum than would someone's experience of seeing the NAMES Project AIDS Memorial Quilt, even though both would be classified as opinions. The Surgeon General is a more

---

✓ *QuickCheck*
Organizing Your Supporting Material

■ Primacy: most important material first
■ Recency: most important material last
■ Specificity: from specific information to general overview or from general overview to specific information
■ Complexity: from simple to more complex material
■ Soft to hard evidence: from opinion or hypothetical illustration to fact or statistic

credible speaker whose analysis is the result of his or her extensive knowledge of and research into the subject.

Soft to hard organization of supporting material relies chiefly on the principle of recency—that the last statement is remembered best.

Develop Signposts

Once you have organized your notes, you have a logically ordered, fairly complete plan for your speech. But if you tried to deliver the speech at this point, you would find yourself frequently groping for some way to get from one point to the next. Your audience might become frustrated or even confused by your hesitations and awkwardness.

Your next organizational task is to develop **signposts**—words and gestures that allow you to move smoothly from one idea to the next throughout your speech, showing relationships between ideas and emphasizing important points. Three types of signposts can serve as glue to hold your speech together:

1. transitions
2. previews
3. summaries

Transitions

Transitions indicate that a speaker has finished discussing one idea and is moving to another. Transitions may be either verbal or nonverbal. Let's consider some examples of each type.

Verbal Transitions   A speaker can sometimes make a verbal transition simply by repeating a key word from an earlier statement or by using a synonym or a pronoun that refers to an earlier key word or idea. This type of transition is often used to make one sentence flow smoothly into the next. The previous sentence itself is an example: "This type of transition" refers to the sentence that precedes it. Other verbal transitions are words or phrases that show relationships between ideas. Note the italicized transitional phrases in the following examples:

- *In addition to* transitions, previews and summaries are *also* considered to be signposts.
- *Not only* does plastic packaging use up our scarce resources; it contaminates them *as well*.
- *In other words*, as women's roles have changed, they have *also* contributed to this effect.
- *In summary*, Fanny Brice is probably the best remembered star of Ziegfeld's Follies.
- *Therefore*, I recommend that you sign the grievance petition.

Simple enumeration (*first, second, third*) can also point up relationships between ideas and provide transitions.

One type of transitional signpost that can occasionally backfire and do more harm than good is one that signals the end of a speech. *Finally* and *in conclusion* give the audience implicit permission to stop listening, and they often do. If the speech has been too long or has otherwise not gone well, the audience may even audibly express relief.

Better strategies for moving into a conclusion include repeating a key word or phrase, using a synonym or pronoun that refers to a previous idea, offering a final summary, or referring to the introduction of the speech.

Internal previews and summaries, which we will discuss shortly, are yet other ways to provide a verbal transition from one point to the next in your speech. They have the additional advantage of repeating your main ideas, thereby enabling audience members to understand and remember them.

Repetition of key words or ideas, the use of transitional words or phrases, enumeration, and internal previews and summaries all provide verbal transitions from one idea to the next. You may need to experiment with several alternatives before you find the smooth transition you seek in a given instance. If none of these alternatives seems to work well, consider a nonverbal transition.

Nonverbal Transitions   Nonverbal transitions can occur in several ways, sometimes alone and sometimes in combination with verbal transitions. A change in facial expression, a pause, an altered

✓ **QuickCheck**
Verbal Transitions

Strategy	Example
Repeating a key word or using a synonym or pronoun that refers to a key word	*"These problems* cannot be allowed to continue."
Using a transitional word or phrase	*"In addition* to the facts that I've mentioned, we need to consider one further problem."
Enumerating	*"Second,* there has been a rapid increase in the number of accidents reported."
Using internal summaries	"Now that we have discussed the problems caused by illiteracy, let's look at some of the possible solutions."

vocal pitch or speaking rate, and a movement all may indicate a transition.

For example, a speaker talking about the value of cardiopulmonary resuscitation began his speech with a powerful anecdote about a man suffering a heart attack at a party. No one knew how to help, and the man died. The speaker then looked up from his notes and paused, while maintaining eye contact with his audience. His next words were "The real tragedy of Bill Jorgen's death was that it should not have happened." His pause, as well as the words that followed, indicated a transition into the body of the speech. Like this speaker, most good speakers use a combination of verbal and nonverbal transitions to move from one point to another through their speeches.

Previews

One significant difference between writing and public speaking is that public speaking is more repetitive. Audience-centered speakers need to remember that the members of their audiences, unlike readers, cannot go back to review a missed point. As its name indicates, a *preview* is a statement of what is to come. Previews help to ensure that audience members will first anticipate and later remember the important points of a speech. Like transitions, previews also help to provide coherence. Two types of previews are usually used in speeches:

■ the preview statement, or initial preview
■ the internal preview

Initial Previews   The preview statement is a statement of what the main ideas of the speech will be. It is usually presented in conjunction with the central idea as a blueprint for the speech at or near the end of the introduction. Sometimes speakers enumerate their main ideas to identify them even more clearly.

Internal Previews   In addition to using previews near the beginning of their speeches, speakers also use them at various points throughout. These internal previews introduce and outline ideas that will be developed as the speech progresses. As noted, internal previews also serve as transitions.

Sometimes speakers couch internal previews in the form of questions they plan to answer. Note how the question in this example provides an internal preview.

> Now that we know about the problem of hotel security and some of its causes and impacts, the question remains, what can we do, as potential travelers and potential victims, to protect ourselves?[3]

Just as anticipating an idea helps audience members remember it, so mentally answering a question helps them plant the answer firmly in their minds.

Summaries

Like previews, summaries provide additional exposure to a speaker's ideas and can help ensure that audience members will grasp and remember them. Most speakers use two types of summaries:

■ the final summary
■ the internal summary

Final Summary   A final summary occurs just before the end of a speech, often doing double duty as a transition between the body and the conclusion. The final summary is the opposite of the preview statement. The preview statement gives an audience their first exposure to a speaker's main ideas; the final summary gives them their last exposure to those ideas.

Internal Summary   Internal summaries, as their name suggests, occur within and throughout a speech. They are often used after two or three points have been discussed, to keep those points fresh in the minds of the audience as the speech progresses.

Like internal previews, internal summaries can help provide transitions. In fact, internal summaries are often used in combination with internal previews to form transitions between major points and ideas. Each of the following examples makes clear what has just been discussed in the speech as well as what will be discussed next:

> Now that we've seen how radon can get into our homes, let's take a look at some of the effects that it can have on our health once it begins to build.[4]

> So now that we are aware of the severity of the disease and unique reasons for college students to be concerned, we will look at some steps we need to take to combat bacterial meningitis.[5]

> It seems as though everyone is saying that something should be done about NutraSweet. It should be retested. Well, now that it is here on the market, what can we do to see that it does get investigated further?[6]

Supplement Signposts with Presentation Aids

Transitions, summaries, and previews are the "glue" that holds a speech together. Such signposts can help you achieve a coherent flow of ideas and help your audience remember those ideas. Unfortunately, however, you cannot guarantee that your audience will be attentive to your signposts. It is possible for your listeners to be so distracted by internal or external noise that they fail to hear or process even your most carefully planned verbal signposts.

One way in which you can increase the likelihood of your listeners' attending to your signposting is to prepare and use presentation aids to supplement your signposts. For example, you could display on an overhead transparency a bulleted or numbered outline of your main ideas as you initially preview them in your introduction, and again as you summarize them in your conclusion.

Some speakers like to use one transparency or PowerPoint slide for each main point. Transitions between points are emphasized as the speaker displays the next transparency or slide. Especially if your speech is long or its organization is complex, you can help your audience remember your main points if you provide visual support for your signposts.

QuickCheck
Develop Signposts

- Use verbal transitions to move from one point to another.
- Repeat key words and ideas.
- Enumerate selected points.
- Provide an initial preview.
- Include internal previews.
- Provide internal summaries.
- Include a final summary.
- Use nonverbal transitions.

A Question of Ethics

In recent years, people have become increasingly conscious of the ways in which our language gives the impression that we are referring only to men when it is more appropriate to refer to both men and women. Has political correctness gotten out of hand? Are we becoming too sensitive to gender issues in our public dialogue? Or are we not sensitive enough? Explain your answer.

Chapter 12

Developing an Introduction

Your speech introduction signals the arrival of your message to your listeners and is vital to achieving your communication goal.

Understand the Purposes of Introductions

Although it makes up only about 10 percent of the total speech you deliver, the introduction provides audiences with important first impressions of speaker and speech. This is too important to the overall success of your speech to be left to chance or last-minute preparation.

Your task as a speaker is to ensure that your introduction convinces your audience to listen to you. Specifically, a good introduction must perform five important functions:

1. Get the audience's attention.
2. Introduce the subject.
3. Give the audience a reason to listen.
4. Establish your credibility.
5. Preview your main ideas.

Get the Audience's Attention

A key purpose of the introduction is to gain favorable attention for your speech. Because listeners form their first impressions of a speech quickly, if the introduction does not capture their attention and cast the speech in a favorable light, the rest of the speech may be wasted on them.

Favorable attention is emphasized for a good reason. It is possible to gain an audience's attention but in so doing to alienate them or disgust them so that they become irritated instead of interested in what you have to say.

Be creative in your speech introductions. But also use common sense in deciding how best to gain the favorable attention of your audience. Alienating them is even worse than boring them.

Introduce the Subject

The most obvious purpose of an introduction is to introduce the subject of a speech. Within a few seconds after you begin your speech, the audience should have a pretty good idea of what you are going to talk about.

The best way to ensure that your introduction does indeed introduce the subject of your speech is to include a statement of your central idea in the introduction.

Give the Audience a Reason to Listen

After you have captured the attention of your audience and introduced the topic, you have to give the audience some reason to want to listen to the rest of your speech. An unmotivated listener quickly tunes out. You can help establish listening motivation by showing the members of your audience how the topic affects them directly.

One criterion for determining the effectiveness of your supporting material is *proximity*, the degree to which the information affects your listeners directly. Just as proximity is important to supporting materials, it is also important to speech introductions. "This concerns me" is a powerful reason to listen.

It does not matter so much *how* or *when* you demonstrate proximity. But it is essential that you do at some point establish that your topic is of vital personal concern to your listeners.

Establish Your Credibility

Credibility is a speaker's believability. A credible speaker is one whom the audience judges to be a believable authority and a competent speaker. A credible speaker is also someone the audience believes they can trust.

As you begin your speech, you should be mindful of your listeners' attitudes toward you. When thinking of your listeners, ask yourself, "Why should they listen to me? What is my background with respect to the topic? Am I personally committed to the issues about which I am going to speak?"

Many people have so much admiration for a political or religious figure, an athlete, or an entertainer that they sacrifice time, energy, and money to hear the celebrity speak. Ordinary people cannot take their own credibility for granted when they speak. If you can establish your credibility early in a speech, it will help motivate your audience to listen.

1. Be well prepared and appear confident. Speaking fluently while maintaining eye contact does much to convey a sense of confidence. If you seem to have confidence in yourself, your audience will have confidence in you.

✔ QuickCheck
Purposes of Introductions

Purpose	Method
Get the audience's attention.	Use an illustration, a startling fact or statistic, a quotation, humor, a question, a reference to a historical event or to a recent event, a personal reference, a reference to the occasion, or a reference to a preceding speech.
Introduce the subject.	Present your central idea to your audience.
Give the audience a reason to listen.	Tell your listeners how the topic directly affects them.
Establish your credibility.	Offer your credentials. Tell your listeners about your commitment to the topic.
Preview your main ideas.	Tell your audience what you are going to tell them.

2. Tell the audience of your personal experience with your topic. Instead of considering you boastful, most audience members will listen to you with respect.

Preview Your Main Ideas

A final purpose of the introduction is to preview the main ideas of your speech. The preview statement usually comes near the end of the introduction, included in or immediately following a statement of the central idea. The preview statement allows your listeners to anticipate the main ideas of your speech, which in turn helps ensure that they will remember those ideas after the speech.

A preview statement is a signpost. Just as signs posted along a highway tell you what is coming up, a signpost in your speech tells the listeners what to expect by enumerating the ideas or points that you plan to present. Identifying your main ideas helps organize the message and enhances listeners' learning.

Write an Effective Introduction

With a little practice, you will be able to write satisfactory central ideas and preview statements. There are several effective methods for developing speech introductions. Not every method is appropriate for every speech, but chances are that you can discover among these alternatives at least one type of introduction to fit the topic and purpose of your speech, whatever they might be.

Use Illustrations or Anecdotes

An illustration or **anecdote** can provide the basis for an effective speech introduction. In fact, if you have an especially compelling illustration that you had planned to use in the body of the speech, you might do well to use it in your introduction instead. A relevant and interesting anecdote will introduce your subject and almost invariably gain an audience's attention. And a personal illustration can help establish your credibility.

If a topic does not lend itself to personal illustrations, illustrations drawn from secondary sources can also be used effectively.

Provide Startling Facts or Statistics

A second method of introducing a speech is to use a startling fact or statistic. Startling an audience with the extent of a situation or problem invariably catches their attention and motivates them to listen further, as well as helping them remember afterward what you had to say.

Use Quotations

Using an appropriate quotation to introduce a speech is a common practice. Often a past writer or speaker has expressed an opinion on your topic that is more authoritative, comprehensive, or memorable than what you can say.

Although a quote can effectively introduce a speech, do not fall into the lazy habit of turning to a collection of quotations every time you need an introduction. There are so many other interesting, and sometimes better, ways to introduce a speech that quotes should be used only if they are extremely interesting, compelling, or very much to the point.

Use Humor

Humor, handled well, can be a wonderful way to get an audience's attention. It can help relax your audience and win their goodwill for the rest of the speech.

If your audience is linguistically diverse or composed primarily of listeners whose first language is not English, you may want to choose an introduction strategy other than humor. Because much humor is created by verbal plays on words, people who do not speak English as their native language may not perceive the humor in an anecdote or quip that you intended to be funny. And humor rarely translates well.

Just as certain audiences may preclude your use of a humorous introduction, so may certain subjects. It would hardly be appropriate to open a speech on world hunger, for example, with a funny story. Nor would it be appropriate to use humor in a talk on certain serious crimes. Used with discretion, however, humor can provide a lively, interesting, and appropriate introduction for many speeches.

Ask Questions

Questions are commonly combined with another method of introduction. Either by themselves or in tandem with another method of introduction, questions can provide effective openings for speeches. When using a question to open a speech, you will generally use a **rhetorical question**, the kind you don't expect an answer to. Nevertheless, your listeners will probably try to answer it mentally. Questions prompt the audience's mental participation in your introduction. Such participation is an excellent way to ensure their continuing attention to your speech. The main advantage of asking a question as an introductory technique is to "hook" the audience by getting them to engage in a mental dialogue with you.

Refer to Historical Events

Perhaps you could begin a speech by drawing a relationship between an historic event that happened on this day and your speech objective. To discover anniversaries of historic events, you can consult Jane M. Hatch's *The American Book of Days* or *Anniversaries and Holidays* by Ruth W. Gregory. Finally, many newspapers have a section that identifies key events that occurred on "this day in history." Your historical reference should be linked clearly to the purpose of your speech.

Refer to Recent Events

If your topic is timely, a reference to a recent event can be a good way to open your speech. An opening taken from a recent news story can take the form of an illustration, a startling statistic, or even a quotation. Referring to a recent event increases your credibility by showing that you are knowledgeable about current affairs.

"Recent" does not necessarily mean a story that broke just last week or even last month. An event that occurred within the past year or so can be considered recent. Even a particularly significant event that is slightly older can qualify.

Use Personal References

A reference to yourself can take several forms. You might reveal your reason for interest in the topic.

You might express appreciation at having been asked to speak. Or you might share a personal experience. Although personal references take a variety of forms, what they do best, in all circumstances, is to establish a bond between you and your audience.

Refer to the Occasion

References to the occasion are often made at weddings, birthday parties, dedication ceremonies, and other such events. It is customary to make a personal reference as well, placing oneself in the occasion. Referring to the occasion can also be combined with other methods of introduction, such as an illustration or a rhetorical question.

Refer to Preceding Speeches

If your speech is one of several being presented on the same occasion, you will usually not know until shortly before your own speech what other speakers will say. Few experiences will make your stomach sink faster than hearing a speaker just ahead of you speak on your topic. Worse still, that speaker may even use some of the same supporting materials you had planned to use. When this happens, you must decide on the spot whether referring to one of these previous speeches will be better than using the introduction you originally prepared.

It may be wise to refer to a preceding speech when another speaker has spoken on a topic so

---

✔ QuickCheck
Techniques for Developing an Effective Introduction

- ■ Use an illustration or anecdote.
- ■ Use a personal anecdote to establish your credibility.
- ■ Present startling facts or statistics.
- ■ Use an appropriate quotation.
- ■ Use humor.
- ■ Begin with a rhetorical question.
- ■ Refer to historical events or recent events.
- ■ Use personal references.
- ■ Refer to the occasion or to preceding speeches.

related to your own that you can draw an analogy. In a sense, your introduction becomes a transition from that earlier speech to yours.

A Question of Ethics

Louis Howe, aide to President Franklin D. Roosevelt, is now thought to have written the famous line from Roosevelt's first inaugural address: "The only thing we have to fear is fear itself." Is it ethical to credit Roosevelt with this line?

Chapter 13

Developing a Conclusion

An effective conclusion is as vital to achieving your communication goal as an introduction. Just as most fireworks displays end with a grand finale, your speech should end, not necessarily with fireworks, but with a conclusion worthy of your well-crafted message.

Understand the Purposes of Conclusions

Your introduction creates an important first impression; your conclusion leaves an equally important final impression. Long after you finish speaking, your audience is likely to remember the effect, if not the content, of your closing remarks.

An effective conclusion will serve four purposes:

1. Summarize the speech.
2. Reemphasize the main idea in a memorable way.
3. Motivate the audience to respond.
4. Provide closure.

Summarize the Speech

A conclusion is your last chance to repeat your main ideas for the audience. Most speakers summarize their speech in the first part of the conclusion or perhaps even in a transition between the body of the speech and its conclusion.

Reemphasize the Central Idea in a Memorable Way

Another purpose of a conclusion is to restate the central idea of the speech in a memorable way. The end of your speech is your last chance to impress the central idea on your audience. Do it in such a way that they cannot help but remember it.

Motivate the Audience to Respond

One of your tasks in an effective introduction is to motivate your audience to listen to your speech. Creating motivation is also a necessary function of an effective conclusion—not motivation to listen, but motivation to respond to the speech in some way. If your speech is informative, you may want the audience to think about the topic or to research it further. If your speech is persuasive, you may want your audience to take some sort of appropriate action—write a letter, buy a product, make a telephone call, or get involved in a cause. In fact, an *action* step is essential to the persuasive organizational strategy called the *motivated sequence*. If audience members feel that they are or could be personally involved or affected, they are more likely to respond to your message.

Provide Closure

Probably the most obvious purpose of a conclusion is to let the audience know that the speech has ended. Speeches have to "sound finished."

You can attain **closure** both verbally and nonverbally. Verbal techniques include using such transi-

---

✓ *QuickCheck*
Purposes of Conclusions

Purpose	Technique
Summarize your speech.	Tell the audience what you told them.
Reemphasize the main idea in a memorable way.	Use a well-worded closing phrase. Provide a final illustration, quotation, or personal reference.
Motivate the audience to respond.	Urge the audience to think about the topic or to research it further. Suggest appropriate action.
Provide closure.	Use verbal and nonverbal transitions. Refer to your introduction.

tions as "finally," "for my last point," and "in conclusion." Use care in signaling your conclusion,
however. Such a cue gives an audience unspoken
permission to tune out. A concluding transition
needs to be followed quickly by the final statement
of the speech. You can also signal closure with one
or more nonverbal cues:

- pausing between the body of your speech and
  its conclusion
- slowing your speaking rate
- moving out from behind the podium to make a
  final impassioned plea to your audience
- indicating with falling vocal inflection that you
  are making your final statement

Develop an Effective Conclusion

Effective conclusions may employ illustrations,
quotations, personal references, or any of the other
methods used for introductions.

- **Illustrations or anecdotes.** An illustration
  or anecdote can provide the basis for an
  effective conclusion. It can help the audience
  focus on the main point of your speech and
  hold their attention. A personal illustration
  used in a conclusion will also reinforce your
  credibility.
- **Startling facts or statistics.** Startling facts and
  statistics can help your audience remember afterward what you had to say.
- **Quotations.** Just as using an appropriate quotation to introduce a speech is a common practice, so too is using a quotation to conclude a
  speech.
- **Humor.** A humorous conclusion puts the audience in a relaxed frame of mind so that they
  leave with a sense of enjoyment at what you
  have told them and goodwill toward you as the
  speaker.
- **Questions.** Using a rhetorical question to open
  a speech focuses the audience's attention. Using

a rhetorical question in your conclusion keeps your speech in the audience's mind as they try to answer the question.

In addition, there are at least two other distinct ways of concluding a speech: with a reference to the introduction and with an inspirational appeal or challenge.

Refer to the Introduction

Finishing a story, answering a rhetorical question, and reminding the audience of the startling fact or statistic you presented in the introduction are excellent ways to provide closure. A related introduction and conclusion provide unified support for the ideas in the middle.

Alluding to the introduction in your conclusion will make your speech memorable and motivate the audience to respond.

Issue an Inspirational Appeal or Challenge

Another way to end your speech is to issue an inspirational appeal or challenge to your listeners, rousing them to a high emotional pitch. The conclusion becomes the climax.

An inspiring conclusion should reemphasize your central ideas in a memorable way, motivate your audience to respond, and provide closure to your speech.

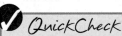

QuickCheck
Techniques for Developing an Effective Conclusion

- ■ Use an illustration or anecdote.
- ■ Use a personal anecdote to reinforce your credibility.
- ■ Present startling facts or statistics.
- ■ Use an appropriate quotation.
- ■ Use humor.
- ■ Use a rhetorical question.
- ■ Refer to the introduction.
- ■ Issue an inspirational appeal or challenge.

A Question of Ethics

Brenda, who is from a rural area in Kentucky, is now a student at a prestigious college in Boston, Massachusetts. She has to deliver a speech to her classmates. Is it ethical for her to deliver her speech using the Boston dialect, even though she uses her original speech patterns with friends and when she returns to Kentucky? Why or why not?

Chapter 14

Outlining and Editing Your Speech

Most speakers find that they need to prepare two types of outline:

1. a preparation outline
2. a delivery outline

Develop a Preparation Outline

Although few speeches are written in paragraph form, most speakers develop a detailed **preparation outline** that includes the following:

- main ideas
- subpoints
- supporting material
- the speech's specific purpose
- introduction
- blueprint
- conclusion
- signposts

To begin your outlining task, you might try a technique known as **mapping** or clustering. Write on a sheet of paper all the main ideas, subpoints, and supporting material for the speech. Then use geometric shapes and arrows to indicate the logical relationships among them.

Whatever technique you choose to begin your outline, your ultimate goal is to produce a plan that lets you judge the unity and coherence of your speech, see how well the parts fit together, and see how smoothly the speech flows. Your finished preparation outline will help you make sure that all main ideas and subpoints are clearly and logically related and adequately supported.

Write Your Preparation Outline in Complete Sentences

Unless you write your preparation outline in complete sentences, you will have trouble judging the coherence of the speech. Moreover, complete sentences will help during your early rehearsals. If you write cryptic phrases, you may not remember what they mean.

Use Standard Outline Form

Although you did not have to use standard outline form when you began to outline your ideas, you need to do so now. **Standard outline form** lets you see at a glance the exact relationships among various main ideas, subpoints, and supporting material in your speech. It is an important tool for evaluating your speech. To produce a correct outline, follow these instructions.

I. First main idea
   A. First subpoint of I
   B. Second subpoint of I
      1. First subpoint of B
      2. Second subpoint of B
         a. First subpoint of 2
         b. Second subpoint of 2
II. Second main idea

Properly indent main ideas, subpoints, and supporting material.

Use at least two subpoints, if any, for each main idea. Logic dictates that you cannot divide anything into one part. If, for example, you have only one piece of supporting material, incorporate it into the subpoint or main idea that it supports. If you have only one subpoint, incorporate it into the main idea above it.

If you have more than five subpoints, you may want to place some of them under another point. An audience will remember your ideas more easily if they are divided into blocks of no more than five.

It is unlikely that you will subdivide beyond the level of lowercase letters (a., b., etc.) in most speech outlines, but next would come numbers in parentheses and then lowercase letters in parentheses.

Write and Label Your Specific Purpose at the Top of Your Outline

Do not work the specific purpose into the outline itself. Instead, label it and place it at the top of the outline. Your specific purpose can serve as a yardstick by which to measure the relevance of each main idea, subpoint, and piece of supporting material. Everything in the speech should contribute to your purpose.

Add the Blueprint, Key Signposts, and Introduction and Conclusion to Your Outline

Place the introduction after the statement of your specific purpose, the blueprint immediately following the introduction, the conclusion after the outline of the body of the speech, and other signposts within the outline.

Analyze Your Preparation Outline

Once you have completed your preparation outline, you can use it to help you analyze and possibly revise the speech. The following questions can help you in this critical thinking task.

- **Does the speech as outlined fulfill the purpose you have specified?** If not, revise the specific purpose or change the direction and content of the speech itself.
- **Are the main ideas logical extensions (natural divisions, reasons, or steps) of the central idea?** If not, revise either the central idea or the main ideas. Like the first question, this one relates to the unity of the speech and is critical to making certain the speech "fits together" as a whole.
- **Do the signposts enhance the comfortable flow of each idea into the next?** If not, change or add previews, summaries, or transitions. If signposts are not adequate, the speech will lack coherence.

> ✓ *QuickCheck*
> *Analyze Your Preparation Outline*
>
> ■ Does the speech as outlined fulfill your specific purpose?
> ■ Are the main ideas logical extensions of the central idea?
> ■ Do signposts enhance the comfortable flow of each idea into the next?
> ■ Does each subpoint provide support for the point under which it falls?
> ■ Is your outline form correct?

■ **Does each subpoint provide support for the point under which it falls?** If not, then either move or delete the subpoint.

■ **Is your outline form correct?**

Having considered these five questions, you are ready to rehearse your speech using the preparation outline as your first set of notes.

Edit Your Speech

Often when you rehearse your speech using your preparation outline, you discover that you have too much information and you have to cut your speech. Here are a few tips to help you edit a speech that is too long.

■ **Review your specific purpose.** With your audience in mind, take a hard look at your specific purpose statement. If, for example, your purpose was to have your audience be able to list and describe five advantages of staying on standard time rather than switching to daylight savings time, you may have to be less ambitious and describe only three—pick your best three.

■ **Consider your audience.** What do audience members really need to hear? Which parts of your message will be most and least interesting to your listeners? Cut those portions that are of least potential interest.

■ **Simply say it.**
  ■ Eliminate phrases that add no meaning to your message, such as "In my opinion" (just

state the opinion) or "Before I begin, I'd like to say" (you've already begun—just say it).

- Avoid narrating your speaking technique. There is no need to say, "Here's an interesting story that I think you will like." Just tell the story.

- Avoid long phrases when a short one will do. Here are some examples:

Instead of saying	Say
So, for that reason	So
Due to the fact	Because
But at the same time	But
In the final analysis	Finally

- **Keep only the best supporting material.** Stories and other types of supporting material help you make your point and maintain interest, so don't reduce your speech to a bare bones outline. But scan your speech for supporting material that can be cut.

- **Ask a listener to help you cut.** Ask a friend to listen to your speech and help you note parts that are less than clear, powerful, or convincing.

- **Look at your introduction and conclusion.** Each should consume no more than about 10 percent of your speaking time. If either exceeds this guideline, see if you can shorten it.

Prepare a Delivery Outline

As you rehearse your speech, you will find that you need your preparation outline less and less. Both the structure and the content of your speech will become set in your mind. At this point, you are ready to prepare a **delivery outline**.

A delivery outline, as the name implies, is meant to give you all you will need to present your speech in the way you have planned and rehearsed. However, it should not be so detailed that it encourages you to read rather than speak to your audience. Here are a few tips:

- **Make the outline as brief as possible.** Write in single words or short phrases rather than complete sentences.

- **Include the introduction and conclusion in much shortened form.** You may feel more comfortable if you have the first and last sentences written in full in front of you. Writing out the first sentence eliminates any fear of a mental block at the outset of your speech. And writing a complete last sentence ensures a smooth ending to your speech and a good final impression.
- **Include supporting material and signposts.** Write out statistics, direct quotations, and key signposts. Writing key signposts in full ensures that you will not grope awkwardly for a way to move from one point to the next. After you have rehearsed the speech several times, you will know where you are most likely to falter and can add or omit written transitions as needed.
- **Do not include your purpose statement in your delivery outline.**
- **Use standard outline form.** That will allow you to easily find the exact point or piece of supporting material you are seeking when you glance down at your notes.

Rehearse Your Delivery Outline

As you rehearse the speech, you will probably continue to revise the delivery outline. You may decide to cut further or to revise signposts. Your outline should provide just enough information to ensure smooth delivery. It should not burden you with unnecessary notes or compel you to look down too often during the speech.

Create Speaking Notes

Many speakers find paper difficult to handle quietly, so they transfer their delivery outlines to note cards. Note cards are small enough to hold in one hand, if necessary, and stiff enough not to rustle. Two or three note cards will give you enough space for a delivery outline; the exact number of cards you use will depend on the length of your speech. Following are some hints for preparing your note cards.

- Type or print your outline neatly on one side, making sure that the letters and words are large enough to read easily.

- You may find it helpful to plan your note cards according to logical blocks of material, using one note card for the introduction, one or two for the body, and one for the conclusion.
- Plan so that you do not have to shuffle note cards midsentence.
- Number the note cards to prevent a fiasco if your notes get out of order.

Instead of using an outline, you might use an alternative format for your speaking notes. For example, you could use a map, or you could use a combination of words, pictures, and symbols. Whatever form your notes take, they should make sense to *you*.

A final addition to your speaking notes will be delivery cues and reminders, such as "Louder," "Pause," or "Move in front of podium." You could write your delivery cues in the margins by hand or, if the entire outline is handwritten, in ink of a different color.

A Question of Ethics

Karl is working in a group with four other people. One group member, José, seems to have taken charge and is making assignments for other group members. Although José's leadership skills are helping to get a lot accomplished, Karl resents his overly zealous efforts to take charge. Should Karl keep quiet and just go along with José, or should he speak up and express his concerns about José's actions?

Chapter 15

Using Words Well

Using language accurately, clearly, and effectively can be a challenge. You must speak clearly and communicate ideas accurately. At the same time, you must present those ideas in such a way that your audience will listen to, remember, and perhaps act on what you have to say.

Oral versus Written Language Style

There are at least three major differences between oral and written language styles.

- **Oral style is more personal.** When speaking, you can look your listeners in the eye and talk to them directly. If you see that they don't like or don't understand what you are saying, you can adjust your statements and explanations to gain greater acceptance. You and your audience can interact, something a writer and a reader cannot do. As a speaker, you are likely to use more pronouns (*I, you*) than you would in writing.

- **Oral style is less formal.** Written communication often uses rather formal language and structure. Spoken communication, by contrast, is usually less formal, characterized by shorter words and phrases and less complex sentence structures. Speakers generally use many more contractions and colloquialisms than writers.

- **Oral style is more repetitious.** When you don't understand something you are reading, you can stop and reread a passage, look up unfamiliar words in the dictionary, or ask someone for help. When you're listening to a speech, those opportunities aren't available. For this reason, an oral style is and should be more repetitious. When you organize a speech, you preview main ideas in your introduction, develop your ideas in the body of the speech, and summarize these same ideas in the conclusion. You build in repetition to make sure that your listener will grasp your message.

Use Words Effectively

Your challenge as a speaker is to use words well so that you can communicate your intended message. Ideally, language should be specific and concrete, simple, and correct.

Use Specific, Concrete Words

Specific words are often concrete words, which appeal to one of our five senses, whereas general words are often abstract words, which refer to ideas or qualities. A linguistic theory known as *general semantics* holds that the more concrete your words, the clearer your communication.

Specific, concrete nouns create memorable images; likewise, specific, concrete verbs can be especially effective. When searching for a specific, concrete word, you may want to consult a **thesaurus**. But in searching for an alternative word, do not feel that you have to choose an obscure or unusual term to vary your description. Simple language can often evoke a vivid image for your listeners.

Use Simple Words

The best language is often the simplest. Your words should be immediately understandable to your listeners. Don't try to impress them with jargon and pompous language. Used wisely, simple words communicate with great power and precision.

Use Words Correctly

Your effectiveness with your audience depends in part on your ability to use the English language correctly. If you are unsure of a grammatical rule, seek assistance from a good English usage handbook. If you are unsure of a word's pronunciation, use a dictionary. Language operates on two levels.

1. The **denotation** of a word is its literal meaning, the definition you find in a dictionary. For example, the denotation of the word *notorious* is "famous."
2. The **connotation** of a word is the meaning we associate with the word, based on our past experiences. *Notorious* connotes fame resulting from some dire deed. *Notorious* and *famous* are not really interchangeable. It is just as important to consider the connotations of the words you use as it is to consider the denotations.

Sometimes connotations are private. For example, the word *table* is defined denotatively as a piece of furniture consisting of a smooth, flat slab affixed on legs. But when you think of the word *table*, you may think of the old oak table your grandparents used to have. This is a private connotation of the word, a unique meaning based on your own past experiences. Private meanings are difficult to predict, but as a public speaker you should be aware of the possibility of triggering audience members' private connotations. This awareness is particularly important when you are discussing highly emotional or controversial topics.

And finally, if your audience includes people whose first language is not English, to whom the nuances of connotation may not be readily apparent, it may be necessary to explain your intentions in more detail, rather than relying on word associations.

Adapt Your Language Style to Diverse Listeners

To communicate successfully with the diverse group of listeners who comprise your audience, make sure your language is understandable, appropriate, and unbiased.

Use Understandable Language

Even if you and all your public-speaking classmates speak English, you probably speak many varieties of the language.

- Perhaps some of your classmates speak in an **ethnic vernacular**, such as "Spanglish," the combination of English and Spanish often heard near the United States–Mexico border.
- Some of you may reflect where you grew up by your use of **regionalisms**, words or phrases specific to one part of the country but rarely used in quite the same way in other places.
- Others of you may frequently use **jargon**, the specialized language of your profession or hobby.

If you give a speech to others who share your ethnic, regional, or professional background, you can communicate successfully with them using these specialized varieties of English. However, if you give a speech to an audience as diverse as the members of your public-speaking class, use **standard U.S. English**. Standard U.S. English is the language taught by schools and used in the media, business, and the government in the United States. "Standard" does not imply that standard U.S. English is inherently right and all other forms are wrong, only that it conforms to a standard that most speakers of U.S. English will readily understand—even though they may represent a variety of ethnic, regional, and professional backgrounds.

Use Appropriate Language

A speaker whose language defames any subgroup—people of particular ethnic, racial, and religious backgrounds or sexual orientations; women; people with disabilities—or whose language might be otherwise considered offensive or risqué runs a great risk of antagonizing audience members.

Use Unbiased Language

Even speakers who would never dream of using overtly offensive language may find it difficult to avoid language that more subtly stereotypes or discriminates. Sexist language falls largely into this second category.

For example, not many years ago, a singular masculine pronoun (*he, him, his*) was the accepted way to refer to a person of unspecified sex:

Everyone should bring his book to class tomorrow.

This usage is now considered sexist and unacceptable. Instead, you may include both a masculine and a feminine pronoun:

Everyone should bring his or her book to class tomorrow.

Or, you may reword the sentence so that it is plural and thus gender neutral:

All students should bring their books to class tomorrow.

Also now considered sexist is the use of the masculine noun *man* to refer to all people. You should monitor your use of such masculine nouns as *waiter*, *chairman*, *fireman*, and *Congressman*. Instead choose such gender-neutral alternatives as *server*, *chair*, *firefighter*, and *member of Congress*.

In addition, you should avoid sexist language that patronizes or stereotypes people. It is not always easy to avoid biased language. For example, suppose that Dr. Pierce is a young, African American, female M.D. If you don't mention her age, race, and gender, you may reinforce your listeners' stereotypical image of a physician as middle-aged, white, and male. But if you *do* mention these factors, you may be suspected of implying that Dr. Pierce's achievement is unusual. There is no easy answer to this dilemma or others like it. You will have to consider your audience, your purpose, and the occasion in deciding how best to identify Dr. Pierce.

✔ QuickCheck
Use Words Well

■ Did you use specific, concrete words?
■ Did you use the English language correctly?
■ Is your language immediately understandable to your listeners?
■ Is your language appropriate for your audience?
■ Is your language unbiased?

Craft Memorable Word Structures

Memorable speeches are stylistically distinctive. They create arresting images. And they have what a marketing-communication specialist has termed "ear appeal."

Create Figurative Images

One way to make your message memorable is to use figures of speech to create arresting images. A **figure of speech** deviates from the ordinary, expected meanings of words to make a description or comparison unique, vivid, and memorable. Common figures of speech include metaphors, similes, and personification.

Use Metaphors and Similes   A **metaphor** is an implied comparison. A **simile** is a less direct comparison that includes the word *like* or *as*.

Speakers often turn to metaphor and simile in times that are especially momentous or overwhelming—times when literal language seems insufficient. In the hours and days after the September 11, 2001, terrorist attacks on the United States, various speakers used metaphorical phrases, including "one more circle of Dante's hell," "nuclear winter," and "the crater of a volcano" to describe the site of the destroyed World Trade Center in New York.[1]

Use Personification   **Personification** is the attribution of human qualities to inanimate things or ideas.

Create Drama

Another way you can make phrases and sentences memorable is to use them to create drama in your speech—to keep the audience in suspense or to catch them slightly off guard by saying something in a way that differs from the way they expected you to say it.

Sentence Length   Use a short sentence to express a vitally important thought. Short, simple sentences can have much the same power as short, simple words.

Omission   Use **omission**. Leave out a word or phrase that the audience expects to hear. But, of course, the words you leave out must be understood by your listeners.

Inversion   Use **inversion**. Reverse the normal word order of a phrase or sentence. John F. Kennedy used inversion by changing the usual subject-verb-object sentence pattern to object-subject-verb in this brief declaration from his inaugural speech: "This much we pledge."[2]

Suspension   Use a key word or phrase at the end of a sentence, rather than at the beginning. When you read a mystery novel, you are held in suspense until you reach the end and learn "who done it." The stylistic technique of verbal suspension does something similar.

Advertisers use the technique of **suspension** frequently. A few years ago, the Coca-Cola Company used suspension as the cornerstone of its worldwide advertising campaign. Rather than saying "Coke goes better with everything," the copywriter decided to stylize the message by making Coke the last word in the sentence. The slogan became "Things go better with Coke." The stylized version was more memorable because it used language in an unexpected way.

Create Cadence

Rhythms are memorable. Take advantage of language rhythms, not by speaking in singsong patterns, but by using such stylistic devices as parallelism, antithesis, repetition, and alliteration.

Parallelism   **Parallelism** occurs when two or more clauses or sentences have the same grammatical pattern. When he delivered the Phi Beta Kappa oration at Harvard in 1837, Ralph Waldo Emerson cast these simple expressions in parallel structures:

> We will walk on our own feet; we will work with our own hands; we will speak our own minds.[3]

Antithesis   The word *antithesis* means "opposition." In language style, a sentence that uses **antithesis** has two parts with parallel structures but contrasting meanings. Speakers have long realized the dramatic potential of antithesis. In Franklin Roosevelt's first inaugural address, he declared,

> Our true destiny is not to be ministered unto but to minister to ourselves and to our fellow men.[4]

An antithetical statement is a good way to end a speech. The cadence will make the statement memorable.

Repetition Repetition of a key word or phrase gives rhythm and power to a message and makes it memorable. In a speech honoring the Tuskegee Airmen and addressing issues of race in the modern U.S. military, former Deputy Secretary of Defense Rudy de Leon claimed that recruitment of minorities is only one part of the task facing the military:

> *Our job is not finished* if we fail to recognize that each generation has its own unique problems and perceptions when it comes to race and ethnicity.
>
> We can ensure our rules and regulations are clear and fair. But *our job is not finished* if people believe that those rules and regulations are not being enforced fairly.
>
> *Our job is not finished* if the rules and regulations work for those in uniform, but they do not reach people in our civilian workforce.[5] [emphasis added]

The repeated mantra, "our job is not finished," rings in one's mind long after hearing or reading the passage.

Alliteration Alliteration is the repetition of a consonant sound (usually an initial consonant) several times in a phrase, clause, or sentence (for example, discipline and direction; confidence and courage). Alliteration adds cadence to a thought. Used sparingly, alliteration can add power to your rhetoric.

A Question of Ethics

Tom is preparing a speech on driver safety. He plans to begin his speech with a series of graphic pictures showing traffic-accident victims who were maimed or killed because they did not use safety belts. Is it ethical to show graphic images that arouse audience fears?

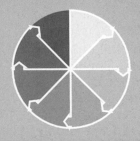

Part 5

Delivering a
Speech

Chapter 16

Methods of Delivery

There are four basic methods of delivery from which a speaker can choose: manuscript speaking, memorized speaking, impromptu speaking, and extemporaneous speaking.

Manuscript Speaking

Reading is usually a poor way to deliver a speech. Although it may provide some insurance against forgetting the speech, **manuscript speaking** is rarely done well enough to be interesting.

However, some speeches should be read. One advantage of reading from a manuscript is that you can choose words very carefully when dealing with a sensitive and critical issue. When possible, during times of crisis, statements to the press by government or business leaders should be carefully crafted rather than tossed off casually. An inaccurate or misspoken statement could have serious consequences.

According to Roger Ailes, a media consultant to Republican presidents and governors, to ensure maximum eye contact if you do have to read from a manuscript, you should type your speech in short, easy-to-scan phrases on the upper two thirds of the paper so that you do not have to look too far down into your notes.[1] Make eye contact at the ends of sentences. He also recommends that you not read a speech too quickly. Finally, use your index finger to keep your place in the manuscript.

The key to giving an effective manuscript speech is to sound as though you are not giving a manuscript speech.

- Speak with vocal variation—vary the rhythm, inflection, and pace of your delivery.

- Be familiar enough with your manuscript that you can make as much eye contact with your audience as possible.
- Use gestures and movement to add interest and emphasis to your message.

Memorized Speaking

Memorized speaking sounds stiff, stilted, and over-rehearsed. You also run the risk of forgetting parts of your speech and awkwardly searching for words in front of your audience. And you won't be able to make on-the-spot adaptations to your listeners if your speech is memorized. Memorized speaking does, however, have the advantage of allowing you to have maximum eye contact with the audience.

The differences between speaking and writing are evident in a memorized speech, just as they can be heard in a manuscript speech. If you are accepting an award, introducing a speaker, making announcements, or delivering other brief remarks, however, a memorized delivery style is sometimes acceptable. But, as with manuscript speaking, you must take care to make your presentation sound lively and interesting.

Impromptu Speaking

You have undoubtedly already delivered many impromptu presentations. Your response to a question posed by a teacher in class and an unrehearsed rebuttal to a comment made by a colleague during a meeting are examples of impromptu presentations. The impromptu method is often described as "thinking on your feet" or "speaking off the cuff." The advantage of **impromptu speaking** is that you can speak informally and maintain direct eye contact with the audience. But unless you are extremely talented or have learned and practiced the techniques of impromptu speaking, your speech itself will be unimpressive. An impromptu speech usually lacks logical organization and thorough research.

When you are called on to deliver an improvised or impromptu speech, the following guidelines can help ease you through it.

- **Consider your audience.** Who are the members of your audience? What are their common characteristics and interests? What do they know about your topic? What do they expect you to say? What is the occasion of your speech? A quick mental review of these questions will help ensure that even impromptu remarks are audience-centered.

- **Be brief.** Your audience knows the situation and will not expect or even want a lengthy discourse. One to three minutes is a realistic time frame for most impromptu situations. Some spur-of-the-moment remarks, such as press statements, may be even shorter.

- **Organize!** Even off-the-cuff remarks need not falter or ramble. Effective impromptu speakers still organize their ideas into an introduction, body, and conclusion. Consider organizing your points using a simple strategy such as chronological order or a topical pattern. A variation on the chronological pattern is the past, present, future model of addressing an issue. You organize your impromptu speech by discussing (1) what has happened in the past, (2) what is happening now, and (3) what may happen in the future.

- **Speak honestly, but with reserve, from personal experience and knowledge.** Because there is no opportunity to conduct any kind of research before delivering an impromptu speech, you will have to speak from your own experience and knowledge. Remember, audiences almost always respond favorably to personal illustrations, so use any appropriate and relevant ones that come to mind. Of course, the more knowledge you have about the subject to be discussed, the easier it will be to speak about it off the cuff. But do not make up information or provide facts or figures you're not certain about. An honest "I don't know" or a very brief statement is more appropriate.

- **Be cautious.** No matter how much knowledge you have, if your subject is at all sensitive or your information is classified, be careful when

> ✓ *QuickCheck*
> *Impromptu Presentations*
> - ■ Consider your audience.
> - ■ Be brief.
> - ■ Organize ideas into an introduction, body, and conclusion.
> - ■ Speak honestly, but with reserve, from personal experience and knowledge.
> - ■ Be cautious about what you say.

discussing it during your impromptu speech. If asked about a controversial topic, give an honest but noncommittal answer. You can always elaborate later, but you can never take back something rash you have already said. It is better to be cautious than sorry!

Extemporaneous Speaking

In **extemporaneous speaking**, you speak from a written or memorized general outline, but you do not have the exact wording in front of you or in memory. You have rehearsed the speech so that you know key ideas and their organization, but not to the degree that the speech sounds memorized.

An extemporaneous style is conversational; it gives your audience the impression that the speech is being created as they listen to it, and to some extent it is. Audiences prefer to hear something live rather than something canned. Seeing something happening *now* provides added interest and excitement. An extemporaneous speech sounds live rather than as though it were prepared yesterday or weeks ago. The extemporaneous method reflects the advantages of a well-organized speech delivered in an interesting and vivid manner.

You develop an extemporaneous style by first rehearsing your speech, using many notes or perhaps looking at your preparation outline. As you continue to rehearse, try to rely less on your notes, but don't try to memorize your message word for word. After going over your speech a few times, you will find that you have internalized the overall structure

Table 16.1 ■ Advantages and Disadvantages of Methods of Delivery

	Advantages	Disadvantages
Manuscript: reading a speech from a prepared text	You can choose words carefully when dealing with sensitive or critical issues; you can be precise.	Rarely done well enough to maintain audience interest.
Memorized: giving a speech from memory without using notes	This method enables you to have maximum eye contact with the audience.	May sound stiff, stilted, and overrehearsed; you may forget parts of your speech; you cannot make on-the-spot adaptations.
Impromptu: delivering a speech without preparing in advance	You can speak informally and maintain direct eye contact with the audience.	May lack logical organization and thorough research; may be unimpressive.
Extemporaneous: speaking from a written or memorized general outline, knowing the major ideas but not the exact wording	Style is conversational; speech sounds live rather than rehearsed, is well organized, and is delivered in an interesting and vivid manner.	Could become repetitive; you may forget certain points; new thoughts may increase the length.

of the speech, although the exact way you express your ideas may vary. You'll rely less on your notes and focus more on adapting your message to your listeners. The final draft of your speaking notes may be an abbreviated outline or a few key words and essential facts or statistics that you want to remember.

See Table 16.1 for an overview of the advantages and disadvantages of the various ways of delivering a speech.

A Question of Ethics

Julie put off preparing for a speech that she now has to deliver in a few days. Because she doesn't have time to do any more preparation, she decides to dress provocatively on the day of the speech in an effort to distract her listeners. Is her behavior ethical?

Chapter 17

Nonverbal Communication

You now know that, for most speaking situations, you should strive for a conversational style. Practice and a focus on communicating your message to your audience are vital for effective communication and great for your confidence.

These six major categories of nonverbal behavior affect delivery:

1. eye contact
2. gestures
3. movement
4. posture
5. facial expression
6. personal appearance

Eye Contact

Eye contact with your audience opens communication, makes you more believable, and keeps your audience interested. Each of these functions contributes to the success of your delivery. Eye contact also provides you with feedback about how your speech is coming across.

When it's your time to speak, walk to the lectern or to the front of the audience, pause briefly, and look at your audience before you say anything. Eye contact nonverbally sends the message "I am interested in you; tune me in; I have something I want to share with you." You should have your opening sentence well enough in mind that you can deliver it without looking at your notes or away from your listeners.

Establish eye contact with the entire audience, not just with those in the front row or only one or two people. Look to the back as well as the front

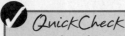

QuickCheck
Benefits of Eye Contact

- Lets your audience know that you are interested in them and that you want to talk to them
- Permits you to monitor audience reaction to your message in order to determine whether your audience is responding to you
- Establishes your credibility
- Helps your audience maintain interest and remember more of your message

and from one side of your audience to the other, selecting an individual to focus on and then moving on to someone else. It's best not to establish a predictable pattern for your eye contact. Look at individuals, establishing person-to-person contact with them—not so long that it will make a listener feel uncomfortable, but long enough to establish the feeling that you are talking directly to that individual. Don't look over your listeners' heads; establish eye-to-eye contact.

Gestures

Important points are emphasized with gestures. You gesture to indicate places, to enumerate items, and to describe objects. Many people who gesture easily and appropriately in the course of everyday conversations aren't sure what to do with their hands when they find themselves in front of an audience.

Cultural expectations can help you make decisions about your approach to using gestures. Listeners from Japan and China, for example, prefer a quieter, less flamboyant use of gestures. British listeners seem to prefer that the speaker stay behind a lectern and use relatively few gestures. Europeans agree that they can spot an American speaker because Americans typically are more animated in their use of gestures, movement, and facial expressions.

Problem Gestures

Following are some common problem poses and gestures.

- **Parade rest.** One common problem is keeping your hands behind your back in a "parade rest" pose. Although you may put your hands behind your back, standing at parade rest during an entire speech looks awkward and unnatural and may distract your audience.
- **Broken wing.** Another common position is standing with one hand on the hip in a "broken wing" pose. Worse than the "broken wing" is both hands resting on the hips in a "double broken wing." Holding that one pose throughout a speech looks unnatural and will keep you from using other appropriate gestures.
- **"Don't worry, Ma."** Few poses are more awkward-looking than when a speaker clutches one arm, as if grazed by a bullet. The audience half expects the speaker to call out reassuringly, "Don't worry, Ma; it's only a flesh wound." Similarly, keeping your hands in your pockets can make you look as if you were afraid to let go of your change or your keys.
- **Fig leaf clutch.** Some students clasp their hands and let them drop in front of them in a distracting "fig leaf clutch."

Gestures can distract your audience in various other ways as well. Grasping the lectern until your knuckles turn white or just letting your hands flop around without purpose or control does little to help you communicate your message.

Functions of Gestures

If you don't know what to do with your hands, think about the message you want to communicate. As in ordinary conversation, your hands should simply help emphasize or reinforce your verbal message. Your gestures can lend strength to or detract from what you have to say by repeating, contradicting, substituting, complementing, emphasizing, or regulating.

- **Repeating.** Gestures can help you repeat your verbal message. For example, you can say "I have three major points to talk about today" while holding up three fingers. Or you can describe an object as 12 inches long while holding your hands about a foot apart. Repeating what you say through nonverbal means can reinforce your message.
- **Contradicting.** Because your audience will believe what you communicate nonverbally sooner than what you communicate verbally, monitor your gestures to make sure that you are not contradicting what you say. You don't want to display behavior that will conflict with your intended image or message, nor do you want to appear stiff and self-conscious. So the crucial thing to keep in mind while monitoring your own behavior is to stay relaxed.
- **Substituting.** Not only can your behavior reinforce or contradict what you say, but your gestures can also substitute for your message. Without uttering a word, you can hold up the palm of your hand to calm a noisy crowd. Flashing two fingers to form a V for "victory" and raising a clenched fist are other common examples of gestures that can substitute for a verbal message.
- **Complementing.** Gestures can also add further meaning to your verbal message. A politician who declines to comment on a reporter's question while holding up her hands to augment her verbal refusal is relying on the gesture to complement or provide further meaning to her verbal message.
- **Emphasizing.** You can give emphasis to what you say by using an appropriate gesture. A shaking fist or a slicing gesture with one or both hands helps emphasize a message. So does pounding your fist into the palm of your hand. Other gestures can be less dramatic but still lend emphasis to what you say. You should try to allow your gestures to arise from the content of your speech and your emotions.

- **Regulating.** Gestures can also regulate the exchange between you and your audience. If you want the audience to respond to a question, you can extend both palms to invite a response. During a question-and-answer session, your gestures can signal when you want to talk and when you want to invite others to do so.

Using Gestures Effectively

Here are some guidelines to consider when working on your delivery.

- **Stay natural.** Gestures should be *relaxed,* not tense or rigid. Your gestures should flow from your message. Avoid sawing or slashing through the air with your hands unless you are trying to emphasize a particularly dramatic point. A pounding fist or forefinger raised in hectoring style will not necessarily enhance the quality of your performance.
- **Be definite.** Gestures should appear *definite* rather than as accidental brief jerks of your hands or arms. If you want to gesture, go ahead and gesture. Avoid minor hand movements that will be masked by the lectern.
- **Use gestures that are consistent with your message.** If you are excited, gesture more vigorously. But remember that prerehearsed gestures are likely to appear awkward and stilted.
- **Vary your gestures.** Strive for variety and versatility in your use of gesture. Try not to use just one hand or one all-purpose gesture. Gestures can be used for a variety of purposes, such as enumerating, pointing, describing, and symbolizing an idea or concept.
- **Don't overdo it.** Gestures should be *unobtrusive*; your audience should focus not on the beauty or appropriateness of your gestures but on your message. Your purpose is to communicate a message to your audience, not to perform for your listeners to the extent that your delivery receives more attention than your message.

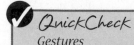

QuickCheck
Gestures

The most effective gestures are
- natural and relaxed
- definite and varied
- consistent with your message
- unobtrusive
- coordinated with what you say
- appropriate to your audience and situation

■ **Coordinate gestures with what you say.** Gestures should be *well timed* to coincide with your verbal message. When you announce that you have three major points, your gesture of enumeration should occur simultaneously with your utterance of the word *three*.

■ **Make your gestures appropriate to your audience and situation.** Gestures must be adapted to the audience. In more formal speaking situations, particularly when speaking to a large audience, bolder, more sweeping, and more dramatic gestures are appropriate. A small audience in a less formal setting calls for less formal gestures.

Keep one important principle in mind: Use gestures that work best for you. Your gestures should fit your personality. It may be better to use no gestures—to just put your hands comfortably at your side—than to use awkward, distracting gestures or to try to counterfeit someone else's gestures. Your nonverbal delivery should flow from your message.

Movement

Should you walk around during your speech, or should you stay in one place? If there is a lectern, should you stand behind it, or would it be acceptable to stand in front of it or to the side? Is it all right to sit down while you speak? Can you move among the audience, as Oprah Winfrey does on her

TV talk show? The following discussion may help you answer these questions.

Purpose, Not Distraction

You may want to move purposefully about while delivering your speech, but take care that your movement does not detract from your message. If the audience focuses on your movement rather than on what you are saying, it is better to stand still. Your movement should be consistent with the verbal content of your message. It should make sense rather than appear as aimless wandering.

Physical Barriers

As you consider incorporating movement into your speech, also be mindful of physical barriers that exist between you and your audience. Barriers such as a lectern, rows of chairs, a chalkboard, an overhead projector, or other audiovisual aids may act as obstacles between you and your audience. If physical barriers make you feel too far removed from your audience, move closer.

Transitions

You may also signal the beginning of a new idea or major point in your speech with movement. As you move into a transition statement or change from a serious subject to a more humorous one, movement can be a good way to signal that your approach to the speaking situation is changing.

Your use of movement during your speech should make sense to your listeners. Avoid random pacing and overly dramatic gestures. Temper the advice about proximity and other delivery variables by adapting to the cultural expectations of your audience.

Posture

Although there have been few formal studies of posture in relation to public speaking, there is evidence that the way you carry your body communicates significant information. Slouching over the lectern, for example, does not project an image of vitality and interest in your audience.

Whereas your face and voice play the major role in communicating a specific emotion, your posture communicates the *intensity* of that emotion. If you are happy, your face and voice reflect your happiness; your posture communicates the intensity of your joy.

The specific stance you adopt should come about naturally, as a result of what you have to say, the environment, and the formality or informality of the occasion. For example, during a very informal presentation it may be perfectly appropriate as well as comfortable and natural to sit on the edge of a desk.

In general, avoid slouched shoulders, shifting from foot to foot, or drooping your head. Your posture should not call attention to itself. Instead, it should reflect your interest in the speaking event and your attention to the task at hand.

Facial Expression

Your face plays a key role in expressing your thoughts, and especially your emotions and attitudes.[1] Your audience sees your face before they hear what you are going to say. Thus, you have an opportunity to set the emotional tone for your message before you start speaking. Do not adopt a phony smile that looks insincere and plastered on your face; try for a pleasant facial expression that helps establish a positive emotional climate. Your facial expression should naturally vary to be consistent with your message. Present somber news with a more serious expression. To communicate interest in your listeners, keep your expression alert and friendly.

Although humans are technically capable of producing thousands of different facial expressions, we most often express only six primary emotions: happiness, anger, surprise, sadness, disgust, and fear. But when we speak to others, our faces are a blend of expressions rather than communicators of a single emotion. According to cross-cultural studies by social psychologist Paul Ekman, the facial expressions of these emotions are virtually universal, so even a culturally diverse audience will be able to read your emotional expressions clearly. When you rehearse your speech, stand in front of a mirror or, better yet, videotape yourself. Note whether you are allowing your face to help communicate the emotional tone of your thoughts.

Personal Appearance

Most people have certain expectations about the way a speaker should look. One of your audience analysis tasks is to identify what those audience expectations are. Appropriate wardrobe varies depending on climate, custom, culture, and audience expectations. There is considerable evidence that your personal appearance affects how your audience will respond to you and your message, particularly during the opening moments of your presentation.

Styles and audience expectations change and are sometimes unpredictable. Therefore, a general rule of thumb to follow is this: When in doubt about what to wear, select something conservative.

A Question of Ethics

McKenzie is planning to give a speech about emergency first aid. Her sister is a registered nurse. Is it ethical for McKenzie to wear her sister's nursing clothes without telling her audience that the clothing belongs to her sister?

Chapter 18

Verbal Communication

Have you ever listened to a radio announcer and imagined what he or she looked like, only later to see a picture and have your image of the announcer drastically altered? Based on verbal communication alone, you make inferences about a person's age, status, occupation, ethnic origin, and other matters. Your voice is one of the most important delivery tools you have as a public speaker for conveying your ideas to your audience.

Vocal Delivery

Your credibility as a speaker and your ability to communicate your ideas clearly to your listeners will in large part depend on your vocal delivery. Vocal delivery includes pitch, speaking rate, volume, pronunciation, articulation, pauses, and general variation of the voice. A speaker has at least two key vocal obligations to an audience: Speak to be understood, and speak with vocal variety to maintain interest.

Speak to Be Understood

To be understood, you need to consider four aspects of vocal delivery: volume, articulation, dialect, and pronunciation.

Volume　The fundamental goal in your vocal delivery is to speak loudly enough that your audience can hear you. The **volume** of your speech is determined by the amount of air you project through your larynx, or voice box. More air equals more volume of sound. Your diaphragm, a muscle in your upper abdomen, helps control sound volume by increasing air flow from your lungs through your voice box.

Breathing from your diaphragm—that is, consciously expanding and contracting your abdomen as you breathe in and out—can increase the volume of sound as well as enhance the quality of your voice.

Articulation   The process of producing speech sounds clearly and distinctly is **articulation**. In addition to speaking loudly enough, say your words so that your audience can understand them. Without distinct enunciation, or articulation of the sounds that make up words, your listeners may not understand you or may fault you for simply not knowing how to speak clearly and fluently. Here are some commonly misarticulated words:[1]

dint	instead of	*didn't*
lemme	instead of	*let me*
mornin	instead of	*morning*
seeya	instead of	*see you*
soun	instead of	*sound*
wanna	instead of	*want to*
whadayado	instead of	*what do you do*

Many errors in articulation result from simple laziness. It takes effort to articulate speech sounds clearly. Sometimes we are in a hurry to express our ideas, but more often we simply get into the habit of mumbling, slurring, and abbreviating. Such speech flaws may not keep your audience from understanding you, but poor enunciation does reflect on your credibility as a speaker.

The best way to improve your articulation of sounds is first to identify words or phrases that you have a tendency to slur or chop. Once you have identified them, practice saying the words correctly. Make sure you can hear the difference between the improper and proper pronunciations. A speech teacher can help you check your articulation.

Dialect   A **dialect** is a consistent style of pronouncing words that is common to an ethnic group or a geographic region such as the South, New England, or the upper Midwest. In the southern part of the United States, people prolong some vowel sounds when they speak. And in the northern Midwest, the word *about* sometimes sounds a bit like "aboat."

Although a speaker's dialect may pigeonhole that person as being from a certain part of the country, it won't necessarily affect the audience's comprehension of the information unless the dialect is so pronounced that the listeners can't understand the speaker's words. Research does suggest, however, that listeners tend to prefer a dialect similar to their own pronunciation style.[2] If your word pronunciation is significantly distracting to your listeners, you might consider modifying your dialect (although radically changing a dialect is difficult and time consuming).

Dialect includes four elements: intonation pattern, vowel production, consonant production, and speaking rate.

■ **Intonation pattern.** A typical North American intonation pattern is predominantly a rising and falling pattern. The pattern looks something like this:

"Good ^{morn}ing.   How ^{are} you?"

Intonation patterns of other languages, such as Hindi, may remain on almost the exact same pitch level; native North American ears find the monotone pitch distracting.

■ **Vowel production.** Many people who speak English as a second language often clip, or shorten, the vowel sounds, which can make comprehension more challenging. Stretching or elongating vowels within words can be a useful skill for such speakers to develop. If this is a vocal skill you need to cultivate, consider taping your speech and then comparing it with the standard American pronunciation you hear on TV or radio.

■ **Consonant production.** Consonant production varies depending on which language you are speaking. It is sometimes difficult to produce clear consonants that are not overdone. Consonants that are so soft as to be almost unheard may produce a long blur of unintelligible sound rather than a crisply articulated sound.

■ **Speaking rate.** People whose first language is not English sometimes speak at too fast a rate in the hope that this will create the impression of being very familiar with English. Slowing the rate just a bit often enhances comprehension for native English speakers listening to someone less familiar with English pronunciation. A rate that is too fast also contributes to problems with clipped vowels, soft or absent consonants, and an intonation pattern that is on one pitch level rather than comfortably varied.

Pronunciation   Whereas articulation relates to the clarity of sounds, **pronunciation** concerns the degree to which the sounds conform to those assigned to words in standard English. Mispronouncing words can detract from a speaker's credibility. Often, however, we are not aware that we are not using standard pronunciation unless someone points it out.

Some speakers reverse speech sounds, saying "aks" instead of "ask," for example. Some allow an *r* sound to intrude into some words, saying "warsh" instead of "wash," or leave out sounds in the middle of a word, as in "ackchally" instead of "actually" or "Febuary" instead of "February." Some speakers also accent syllables in nonstandard ways; they say "po′ lice" instead of "po lice′" or "um′brella" rather than "um brel′la."

If English is not your native language, you may have to spend extra time working on your pronunciation and articulation. Here are two useful tips to help you. First, make an effort to prolong your vowel sounds. Speeeeak tooooo prooooolooooong eeeeeeach vooooooowel soooooound yooooooooou maaaaaaaake. Second, to reduce choppy-sounding word pronunciation, blend the end of one word into the beginning of the next. Make your speech flow from one word to the next, instead of separating it into individual chunks of sound.[3]

Speak with Variety

To speak with variety is to vary your pitch, rate, and pauses. It is primarily through the quality of our voices, as well as our facial expressions, that we communicate whether we are happy, sad, bored, or excited. If your vocal clues suggest that you are bored with your topic, your audience will probably be bored also. Appropriate variation in vocal pitch and rate, as well as appropriate use of pauses, can add zest to your speech and help maintain audience attention.

Pitch   Vocal **pitch** is how high or low your voice sounds. You can sing because you can change the pitch of your voice to produce a melody. Lack of variation in pitch has been consistently identified as one of the most distracting characteristics of ineffective speakers. A monotone is boring.

Everyone has a habitual pitch. This is the range of your voice during normal conversation. Some people have a habitually high pitch, whereas others have a low pitch.

Your voice has **inflection** when you raise or lower the pitch as you pronounce words or sounds. Your inflection helps determine the meaning of your utterances. A surprised "ah!" sounds different from a disappointed "ah" or "ah?" Your vocal inflection is thus an important indicator of your emotions and gives clues as to how to interpret your speech.

In some cultures, vocal inflection plays a major role in helping people interpret the meaning of words. For example, Thai, Vietnamese, and Mandarin Chinese languages purposely use monotone and low, falling, high, and rising pitches.[4] If you are a native speaker of a language in which pitch influences meaning, be mindful that listeners do not expect this in many Western languages, although all languages rely on inflection to provide nuances of meaning.

The best public speakers vary their inflection considerably. Variation in your vocal inflection and overall pitch helps you communicate the subtlety of your ideas.

Record your speech as you rehearse, and evaluate your use of pitch and inflection critically. If you are not satisfied with your inflection, consider practicing your speech with exaggerated variations in vocal pitch. Although you would not deliver your speech this way, it may help you explore the expressive options available to you.

Rate   How fast do you talk? Most speakers average between 120 and 180 words per minute. There is no one "best" speaking rate. The best rate depends on two factors: your speaking style and the content of your message.

One symptom of speech anxiety is the tendency to rush through a speech to get it over with. Relying on feedback from others can help you determine whether your rate is too rapid. Tape-recording your message and listening critically to your speaking rate can help you assess whether you are speaking at the proper speed.

Fewer speakers have the problem of speaking too slowly, but a turtle-paced speech will almost certainly make it more difficult for your audience to maintain interest. Remember, your listeners can grasp information much faster than you can speak it.

You need not deliver your entire speech at the same pace. It is normal to speak more rapidly when talking about something that excites you. You slow your speaking rate to emphasize key points or ideas. Speaking rate is another tool you can use to add variety and interest to your vocal delivery. The pace of your delivery, however, should make sense in terms of the ideas you are sharing with your listeners.

Pauses   An appropriate pause can often do more to accent your message than any other vocal characteristic. President Kennedy's famous line "Ask not what your country can do for you; ask what you can do for your country" was effective not only because of its language but also because it was delivered with a pause dividing the two thoughts. Try delivering that line without the pause; without it, that statement just doesn't have the same power.

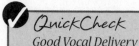

QuickCheck
Good Vocal Delivery

- Use adequate volume.
- Articulate speech sounds clearly and distinctly.
- Pronounce words accurately.
- Vary your pitch.
- Vary your speaking rate.
- Pause to emphasize ideas.

Effective use of pauses, also known as effective timing, can greatly enhance the impact of your message. Whether you are trying to tell a joke, a serious tale, or a dramatic story, your use of a pause can determine the effectiveness of your anecdote.

Beware, however, of the vocalized pause. Many beginning public speakers are uncomfortable with silence, and so, rather than pausing where it seems natural and normal, they vocalize sounds such as "umm," "er," "you know," and "ah."

One research study counted how frequently certain people use "uh."[5] Science professors in this study said "uh" about 1.4 times a minute; humanities professors timed in at 4.8 times a minute—almost 3.5 times more.

As a public speaker, you don't want to have the most "uhs" and "ums" when you speak. Vocalized pauses will annoy your audience and detract from your credibility; eliminate them.

Silence can be an effective tool in emphasizing a particular word or sentence. A well-timed pause coupled with eye contact can powerfully accent your thought. Silence is a way of saying to your audience, "Think about this for a moment." In speech, an effective use of a pause can add emphasis and interest.

Using a Microphone

No matter how polished your gestures or well-intoned your vocal cues, if you are inaudible or use a microphone awkwardly, your speech will not have the desired effect.

There are three kinds of microphones. The **lavaliere microphone** is the clip-on type often used by news people and interviewees. Worn on a collar or lapel, it requires no particular care other than not thumping it or accidentally knocking it off. The **boom microphone**, used by makers of movies, hangs over the heads of the speakers and is remote-controlled.

The most common microphone is the **stationary microphone**. This is the type that is most often attached to a lectern, sitting on a desk, or standing on the floor. Generally, the stationary microphones used today are multidirectional. You do not have to remain frozen in front of a stationary mike while delivering your speech. However, you do need to take some other precautions when using one.

- First, if you have a fully stationary microphone, rather than one that converts to a hand mike, you will have to remain behind the microphone, with your mouth about the same distance from the mike at all times to avoid distracting fluctuations in the volume of sound. You can turn your head from side to side and use gestures, but you will have to limit other movements.
- Second, microphones amplify sloppy habits of pronunciation and enunciation. Therefore, you need to speak clearly and crisply when using a mike.
- Third, if you must test a microphone, ask the audience whether they can hear you. Blowing on a microphone produces an irritating noise! Do not tap, pound, or shuffle anything near the microphone. If you are using note cards, quietly slide them aside as you progress through your speech. Notes on paper are more difficult to handle quietly, but do so with as little shuffling as you can manage.
- Finally, when you are delivering your speech, speak directly into the microphone, making sure that your words are appropriately amplified. Some speakers lower their volume and become inaudible when they have a microphone in front of them.

Under ideal circumstances, you will be able to practice before you speak with the type of microphone you will use. If you have the chance, figure out where to stand for the best sound quality and how sensitive the mike is to extraneous noise. Practice will accustom you to any voice distortion or echo that might occur so that these sound qualities do not surprise you during your speech.

Rehearsing Your Speech: Some Final Tips

Knowing some of the characteristics of effective speech delivery will not make you a better speaker unless you can put these principles into practice. Effective public speaking is a skill that takes practice. Practicing takes the form of rehearsing. Rehearsing your speech prepares you to deliver your speech to an audience. The following suggestions can help you make the most of your rehearsal time.

■ Finish drafting your speech outline at least two days before your speech performance. The more time you have to work on putting it all together, the better.

■ Before you prepare the speaking notes to use in front of your audience, rehearse your speech aloud to help determine where you will need notes to prompt yourself.

■ Revise your speech as necessary to keep it within the time limits set by your instructor or whoever invited you to speak.

■ Prepare your speaking notes. Use whatever system works best for you. Some speakers use pictorial symbols to remind themselves of a story or an idea. Others use complete sentences or just words or phrases in an outline pattern to prompt them. Most teachers advocate using note cards for speaking notes.

■ Rehearse your speech standing up so that you can get a feel for your use of gestures as well as your vocal delivery. Do not try to memorize your speech or choreograph specific gestures. As you rehearse, you may want to modify your speaking notes to reflect appropriate changes.

- If you can, present your speech to someone else so that you can practice establishing eye contact. Seek feedback from your captive audience about both your delivery and your speech content.

- If possible, tape-record or videotape your speech during the rehearsal stage so that you can observe your vocal and physical mannerisms and make necessary changes. If you don't have a video camera, you may find it useful to practice before a mirror so that you can observe your body language—it's low-tech, but it still works.

- Rehearse using all your presentation aids. Don't wait until the last minute to plan, prepare, and rehearse with flipcharts, slides, overhead transparencies, or other aids that you will need to manipulate as you speak.

- Your final rehearsals should re-create, as much as possible, the speaking situation you will face. If you will be speaking in a large classroom, find a large classroom in which to rehearse your speech. If your audience will be seated informally in a semicircle, then this should be the context in which you rehearse your speech. The more realistic the rehearsal, the more confidence you will gain.

- Practice good delivery skills while rehearsing. Remember this maxim: Practice makes perfect if practice is perfect.

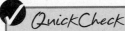

QuickCheck
Effective Delivery

- Strive for a natural, conversational tone.
- Have good eye contact with your listeners.
- Use appropriate gestures.
- Avoid distracting mannerisms such as jingling change in your pockets or playing with your hair.
- Vary the pitch and inflection of your voice.

Responding to Questions

During a question and answer session, your delivery method changes to impromptu speaking. Here are some tips to make the question and answer period less challenging.

- **Prepare.** Anticipate what questions you may be asked. Analyze your audience. Think of possible questions those particular listeners might ask you, and then rehearse your answers.
- **Repeat or rephrase the questions.** Repeating a question ensures that everyone can hear the question. It also ensures that you understand the question before you give an answer. You can succinctly summarize a rambling question. And, repeating the question gives you just a bit of time to think about your answer.
- **Stay on message.** If a listener asks a question unrelated to your talk, you'll want to find a way to guide your questioner back to the message you have prepared. Keep bringing the audience back to your central idea. Your answers, rather than the questions, are what is important.
- **Ask yourself the first question.** Ask yourself a challenging question first. Doing this gives you a comfortable way to make a transition between the speech and the Q&A period.
- **Listen nonjudgmentally.** Keep your eyes focused on the person asking the question, lean forward slightly, and give your full attention to the questioner. Audience members expect speakers to be polite and attentive. Listen and respond courteously.
- **Neutralize hostile questions.** Every hostile question gives you an opportunity to score points with your listeners. Restate the question and focus on the essence of the issue.
- **When you don't know, admit it.** If you don't know the answer to a question, just say so. You can promise to find out more information and then get back to the person later. However, if you make a promise, follow through on it.

- **Be brief.** Even if you've anticipated questions and have a "double-barreled" talk, make your answers short and to the point.
- **Use organized signposts.** Quickly organize your responses. If you have two responses to a question, let your listeners know by using a verbal signpost. Say, "I have two responses. First. . . ." Then when you get to your second point, say, "My second point is. . . ."
- **Indicate when the Q&A period is ending.** To let them know that the Q&A session will soon conclude, tell your audience, "I have time for two more questions."

A Question of Ethics

During a large convention, the after-dinner speaker was seen having several drinks before dinner. Some people thought he was inebriated. Should he be allowed to deliver his speech? Why or why not? Explain your answer.

Chapter 19

Delivering Your Speech

Y ou've worked hard on your speech, and you are ready. Using information about your audience as an anchor, you have developed a speech with an interesting topic and a fine-tuned purpose. Your central idea is clearly identified. You have gathered interesting and relevant supporting material (examples, illustrations, statistics) and organized it well. Your speech has an appropriate introduction, a logically arranged body, and a clear conclusion that nicely summarizes your key theme. You have rehearsed your speech several times; it is not memorized, but you are comfortable with the way you express the major ideas.

Prepare for a Successful Performance

Your last task is to calmly and confidently communicate with your audience. You are ready to deliver your speech. As the time for presenting your speech to your audience approaches, consider the following suggestions to help you prepare for a successful performance.

- **Get plenty of rest before your speech.** Last-minute, late-night final preparations can take the edge off your performance. Many professional public speakers also advocate that you watch what you eat before you speak; a heavy meal or too much caffeine can have a negative effect on your performance.
- **Review the suggestions in Chapter 4 for becoming a confident speaker.** It is normal to have prespeech jitters. But if you have developed a well-organized, audience-centered message on a topic of genuine interest to you, you're doing all

the right things to make your speech a success. Remember some of the other tips for developing confidence: Re-create the speech environment when you rehearse. Use deep breathing techniques to help you relax. Also, make sure you are especially familiar with your introduction and conclusion. Act calm to feel calm.

■ **Arrive early for your speaking engagement.** If the room is in an unfamiliar location, give yourself plenty of time to find it. You may want to rearrange the furniture or make other changes in the speaking environment. If you are using audiovisual equipment, check to see that it is working properly and set up your support material carefully. You might even project a slide or two to make sure they are in the tray right side up. Relax before you deliver your message; budget your time so that you do not spend the moments before you speak hurriedly looking for a parking place or frantically trying to attend to last-minute details.

■ **Visualize success.** Picture yourself delivering your speech in an effective way. Also, remind yourself of the effort you have spent preparing for your speech. A final mental rehearsal can boost your confidence and help ensure success.

Even though there are many time-tested methods for enhancing your speech delivery, keep in mind that speech delivery is an art rather than a science. The manner of your delivery should reflect your personality and individual style.

Adapt Your Delivery to a Diverse Audience

You need to adapt your presentation to the expectations of your listeners, especially those from different cultural backgrounds. Consider the following suggestions to help you develop strategies for adapting both your verbal and your nonverbal messages for a culturally diverse audience.

Avoid an Ethnocentric Mind Set

Ethnocentrism is the assumption that your own cultural approaches are superior to those of other cultures. When considering how to adapt your delivery style to your audience, try to view different approaches and preferences not as right or wrong but merely as different from your own.

Use a Less Dramatic Style for High-Context Listeners

Because a high-context culture places considerable emphasis on unspoken messages, you need not be overly expressive for a high-context audience. For example, to many Japanese people, a delivery style that includes exuberant gestures, overly dramatic facial expressions, and frequent movements might seem overdone. A more subtle, less demonstrative approach would create less "noise" and be more effective.

Consult with Other Speakers

Talk with people you know who are familiar with the cultural expectations of the audience you will address. Ask specific questions:

- What are audience expectations about where I should stand while speaking?
- Do listeners like direct eye contact?
- When will the audience expect me to start and end my talk?
- Will listeners find movement and gestures distracting or welcome?

Monitor Your Level of Immediacy with Your Audience

Speaker **immediacy** depends on how close you are to your listeners, the amount of eye contact you display, and whether you speak from behind or in front of a lectern. According to the immediacy principle, we move closer to things we like, and we move away from things we don't like.[1]

Some cultures may expect less immediacy; the key is not to violate what listeners expect.[2] For example, Japanese audiences don't expect speakers to move from behind a lectern and stand very close to listeners.

Monitor Your Expression of Emotion

Not all cultures interpret and express emotions the same way. People from the Middle East and the

Mediterranean are typically more expressive and animated in their conversation than are Europeans.[3] People from a high-context culture—a culture in which nonverbal messages are exceptionally important (such as Japanese or Chinese culture)—place greater emphasis on your delivery of a message than do people from a low-context culture (such as North Americans).[4]

Remember, however, that even though you may be speaking to an audience from a low-context culture—a culture that places a high value on verbal messages—you do not have license to ignore how you deliver a message. Delivery is always important. But audience members from a high-context culture will rely heavily on your unspoken message to help them interpret what you are saying.

Know the Code

Communication occurs when both speaker and listener share the same code system—both verbal and nonverbal. Even subtle nonverbal messages communicate feelings, attitudes, and cues about the nature of the relationship between you and your audience, so it is important to avoid gestures or expressions that would offend your listeners.

Keep cultural expectations in mind when you rehearse and deliver a speech. Become sensitive and responsive to cultural differences. There is no universal dictionary of nonverbal meaning, so spend some time asking people who are from the same culture as your prospective audience about what gestures and expressions your audience will appreciate.

A Question of Ethics

John believes that the U.S. invasion of Iraq was unethical and that President Bush lied to the American people about weapons of mass destruction in Iraq in order to persuade them to support this war. At an anti-war rally, John presented his argument and supported it with PowerPoint slides that showed young soldiers wounded and killed in battle. Was this approach ethical?

Chapter 20

Selecting Presentation Aids

A **presentation aid** is any object that reinforces your point visually so that your audience can better understand it.

The Value of Presentation Aids

Presentation aids help your audience understand and remember your message, communicate the organization of your ideas, gain and maintain attention, and illustrate a sequence of events or procedures.[1]

Presentation Aids Enhance Understanding To many people, seeing is believing. Because your audience is accustomed to visual reinforcement, it is wise to consider how you can increase their understanding of your speech by using presentation aids.

Presentation Aids Enhance Memory Your audience will not only have an improved understanding of your speech but also better remember what you say as a result of visual reinforcement.[2] It is well known that you remember most what you understand best.

Presentation Aids Help Listeners Organize Ideas Even if you clearly lay out your major points, use effective internal summaries, and make clear transition statements, your listeners will welcome additional help. Listing major ideas on a chart, a poster, or an overhead transparency can add clarity to your talk and help your audience grasp your main ideas.

Presentation Aids Help Gain and Maintain Attention
Presentation aids not only grab the attention of

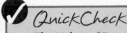

QuickCheck
The Value of Presentation Aids

Do your presentation aids
- help your audience understand your message?
- help your audience remember your message?
- communicate the organization of your message?
- gain and maintain audience attention?
- illustrate a sequence of events or procedures?

your listeners but also keep their interest when words alone might not.

Presentation Aids Help Illustrate a Sequence of Events or Procedures   Demonstrating step-by-step procedures helps your audience understand them.[3] When demonstrating how to make something, you can prepare an example of each step of the process and show the audience the example as you describe the relevant step. A climax to your speech could be to unveil a finished product. If time is limited, you could have on hand a series of diagrams and photographs to illustrate each step of the procedure.

Types of Presentation Aids

Charts, photographs, posters, drawings, graphs, slides, movies, and videos are just some types of presentation aids. Some of these, such as movies and videos, call on sound as well as sight to help you make your point.

Objects

Objects add interest because they are tangible. They can be touched, smelled, heard, and even tasted, as well as seen. Objects are real, and audiences like the real thing.

If you use an object to illustrate an idea, make sure that you can handle the object with ease. If an object is too large, it can be unwieldy and difficult to show to your audience. Tiny objects can be seen only close up. Other objects can be dangerous to handle.

Models

If it is not possible to bring the object you would like to show your audience, consider showing them a **model**. Make sure, however, that any model you use is large enough to be seen by all members of your audience.

People

Using people to illustrate your message can be tricky. Before your presentation, choose someone you trust so that you can fully inform him or her about what needs to be done. Rehearse your speech using your live presentation aid.

If you don't need the person to demonstrate something during your opening remarks, wait and introduce the person to your audience when needed. Remember, your presentation aids are always subordinate to your speech. You must remain in control.

Drawings

Drawings are popular and often-used presentation aids because they are easy and inexpensive to make. Drawings can be tailored to your specific needs. As a rule, large and simple line drawings are more effective for stage presentations than are detailed images.

Photographs

Photographs can show objects or places that cannot be illustrated with drawings or that an audience cannot view directly. To be sure that a printed photograph will be effective as a presentation aid for a large audience, enlarge it or project it.

Slides

Because of the increased use of computer-graphics programs such as PowerPoint, fewer speakers use slides today than just a few years ago. However, if you still have access to a slide projector and a screen, slides can help illustrate your talk. Automatic programming and remote-control features on many modern projectors allow you to change from one slide to the next without relying on anyone else for help. And audiences generally enjoy illustrated talks, which have an inherent attention factor that a speaker can use to advantage.

Working with slides can, however, present problems. Projector bulbs can burn out, and slides can jam in the projector. Moreover, with the lights out, you are less able to receive nonverbal feedback, and you cannot maintain eye contact with your audience.

Giving a slide lecture, therefore, requires considerable preparation.

■ First, know in which direction the slide carousel moves as it feeds the projector so that you will know how to load it.
■ Second, be sure the slides are right side up and in the order in which you want to show them during your speech.
■ Third, know how to operate the programming feature or the remote-control switch so that you can move back and forth among your slides, if you wish.

Graphs

A **graph** is a pictorial representation of statistical data in an easy-to-understand format. Most listeners find that graphs help make data more concrete. Graphs are particularly effective in showing overall trends and relationships among data. The four most common types of graphs are bar graphs, pie graphs, line graphs, and picture graphs.

■ A **bar graph** consists of flat areas—bars—whose various lengths represent information.
■ A **pie graph** shows the general distribution of data. Pie graphs are especially useful in helping your listeners to see quickly how data are distributed in a given category or area.
■ **Line graphs** show relationships between two or more variables. Like bar graphs, line graphs organize statistical data to show overall trends. A line graph can cover a greater span of time or numbers than a bar graph without looking cluttered or confusing. A simple line graph communicates better than a cluttered one.

- **Picture graphs** look somewhat less formal and less intimidating than other kinds of graphs. One of the advantages of picture graphs is that they need few words or labels, which makes them easier for your audience to read.

Charts

Charts summarize and present a great deal of information in a small amount of space. They are easy to use, reuse, and enlarge. They can also be displayed in a variety of ways. You can use a flipchart, a poster, or an overhead projector, which can project a giant image of your chart on a screen. Charts must be simple. Do not try to put too much information on one chart.

- If your chart looks at all cramped or crowded, divide the information into several charts and display each as needed.
- Do not handwrite the chart.
- Consider using a computer that has the software capability to prepare large charts or graphs.
- Make sure that your letters are large enough to be seen clearly in the back row.
- Use simple words or phrases, and eliminate unnecessary words.

Flipcharts

A flipchart consists of a large pad of paper resting on an easel. You can either prepare your visual aids on the paper before your speech or draw on the paper while speaking. Flipcharts are easy to use; during your presentation, you need only flip the page to reveal your next visual. Flipcharts are best used when you have brief information to display or when you want to summarize comments from audience members during a presentation.

Overhead Transparencies

Overhead projectors project images drawn on clear sheets of plastic, called transparencies, onto a screen so that the images can be seen by a large group. They enable you to maintain eye contact with your audience, yet still see your visual, as they don't require that you turn off the lights in the room. You may wish to dim the lights a bit, but most images can be seen clearly in normal room light. Overhead projectors also permit you to prepare your transparencies ahead of time and to mark on them during your presentation. If you do write on your transparencies during your speech, limit yourself to a few short words or to underlining key phrases.

Videotapes and Movies

VCRs permit stop-action, freeze-frame viewing, and some have a slow-motion function. You can also replay a scene several times if you want your audience to watch subtle movement or action.

Before you decide to use a videotape, think about whether it will really enhance your speech. Although movies can dramatically capture and hold your audience's attention, they are not really designed as supporting material for a speech. Unless you show only short excerpts, they can quickly overwhelm your speech. Be sure to rehearse with the equipment until you can handle it smoothly.

CDs and DVDs

CDs and DVDs (digital video disks) are compact disks that can include words, images, and audio or video clips. The files on a CD can be displayed with a large-screen video projector or an LCD panel connected to an overhead projector. DVD players can be connected directly to a TV set, or they can be connected to a computer. Many computers come equipped with DVD capabilities. Because you can stop and start a DVD at a precise place, you can be more confident that your movie or video will start exactly where you want it to start when you are ready to show it to an audience.

Audio Aids

Tapes or audio CDs can complement a visual display—you might play a few measures of Bach's *Toccata and Fugue in D Minor* on tape or CD to illustrate a point.

Probably the easiest to use and least expensive audio aid is a tape recorder that uses cassettes. It is small enough to handle easily, can be held up to a microphone to amplify the sound for a large audience, and can be cued to start exactly where you want it to. Mini CD recorders can record either voices or music; their small size makes them easy to handle, and the digital quality produces crystal-clear sound.

As with movies and videos, use audio aids sparingly. You do not want your speech's electronic soundtrack to interfere with your message.

Select the Right Presentation Aids

Because there are so many choices, you may wonder, "How do I decide which presentation aid to use?" Here are some suggestions:

■ **Consider your audience.** If you have a large audience, do not choose a presentation aid that everyone will not be able to see clearly. The age, interests, and attitudes of your audience should also affect your selection of audiovisual support.

■ **Think of your speech objective.** Don't select a presentation aid until you have decided on the purpose of your speech.

■ **Take into account your own skill and experience.** Use only equipment with which you are comfortable or have had practical experience.

✓ *QuickCheck*
Evaluate Your Presentation Aids

■ Are they easy to see?
■ Are they simple and uncluttered?
■ Are they attractive and carefully prepared?
■ Do they suit your audience, speech objectives, and speech environment?

■ **Know the room in which you will speak.** If the room has large windows with no shades and no other way to dim the light, do not consider using visuals that require a darkened room.

A Question of Ethics

If a speaker has a statistic that offers overwhelming evidence of the severity of a given problem, is it ethical for the speaker to save that statistic for last, or should the speaker reveal immediately to the audience how severe the problem really is? In other words, is there an ethical distinction between primacy and recency? Discuss your answer.

Chapter 21

Designing Presentation Aids

The audience should be your first consideration when determining what sort of a presentation aid would enhance your presentation. Presentation aids are intended to help listeners understand, remember, or attend to a message. They can also help organize a message or illustrate a sequence of events or procedures.

Preparing Presentation Aids

It is helpful to know the basic principles that govern good design so that you can specify what you want in the final product. The strategies that follow apply to preparing graphic materials in any medium. Keeping these guidelines in mind will enable you to produce visual aids that are attractive, instructive, and memorable.

Make Them Easy to See

To communicate your ideas clearly, make your presentation aids easy to see. Make sure your presentation aids are large enough to be seen by all of your audience.

Include a Manageable Amount of Information

Simple presentation aids usually communicate best. Words should be limited to key words or phrases. If you have a great deal of information, use two or three simple charts or overhead transparencies rather than putting all your words on one visual.

The text you include on your presentation aid should convey enough information to tell your audience what you think is most important, but your speech should provide your message. Each presentation aid should also make sense on its own.

Graphics Programs

⟶ Begin
⟶ Develop
⟶ Enter
⟶ Design

Figure 21.1 ■ Presentation aid with too little information.

Figure 21.1 does not provide enough information to give the audience an idea about the topic.

In Figure 21.2, the key words in each step are obscured by the extra words that surround them. Such a graphic creates interference. Instead of focusing easily on your words, audience members have to struggle to read the information in the graphic, which makes them stop listening. In addition, if there are too many words for audience members who take notes to jot down quickly, they tune out and concentrate on writing.

Figure 21.3 provides the audience with enough information that they can listen without distraction as you speak about each step. The key words receive proper emphasis, and note-takers can use the

How to Use PowerPoint

⟶ Begin with an idea that will form
   the basis of your presentation.
⟶ Develop an outline of all the main points.
⟶ Enter the outline in the program's outline
   feature.
⟶ Design slides with either custom or stock
   backgrounds, clip art, and text color.

Figure 21.2 ■ Presentation aid with too much detail.

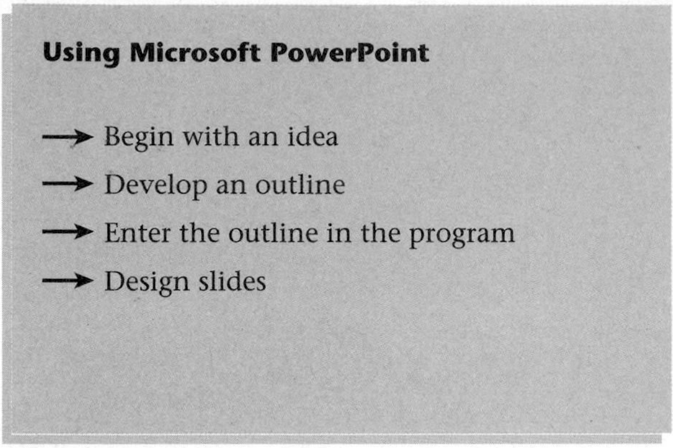

Using Microsoft PowerPoint

⟶ Begin with an idea
⟶ Develop an outline
⟶ Enter the outline in the program
⟶ Design slides

Figure 21.3 ■ Presentation aid with a manageable amount of information.

key words as headings and fill in the details as they listen to you speak.

Use Simple Drawings or Pictures

Simple, well-designed, and well-planned drawings and pictures can be valuable additions to your presentation. If your presentation contains dry or complex information that might be tedious to absorb in large amounts, consider breaking up the pace by using drawings or pictures instead of text on some of your presentation aids. Your audience will find your presentation more understandable and enjoyable if you vary the types of graphics that you show.

If you are using a computer to create your visual aids, you can insert images directly into the graphics program. If you will be converting your images to slides, you can add photographs to the collection of slides. However, when you incorporate a drawing or picture into your presentation, be careful to ensure that the image you display complements the mental image created by your spoken words.

Presentation graphics should be simple and uncluttered. You may be tempted to load up your graphics with fancy fonts, clip art, and outlandish colors. Resist that temptation. Such visuals can quickly become distracting and hard to read. Instead of supporting your presentation, they will actually confuse your audience and detract from your message.

Each element in your visual aid should serve a clear and specific purpose that is appropriate to your audience, topic, and setting.

Group Related Elements into Visual Units

By grouping related points, you can help your audience grasp key concepts and understand relationships as you convey information. Grouping points frees up space. This space, in turn, highlights the text blocks and also provides a resting place for the eye.

The **alignment** you choose for your text and images also affects the open space on the visual aid and directs the reader's gaze. Alignment can be flush left, flush right, or centered. Centered alignment is often effective for titles, but centered body text can look ragged and disorderly. A flush left or flush right alignment makes the text look crisp and allows the eye to flow easily from point to point.

Establish a Consistent Graphic Theme

Choose a basic design and color scheme and use it throughout your presentation. If you are designing a series of graphics, try to repeat a word, a symbol, styles, or a font throughout the presentation to convey a sense of unity. To carry out a consistent **theme**, choose a symbol other than a round bullet to use for emphasis, maintain a consistent color scheme, and use consistent spacing.

Repetition can be boring, so you may want to vary your visuals a little, but keep in mind that a consistent graphic theme will help your audience process and remember complex information.

Show Numerical Data Graphically

A well-drawn graph can often convey the information that you wish to present without requiring your audience to absorb and interpret complex numerical data. The type of data you have and the message you wish to convey will help you determine which type of graph is the most appropriate for your purposes. If your audience requires detailed numerical information in addition to your graph, consider supplying it in a handout that they will be able to study in detail at their leisure.

Vary Fonts and Font Sizes with Care

A **font** is a typeface of a particular style and design. **Font size** is measured in **points**; a point is 1/72 of an inch. The larger the point size, the larger the letters. Combine typefaces carefully so that your choices complement instead of conflict with one another. The strategies that follow should help you avoid conflict in your design.

Choosing a Font   A single font (typeface) includes a collection of all upper- and lowercase letters, as well as numbers, symbols, and punctuation that have a consistent structure and form. Each font has a name, and many have variations in size, weight, and spacing.

Fonts can be divided into four types: serif, sans serif, script, and decorative (or ornamental).

1. **Serif fonts** have lines (serifs) at the tops and bottoms of the letters. Serif fonts are easier to read for longer passages because the serifs guide the eye from one letter to the next.
2. **Sans serif fonts** do not have extra lines, and all the lines in the letters are of uniform thickness.
3. **Script fonts** imitate handwriting, but are precise and uniform. They can be fancy and compli-cated as well as hard to read, so be cautious about using them.
4. **Decorative fonts** are designed to convey a feel-ing or tone. The letters in decorative fonts may even be stylized drawings (e.g., flowers) in the shape of letters. Use these fonts sparingly for emphasis.

Most designers agree that you should not use more than two fonts on a single visual aid and that the fonts should be from two different font cate-gories. The most common combination is a sans serif font for a title and a serif font for a subtitle or text. This choice is driven by considerations of readability and clarity. A sans serif font is clean and clear. It can convey a feeling of strength as long as there is not too much text. Serif fonts are more readable, so they are a better choice for body text or subtitles.

Choosing a Font Size Your visuals must be big enough to be seen by people in the back row of your audience. Use 44-point type for titles, 32-point type for subtitles or for text if there is no subtitle, and 28-point type for the text if there is also a subtitle.

Avoid using all uppercase letters for emphasis, except in short titles. Longer stretches of text in all caps are hard to read, because our eyes are accustomed to seeing contrasting letter shapes. When we read, we recognize not only the individual letters, but also the shapes of the words. For example, when you drive along a highway, you can probably recognize the words on the sign for your exit long before you are close enough to make out the individual letters, because you recognize the shape of the words.

Use Color to Create a Mood and Sustain Attention

Graphic designers have long known that **warm colors** (oranges and reds) communicate excitement and interest. **Cool colors** such as green and blue have a more calming effect on viewers. Warm colors tend to come forward, whereas cool colors recede into the background. Consider using warm colors for positive messages (for example, "Profits are up") and cool colors for more negative messages ("We're losing money").

Avoiding Conflicting Colors It is also important to choose colors for backgrounds and text or graphics that contrast with one another but do not conflict. The use of yellow against a blue background is effective; the colors are contrasting yet harmonious. The use of purple against a blue background is not effective because both colors are dark and the purple letters do not stand out from the background.

Be cautious about using green and red combinations. Some audience members may have a type of color blindness that makes these two colors indistinguishable. Even for those without color blindness, this combination is not effective. Red type against a green background is difficult to read. The colors are not harmonious and do not contrast effectively, making the text and graphics hard on the eyes.

Designing for Contrast If you're designing overheads, consider using dark text on a light background. You might use black, dark blue, or dark red text that will stand out crisply from a white, light gray, or light yellow background. Each color will be distinctive and will provide excellent contrast for high readability. However, if your visual aids will be computer-generated and projected, light text on a dark background will produce better results. Yellow and white text on a black, dark blue, or dark green background will produce the contrast you need for an attention-getting presentation.

Attractive and harmonious color combinations will get and hold your listeners' attention. Two different colors of text on one background color should be sufficient. To unify your presentation, consider using the same color for all of your backgrounds, and then vary the complementary colors

QuickCheck
Prepare Presentation Aids

- Use simple drawings or pictures.
- Be sure that each element in your visual aid serves a clear and specific purpose that is appropriate to your audience, topic, and setting.
- Ensure that the image you display complements the mental image created by your spoken words.
- Include a manageable amount of information.
- Group related elements into visual units.
- Establish a consistent graphic theme.
- Choose a basic design and color scheme and use it throughout your presentation.
- Show numerical data graphically.
- Vary fonts and font sizes with care.
- Avoid using all uppercase letters for emphasis except in short titles.
- Use color to create a mood and sustain attention.
- For backgrounds and text or graphics, choose colors that contrast with one another but do not conflict.
- Save your most dramatic color contrasts for the most important points.
- Use black and white effectively.

you use for the text. For example, if you choose dark green for your background color, you could use white, yellow, and a very light gray for text. Save your most dramatic color contrasts for the most important points.

Using Black and White Effectively If your budget or equipment limits you to black and white, you can still use contrast to create attractive graphics. By choosing contrasting typefaces, spacing text widely or more compactly, using larger or smaller text, and using both bold and lightface text, you can create differences in textual color.

Using Storyboarding

Storyboarding is a planning technique that combines words and pictures to create a presentation. Each page in the storyboard supports a single point in the presentation, which is described in sentences, phrases, or key words and then illustrated with rough sketches. The verbal components might include facts, statistics, anecdotes, quotes, references to sources, or transition statements to move your presentation from one point to the next.

Storyboards as Outlines

Experienced public speakers may use storyboards as a substitute for a detailed formal outline when they are preparing a presentation. But until you have logged in hours of successful public presentations, you should probably consider storyboarding as a preliminary step to coordinate your visual ideas with your words. You can then work from your storyboards to construct a more polished outline.

The Storyboarding Process

First, consider your audience and fine-tune your persuasive objective. Then make a list of the main points you'd like to cover, knowing that each one will become a page of your storyboard.

Once you have decided on your main points, you can begin creating your storyboards. Divide a piece of paper down the middle and label it "Storyboard." In the left column, write the main idea followed by notes about supporting points.

Next, in the right column, sketch the visuals you plan to include. Don't worry if you are not a fabulous artist. These sketches are placeholders for the finished visual aids that you will prepare later.

When you do your sketches, be conservative about the number of visuals you plan. Select key supporting points to be illustrated with a few memorable words or images. No matter what medium you plan to use, you should give your audience enough time to absorb what you place in front of their eyes and to listen carefully to your verbal information before asking them to shift their attention to another image.

When you finish your storyboards, convert them into a more formal presentation outline. Prepare your visuals; then practice with your outline and visuals to ensure that your visuals are large enough, that they communicate your key points, and that you talk about them as you show them.

A Question of Ethics

Markita wants to convince her classmates, a captive audience, that they should join her in a 24-hour sit-in at the university president's office to protest the recent increase in tuition and fees. The president has made it clear that any attempt to occupy her office after closing hours will result in arrests. Is it appropriate for Markita to use a classroom speech to encourage her classmates to participate in the sit-in? Explain your answer.

Chapter 22

Using Presentation Aids

Here are some tips to help you use presentation aids for maximum audience impact.

Rehearse with Your Presentation Aids

Your appearance before your audience should not be the first time you deliver your speech while holding up your chart, turning on the overhead projector, operating the slide projector, or using the flipchart. Practice with your presentation aids until you feel at ease with them.

Do Not Use Dangerous or Illegal Presentation Aids

Dangerous or illegal presentation aids may either shock your audience or physically endanger them. These types of aids will also detract from your message. They are never worth the risk of a ruined speech or an injured audience member. If your speech seems to call for a dangerous or illegal object or substance, substitute a model, picture, chart, or other representational device.

Make Eye Contact with Your Audience, Not with Your Presentation Aids

You may be tempted to talk to your presentation aid rather than to your audience. Your focus, however, should remain on your audience. Of course, you will need to glance at your visual aid to make sure that it isn't upside down or that it is the proper one. But do not face it while giving your talk. Keep looking your audience in the eye.

Explain Your Presentation Aids

Visual support performs the same function as verbal support. It helps you communicate an idea. Make sure that your audience knows what that idea is. Don't just unceremoniously announce "Here are the recent statistics on birth rates in the United States" and hold up your visual without further explanation. Tell the audience how to interpret the data. Always set your visuals in a verbal context.

Do Not Pass Objects among Members of Your Audience

What can you do if your object is too small to be seen without passing it around? If no other speaker follows your speech, you can invite audience members to come up and see your object when your speech is over. If your audience is only two or three rows deep, you can even hold up the object and move in close to the audience to show it while you maintain control.

Use Animals with Caution

Most actors are unwilling to work with animals—and for good reason. At best, they may steal the show. And most often, they are unpredictable. You may think you have the smartest, best-trained dog in the world, but you really do not know how your dog will react to a strange environment and an unfamiliar audience. The risk of having an animal detract from your speech may be too great to make planning a speech around one worthwhile.

Use Handouts Effectively

Many speech instructors believe that you should not distribute handouts during a speech—handing out papers during your presentation will only distract your audience. However, many audiences in business and other types of organizations expect a summary of your key ideas in written form. If you do find it necessary to use written material to reinforce your presentation, keep the following suggestions in mind.

- Don't distribute your handout during the presentation unless your listeners must refer to the material while you're talking about it. Do not distribute handouts that have only a marginal relevance to your verbal message. They will defeat your purpose.
- If you do need to distribute a handout and you see that your listeners are giving the written material more attention than they are giving you, tell them where in the handout you want them to focus. For example, you could say, "I see that many of you are interested in the second and third pages of the report. I'll discuss those items in just a few moments. I'd like to talk about a few examples before we get to page 2."
- After distributing your handouts, tell audience members to keep the material face down until you're ready to talk about the material; this will help listeners not be tempted to peek at your handout instead of keeping their focus on you and your message.
- Make sure you clearly number the pages on your handout material. This will make it easy for you to direct audience members to specific pages.
- To make sure your listeners know what page of your handouts you want them to focus on, prepare an overhead transparency of each page. You'll be able to display the specific page you're talking about. With a transparency you can also quickly point to the paragraph or chart you want them to focus on. It's not a good idea, however, to economize by only displaying material designed to be used as handouts on an overhead projector and not providing handouts. The print will undoubtedly be too small to be seen clearly.
- If your listeners do not need the information during your presentation, tell them that you will distribute a summary of the key ideas at the end of your talk. Your handout might refer

to the specific action you want your audience to take, as well as summarize the key information you have discussed.

Time the Use of Visuals to Control Your Audience's Attention

A skillful speaker knows when to show a supporting visual and when to put it away. For example, it's not wise to begin your speech with all your charts, graphs, and drawings in full view unless you are going to refer to them in your opening remarks. Time the display of your visuals to coincide with your discussion of the information contained in them.

Here are a few more suggestions for timing your presentation aids.

■ Remove your presentation aid when you move to your next point, unless the information it contains will also help you communicate your next idea.
■ Have your overhead transparency already in place on the projector. When you are ready to show your visual, simply turn on the projector to reveal your drawing. Change to a new visual as you make your next point. Turn the projector off when you are finished with your visual support.
■ Consider asking someone beforehand to help you by holding your presentation aid, turning the pages of your flipchart, or changing the slides on the projector. Make sure you rehearse with your assistant so that all goes smoothly during your presentation.

Use Technology Effectively

You may be tempted to use some of the new technologies we have described because of their novelty rather than because of their value in helping you communicate your message. Most of them, however, are expensive. And some novice speakers are tempted to overuse presentation aids simply because they can quickly produce eye-catching visuals. Resist this temptation.

Also consider that many classrooms and lecture rooms are not equipped with the necessary hardware. And realize that to project images from large-screen projectors or LCD panels, you may have to dim the lights or turn the overhead lights completely off. When you use audiovisual equipment that requires a dark room, you lose vital visual contact with your listeners.

Remember Murphy's Law

According to Murphy's Law, if something can go wrong, it will. When you use presentation aids, you increase the chances that problems or snags will develop when you present your speech. Don't be a pessimist; just have backup supplies and a backup plan in case your best-laid plans go awry.

If something doesn't go as you planned, do your best to keep your speech on track. If a chart falls over, simply pick it up and keep talking; don't offer lengthy apologies. If you can't find the chalk you will need and it is your turn to speak, quietly ask a friend to go on a chalk hunt in another room. A

QuickCheck
Use Presentation Aids Effectively

- Rehearse with your presentation aids until you feel at ease with them.
- Make eye contact with the audience, not with your presentation aid.
- Explain your presentation aids; always set your visuals in a verbal context.
- Do not pass objects among members of your audience.
- Use animals with caution.
- Use handouts effectively.
- Time the use of your visuals to control your audience's attention.
- Use technology effectively.
- Remember Murphy's Law.

thorough rehearsal, a double-check of your equipment, and extra supplies such as extension cords, projector bulbs, or masking tape can help repeal Murphy's Law.

A Question of Ethics

The American Tobacco Institute has hired a physician to represent the organization at a meeting to discuss the relationship between tobacco and diseases. The physician has been instructed to support the institute's position. Is it ethical for the physician not to mention that the institute is paying him or her? Explain your answer.

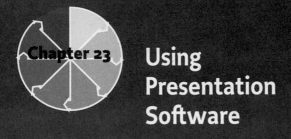

Chapter 23

Using Presentation Software

Many audiences have come to expect to see computer-generated graphics created with such popular software as PowerPoint®. Computer-generated graphics are images, words, charts, and graphs designed and presented with the help of a computer and special computer software. Although computer-generated graphics can be overused and can distract from your message if used improperly, they provide professional-looking possibilities for illustrating your speech.

Designing Computer-Generated Presentation Aids

Using a program such as PowerPoint, you can design and create complete presentation aids on your personal computer. You can then use the computer to display the presentation to your audience by connecting your computer to a special large-screen projector or a liquid crystal display (LCD) panel. You can run the program manually, using a mouse or the keyboard to advance the images as you speak, or you can set the program to run automatically.

Even if you don't have access to a computer to use for your presentation, you can create the graphic images you need using a computer at a commercial copy center or campus computer lab and then transfer the images to slides or overhead transparencies. Or you can print the images on paper and develop dazzling posters to display on an easel.

Consider Software Resources

The various presentation software packages are designed to let you easily include a variety of aids in your presentation. For instance, you can develop a key word or phrase outline to emphasize your main points as you speak. You can create graphs, charts, or drawings to incorporate into the presentation to display statistical information or illustrate particular points. You can also use a scanner to convert into digital format photographs or drawings, which you can then incorporate as visual images in your presentation.

Presentation software can even incorporate video or audio clips. As with any presentation aid, the images or clips that you choose to display must help develop your central idea; otherwise, do not include them.

There is an art to developing effective computer-generated graphics. But you don't have to be a professional artist. That's the advantage of using presentation software programs—virtually anyone can use them to craft professional-looking images. In addition to learning the mechanics of the software program, keep the following tips in mind when designing computer graphics.[1]

Keep Sights and Sounds Simple

In most aspects of communication, simple is better. Keep in mind that presentation aids support your message; they are not your message.

Most graphics software lets you add sound effects to highlight your message. Cute sounds lose their novelty after the first slide or two and can become irritating. You should be the soundtrack, not your computer.

Repeat Visual Elements to Unify Your Presentation

Use a common visual element, such as a bullet or visual symbol, at the beginning of each word or phrase on a list. Use common color schemes and spacing to give your visuals coherence. Also, avoid mixing and matching different fonts. You get a professional, polished look when you use a similar visual style for each of your images.

Clip art consists of pictures and images that are either in printed form or stored as electronic images in a computer file. You can incorporate these images into your visuals. Clip art can give your visuals and graphics a professional touch even if you did not excel in art class. Repeating the visual image can lend a consistent look and feel to your presentation.

Choose a Font with Care

You'll be able to choose from among dozens of fonts. Make an informed choice. Serif fonts are easier to read for longer passages. Sans serif fonts are more appropriate for titles.

Although interesting and dramatic, script fonts should be used sparingly because they are harder to read. Use decorative fonts only when you want to communicate a certain special tone or mood. Regardless of which font style you use, don't use more than one or two on a single visual.

Make Informed Decisions about Using Color

Color communicates. Think about the topic and purpose of your speech, and choose colors that will support and reinforce those. To unify your presentation, use the same background color on all visuals and no more than two colors for words. Using a dark background with lighter-colored words can have a pleasing effect and make the words easy to see.

QuickCheck
Design Effective Computer-Generated Aids

- Keep sights and sounds simple.
- Repeat visual elements to unify your presentation.
- Use clip art to give your visuals and graphics a professional touch.
- Choose a typeface with care.
- Avoid mixing many different fonts.
- Make informed decisions about using color.
- Prepare your presentation aids well in advance of your speaking date so that you can make them as attractive and polished-looking as possible.

Allow Plenty of Time to Prepare Your Presentation Aids

Prepare your presentation aids well in advance of your speaking date so that you can make them as attractive and polished-looking as possible. A sloppy, amateurish presentation aid will convey the impression that you are not a credible speaker, even if you have spent many hours preparing the verbal part of your speech.

If you haven't used computer-generated graphics before, don't expect to whip out the software manual and produce professional-looking images the night before your presentation. Focus your final hours on rehearsing, not on learning a computer program.

Preparing a Presentation with PowerPoint

When you first open PowerPoint, the program displays a dialog box with four options—AutoContent Wizard, Templates, Blank Presentation, and Open an Existing Presentation.

AutoContent Wizard

You can start by working with the **AutoContent Wizard,** which provides suggestions and ideas for your presentation. The AutoContent Wizard guides you through the design and layout process by asking specific questions about your presentation. It also provides you with a variety of sample presentations from which to choose.

The Wizard asks you how your presentation will be used and what type of output you want—slides, overheads, handouts, etc. Once you provide this information, the Wizard sets up an outline for titles, subtitles, main points, and subpoints and displays a slide design.

Templates

PowerPoint comes with a variety of professional presentations as well as professionally designed **templates** that contain color schemes, slide and title masters with custom formatting, and styled fonts designed for a particular "look." Different versions of PowerPoint provide different selections and numbers of templates. Click on a template to pre-view it; then choose one you like.

Blank Presentation

You can also begin with an outline you import from another application, such as Microsoft Word, or with a blank presentation that has neither suggested content nor design. **Blank Presentation** enables you to create your own slide design. You choose a lay-out, colors, graphics, fonts, and how the content is organized.

Open an Existing Presentation

With PowerPoint you can also open, edit, or view existing presentations in many different locations—including on your hard drive, on a network drive that you are connected to, or on an Internet site.

Save a Presentation

You can save a presentation, whether it's new or has been saved before. You can also save it with a dif-ferent name or in a different location. You can save a presentation in HTML format so it can be viewed and used on the Internet. You can also save a pres-entation so that whenever you open it, it always starts as a slide show.

View a Presentation

There are several different ways you can view the presentation aids you create: slide view, outline view, master view, slide sorter view, black-and-white view, and notes page view.

Slide View   In **slide view**, you can see an entire slide or zoom in to magnify a portion of the slide for de-tailed work. You can add both text and art to indi-vidual slides.

Outline View   **Outline view** displays text in an out-line format so you can see how your main points flow from slide to slide. Use outline view when you need to organize and develop the content of your presentation.

Master View   To add such items as a company logo or formatting that you want to appear on every slide, notes page, or handout, use **master view** and make your changes on the appropriate master. The master text determines the format of text on all slides. If you make a change to the slide master, the change affects all slides in your presentation that are based on that master.

Slide Sorter View   In **slide sorter view,** you see miniature versions of all the slides in your entire presentation so you can easily add, delete, and reorder slides. You can also add transitions and animation effects and set the timings for electronic slide shows.

Black-and-White View   When you're creating a presentation in color, you might want to print handouts in black and white. When you switch to **black-and-white view**, the objects in your presentation appear on screen and print in shades of black and white.

Notes Page View   To display the notes page for selected slides, switch to **notes page view,** where you can type speaker notes to use during your presentation. You can also move or resize the slide image and the notes box and print a copy of your notes for reference.

Create a Consistent Look

PowerPoint is designed to give your presentations a consistent appearance. In addition to the menu of design templates, you can use the program's slide master and color schemes to control the look of your slides.

The **slide master** controls the format and placement of the titles and text you type on slides, while the **title master** controls the format and placement of the title slide and any other slide you designate as a title slide. Masters also hold background items such as graphics that you want to appear on every slide. Any change you make to a slide master is reflected on each slide.

Color schemes are sets of eight balanced colors designed to be used as the main colors of a slide presentation—for text, background, fill, accents, and so on. Each different element on a slide is automatically given a color in the scheme. You can pick a color scheme for an individual slide or for an entire presentation.

However, if you create unique slides—for example, slides with backgrounds that differ from the master or fill colors that aren't part of the master color scheme—these slides retain their uniqueness even when you change the master. If you change your mind later, you can always restore slides you altered to the master format.

Add Text

The easiest way to add text to a slide is to type directly into any placeholder on the slide. When you want to add text outside a placeholder or shape, you can use the Text Box tool on the Drawing toolbar. To add text that doesn't wrap, click the tool, click where you want to add the text, and start typing. To add text that does wrap, click the tool, drag it to where you want to add text, and then start typing.

To add text to an AutoShape (a basic shape provided in PowerPoint), just click the shape and type the text. The text attaches to the shape and moves or rotates with the shape as the shape moves or rotates. You can add text to most AutoShapes, except lines, connectors, and free forms.

Insert Pictures

PowerPoint comes with its own set of pictures in the **Clip Gallery**. The Clip Gallery includes a wide variety of clip art that makes it easy for you to dress up your presentations with professionally designed images.

Select a picture by clicking Insert Clip Art and then clicking the Clip Art or Pictures tab. The Clip Gallery includes a handy Find feature to help you locate just the right images for your presentation.

The AutoClipArt command on the Tools menu searches your presentation for concepts and then suggests images in the Clip Gallery you might use to express your ideas.

You can also insert pictures and scanned photographs from other programs and locations. To insert a picture from another program, point to Picture on the Insert menu and then click From File. When you select a picture, the Picture toolbar appears with tools you can use to crop or recolor the picture, add a border to it, and adjust its brightness and contrast. To insert a scanned photograph, point to Picture on the Insert menu and then click From Scanner. You can also draw your own pictures using PowerPoint drawing tools.

Insert Charts and Graphs

PowerPoint includes programs you can use to add charts, scanned pictures, and equations to your presentations. Organization Chart, Graph, Photo Editor, and Equation Editor all create embedded objects that you can insert into a presentation. By **embedding** data in a document, you can edit it in your document without having to return to the source files. When you create or modify a chart, scanned picture, or equation in your presentation, the program's menus and toolbars replace the PowerPoint menus and toolbars.

Print a Presentation

You can print your entire presentation—the slides, outline, speaker notes, and audience handouts—in either color or black and white. To print your presentation, open the file and choose whether you want to print slides, handouts, notes pages, or an outline. Then identify the slides to be printed and the number of copies you want.

You can also make color or black-and-white overhead transparencies or create 35mm slides. When you print handouts, you can print one, two, three, or six slides on a page; or you can use the Microsoft Word Send To command (under the File menu), and then use Word to print other layout variations.

Create Speaker Notes and Handouts

You can create notes pages while you're creating your presentation and then use these pages as speaker notes when you give a slide show. You can also create handouts of slides for the audience.

In addition, you can send your notes and slide images to Microsoft Word and use Word features to enhance their appearance, or you can send them there to become the starting point for a more detailed handout, such as a training manual.

When you want to show only the content of the slides, use handouts. Use notes pages when you want to include the speaker notes with the slides.

Use Special Effects

Transitions and **animations**, when used sparingly, can add interest to your presentation, help highlight important points, and control the flow of information. PowerPoint comes with music, sounds, and videos you can play during your slide shows. You can also animate text, graphics, and other objects. You can insert a sound or video clip on a slide where you want it to play during a slide show. However, you will need special equipment on your computer to play music, sounds, and videos.

You can change the order and timing of animations and set them to occur automatically. Text can appear one letter, one word, or one paragraph at a time. Graphic images and other objects can appear progressively; the elements of a chart can be

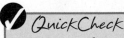

QuickCheck
Be Prepared

- Save all files you create for your visual aids.
- Save your presentation on the hard drive, but also make backup disks.
- Keep the size of your files manageable.
- Plan to rehearse the presentation on the equipment that you will actually use for your presentation.
- Bring copies of the backup disk for your presentation.
- Check the equipment before you begin your presentation to ensure that it works correctly.
- Have a backup plan in case there are problems; either make a set of transparencies that you can show on an overhead projector or print your slides for use as handouts.

animated; the order in which objects appear on a slide can be altered; and you can set timings for each object.

A Question of Ethics

You plan to give a persuasive speech to convince your class-mates that term limits should be imposed for senators and members of Congress—even though you are personally against term limits. Is it ethical to develop a persuasive message based on a proposition with which you personally disagree? Why or why not?

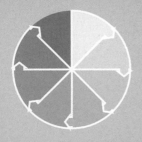

Part 6

Types of Speeches

Chapter 24

Informative Speaking

A speech to inform shares information with others to enhance their knowledge or understanding of the concepts and ideas presented. When you inform someone, you assume the role of a teacher by defining, illustrating, clarifying, or elaborating on a topic.

Goals of Informative Speaking

When trying to help listeners make sense of information, speakers often have one or more of the following goals in mind: to enhance understanding, to gain and maintain interest, or to ensure that listeners can remember what was said.

Speak to Enhance Understanding

Understanding occurs when a listener accurately interprets the intended meaning of a message. Even when your speaking goal is to enhance understanding, the words you select to improve understanding may actually hinder the listener from accurately interpreting your meaning.

When your speaking goal is to enhance understanding, you must first make sure you are using words that your listeners will interpret in the same way as you do. How do you do this? Be audience-centered. The stories you tell, the examples you use, and the statistics you cite will make sense to listeners only if you and they have a common understanding of the words you speak. Without a common framework, your message won't make sense.

Speak to Maintain Interest

You may have carefully selected words, examples, and illustrations that your listeners understand, but if your listeners are bored and not focusing on your message, you won't achieve your informative-speaking goal.

People may be interested in you and your topic for a variety of reasons. They often listen to what affects them directly, adds to their knowledge, satisfies their curiosity, or entertains them. If audience members feel they will benefit from your speech in some way, your speech will interest them. And an interesting speech commands attention as well as respect.

Speak to Be Remembered

One day after hearing a presentation, most audience members will remember only about half of what they were told. And they will recall only about 25 percent two weeks later. Your job as an informative speaker is to improve on those statistics.

Being organized, being appropriately redundant by using internal summaries and a final summary, and relating the message to listeners' interests are all useful methods of helping your audience increase their retention of the message you've worked so hard to develop.

Types of Informative Speeches

Informative speeches can be classified according to the subject areas they cover (see Table 24.1). Classifying your speech can help you decide how to organize the information you want to present. Good organization will help your audience process your message.

Strategies to Enhance Audience Understanding

How do you enhance someone's knowledge or understanding? At the heart of creating understanding in someone is the ability to describe both old and new ideas to the person.

Speak with Clarity

To speak with clarity is to express ideas so that the listener understands the intended message accurately. Speaking clearly is an obvious goal of an

Table 24.1   Types of Informative Speeches

	Description	Typical Organization Patterns	Sample Topics
A Speech about Objects	Presents information about tangible things	Topical Spatial Chronological	The Rosetta Stone Museums International space station Voting machines
A Speech about Procedures	Reviews how something works or describes a process	Chronological Topical Complexity	How to . . . Fix a carburetor Operate a nuclear power plant Buy a quality used car Trap lobsters
A Speech about People	Describes either famous people or personal acquaintances	Chronological Topical	Sojourner Truth Nelson Mandela Indira Gandhi Your granddad Your favorite teacher
A Speech about Ideas	Presents abstract information or discusses principles, concepts, theories, or issues	Topical Complexity Chronological	Communism Success Buddhism Reincarnation
A Speech about Events	Describes an event that either has happened or will happen	Topical Spatial	The 2005 Southeast Asian tsunami Inauguration Day Cinco de Mayo

informative speaker. Communication researcher Joseph Chesebro has summarized several research-based strategies you can use to enhance message clarity.[1]

- Preview your main ideas in your introduction.
- Tell your listeners how what you present relates to a previous point.
- Frequently summarize key ideas.
- Provide a visual outline to help listeners follow your ideas.
- Provide a handout prior to your talk with the major points outlined; leave space so that listeners can jot down key ideas.
- Once you announce your topic and outline, stay on message.
- Don't present too much information too quickly.

Use Principles and Techniques of Adult Learning

Andragogy is the art and science of teaching adults. What are some effective andragogical, or adult-learning, principles found by researchers and scholars?

Give Adults Information They Can Use Immediately Each of us has a kind of mental "in-basket," an agenda for what we want or need to accomplish. If you present adult listeners with information that they can apply immediately to their "in-basket," they are more likely to focus on and understand your message.

Actively Involve Adult Learners in the Learning Process Rather than having your listeners sit passively as you speak, consider asking them questions to think about or, in some cases, to respond to on the spot.

Connect Adult Learners' Life Experiences with the New Information Adult listeners are more likely to understand your message if you help them connect the new information with their past experiences. First, know the kinds of experiences that your listeners have had, and then refer to those experiences as you present your ideas.

Explain How New Information Is Relevant to Adult Learners' Needs and Lives   When speaking to an adult audience, realize that any information or ideas you share will more likely be heard and understood if you relate what you say to their chock-full-of-activity lives. Busy people need to be shown how the ideas you share relate to their lives.

Seek Ways to Relate the Ideas You Present to Listeners' Problems   People will be more likely to pay attention to information that helps them better understand and solve their problems.

Clarify Complex Processes

Research suggests that you can demystify a complex process if you first provide a simple overview of the process with an analogy, model, picture, or vivid description.[2]

Before going into great detail, give listeners the "big picture" or convey the gist of the process.[3] *Analogies* (comparisons) are often a good way to do this.[4]

You can also *describe* the process, providing more detail than when you just define something. Descriptions answer questions about the who, what, where, why, and when of the process. Who is involved? What is the process, idea, or event that you want to describe? Where and when does it take place? Why does it occur, or why is it important to the audience? (Not all of these questions apply to every description.)

Or you can clarify a process with a *word picture*. Word pictures are lively descriptions that help your listeners form a mental image by appealing to their senses of sight, taste, smell, sound, and touch. The following suggestions will help you construct effective word pictures.

■ Form a clear mental image of the person, place, or object before you try to describe it.
■ Describe the appearance of the person, place, or object. What would your listeners see if they were looking at it? Use lively language to describe the flaws and foibles, bumps and beauties of the people, places, and things you want your

audience to see. Make your description an invitation to the imagination.

■ Describe what your listeners would hear. Use colorful, onomatopoeic words, such as *buzz, snort, hum, crackle,* or *hiss.* These words are much more descriptive than the more general term *noise.* Imitate the sound you want your listeners to hear mentally. For example, instead of saying "When I walked in the woods, I heard the sound of twigs breaking beneath my feet," you might say, "As I walked in the woods, I heard the crackle of twigs underfoot."

■ Describe smells, if appropriate. What fragrance or aroma do you want your audience to recall? For example, Thanksgiving would not be complete without the rich aroma of roast turkey. The associated smell greatly enhances the overall word picture.

■ Describe how an object feels when touched. Use words that are as clear and vivid as possible. Rather than saying that something is rough or smooth, use a simile, such as "The rock was as rough as sandpaper" or "The pebble was as smooth as a baby's skin." These descriptions appeal to both the visual and the tactile senses.

■ Describe taste, one of the most powerful sensory cues, if appropriate. Thinking about your grandmother may evoke for you memories of her rich homemade noodles; her sweet, fudgy nut brownies; and her light, flaky, buttery pie crust. Descriptions of these taste sensations would be welcomed by any audience. More important, such description can help you paint an accurate, vivid image of your grandmother.

■ Describe the emotion that a listener might feel if he or she were to experience the situation you relate. If you experienced the situation, describe your own emotions. Use specific adjectives rather than general terms such as *happy* or *sad.* One speaker, talking about her first speech assignment, described her reaction this way: "My heart stopped. Panic began to rise up inside. For the next week, I lived in dreaded anticipation of the event."[5] Note how effectively her choices of such words and phrases as "my heart stopped,"

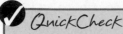

QuickCheck
Strategies to Enhance Audience Understanding

- Speak with clarity.
- Use principles and techniques of adult learning.
- Clarify complex processes.
- Use effective visual reinforcement.

"panic," and "dreaded anticipation" describe her terror at the prospect of making a speech—much more so than if she had said, "I was scared." The more vividly and accurately you can describe emotion, the more intimately involved in your description the audience will become.

Use Effective Visual Reinforcement

Pictures, graphs, posters, and computer-generated graphics can help you gain and maintain audience members' attention, as well as increase their retention.

Strategies to Maintain Audience Interest: Establishing a Motive for Listening

Before you can inform an audience, you must gain and maintain their interest. No matter how carefully crafted your definitions, skillfully delivered your description of a process, or visually reinforcing your presentation aid, if your listeners aren't paying attention, you won't achieve your goal. Strategies for gaining and holding interest are vital in achieving your speaking goal.

Don't assume that your listeners will be automatically interested in what you have to say. Pique their interest with a rhetorical question. Tell them a story. Tell them how the information you present will be of value to them.

Tell a Story

Good stories with interesting characters and riveting plots have fascinated listeners for millennia; the words "Once upon a time" are usually a sure-fire attention getter. A good story is inherently interesting.

The characteristics of a well-told tale are simple yet powerful. Stories are also a way of connecting your message to people from a variety of cultural backgrounds. A good story includes conflict, incorporates action, creates suspense, and may also include humor.

- **Conflict.** Stories that pit one side against another and describe opposing ideas and forces in government, religion, or personal relationships foster attention.
- **Action.** An audience is more likely to listen to an action-packed message than to one that listlessly lingers on an idea too long. Good stories have a beginning that sets the stage, a heart that moves to a conclusion, and then an ending that ties up all the loose ends. The key to interest is a plot that moves along to hold attention.
- **Suspense.** Suspense is created when the characters in the story may do one of several things. Keeping people on the edge of their seats because they don't know what will happen next is an element in good storytelling.
- **Humor.** Using a bit of humor makes the point while holding the listener's attention. Not all stories have to be funny. Stories may be sad or dramatic without humor. But adding humor at appropriate times usually helps maintain interest and attention.

Present Information That Relates to Listeners

Being an audience-centered informative speaker means being aware of information that your audience can use. If, for example, you are going to teach your audience about recycling, be sure to talk about specific efforts on your campus or in your community. Adapt your message to the people who will be in your audience.

Strategies to Enhance Audience Recall

Some speakers are better than others at presenting information in a memorable way. Here are some strategies that will help your audiences remember you and your message.

Build In Redundancy

When you speak, repeat key points. Give a clear preview at the beginning of your talk as well as a summary statement in your conclusion. Include internal summaries—short summaries after key points during your speech—to help audiences remember key ideas. Use numeric signposts (numbering key ideas verbally by saying "My first point is. . . . My second point is. . . .") to make sure your audience can identify and remember key points.

A reinforcing visual aid that displays your key ideas can also enhance recall. If you really want to ensure that listeners come away from your speech with essential information, consider preparing a handout or an outline of key ideas.

Pace Your Information Flow

Organize your speech so that you present an even flow of information, rather than bunching up a number of significant details around one point. If you present too much new information too quickly, you may overwhelm your audience.

Make sure that your audience has time to process any new information. Use supporting materials both to help clarify new information and to slow down the pace of your presentation. Do not try to see how much detail and content you can cram into a speech.

Reinforce Key Ideas Verbally

You can reinforce an idea by using such phrases as "This is the most important point" or "Be sure to remember this next point." Suppose you have four suggestions for helping your listeners avoid a serious sunburn, and your last suggestion is the most important. How can you make sure your audience knows that? Just tell them. "Of all the suggestions I've given you, this last tip is the most important one. The higher the SPF level on your sunscreen, the better." Be careful not to overuse this technique. If you claim that every other point is a key point, soon your audience will not believe you.

Reinforce Key Ideas Nonverbally

You can also signal the importance of a point with nonverbal emphasis. Gestures serve the purpose of accenting or emphasizing key phrases, as italics do in written communication.

■ A well-placed pause can provide emphasis and reinforcement to set off a point. Pausing just before or just after making an important point will focus attention on your thought.

■ Raising or lowering your voice can also reinforce a key idea.

■ Movement can help emphasize major ideas. Moving from behind the lectern to tell a personal anecdote can signal that something special and more intimate is about to be said.

■ Your movement and gestures should be meaningful and natural, rather than seemingly arbitrary or forced.

■ Your need to emphasize an idea can provide the motivation to make a meaningful movement.

Choosing a Speech Topic

by Roger Fringer

The following sample speech illustrates the principles and strategies of effectively informing others. Note how Roger Fringer[6] uses many of the approaches to crafting an informative speech.

Roger cleverly captures attention by purposefully starting with an unimaginative topic and using halting delivery that makes listeners wonder, "What's this really about?"

Today I'd like to talk to you about [pause] tables. Tables are wood . . . usually . . . and they are. . . . How often do we sit in a class and feel the intelligence draining out of us? In a speech class, we are given the opportunity to add to that feeling or to add to the intelligence. Selecting a meaningful speech topic will make our speeches interesting, important, as well as being informative. As students, we've all been in the situation of being more anxious than necessary because we are talking about an unfamiliar or uninteresting speech topic.

Roger establishes a common bond with his listeners by relating to them as fellow students who are often confronted with the same problem: how to select a topic for a speech.

In our public speaking class, we spend a number of hours giving speeches and listening to them. If we have four days of speeches, at what—seven speech topics, that equals 28 hours spent listening to speeches. Let's not forget that we are paying to listen to those speeches. If our tuition is, say, $15,000 a year, that's $875 that we have spent listening to those 28 hours of speeches. We work hard for our tuition, so we should spend it wisely. Spending it wisely means we don't waste our time. We don't waste our own time on preparing and giving the speeches, and we don't waste our classmates' time who have to listen to our speeches. The solution is simple if we take choosing our topic seriously.

Rather than just saying we waste time and money when listening to speeches, Roger uses statistics specifically adapted to the audience to whom he is speaking; this is a good example of being audience-centered.
He clearly previews his major ideas and links each idea together by introducing each point with a word that begins with I.

I recommend that we choose topics following *The Three I's* to guide us. The first *I* is to make speeches *interesting*. By doing so, we can alleviate the boredom that so often permeates the public speaking classroom. If the topic is interesting to us, we will present it in a manner that shows our interest. We will also keep our audience's attention when we know, as students, they can be thinking about a million other things. Choosing an interesting topic will also alleviate some of the angst, anxiety we feel while giving the speech topic.

Here he uses a signpost to clearly note he's moved to his second point.

The second *I* is to make the speech *important.* The speech should not only be interesting but important to us. It should be relevant to our lives now or in the future.

Again he uses a verbal signpost, this time to indicate that this is his third point.

The third *I* is to make the speech *informative.* Let's not waste our tuition money by not learning anything new in those 28 hours of class time. This is our opportunity to learn from each other's experiences and expertise.

Although Roger's primary purpose is to inform, he uses a hypothetical example to tell the audience how the information he has given them will help them solve a problem—how to find a good speech topic.

Now just picture yourself putting these ideas into practice. Imagine sitting in a classroom, listening to your classmates talk about issues or ideas that are important to them. You're learning from their life experiences, experiences that you would not have had the opportunity to learn about if it had not been for their speech. Then, imagine being able to talk about the experiences and knowledge that are important to you. Sometimes you only have seven minutes to express what is most important to you. Besides that, it's to a captive audience that has no choice but to listen to you. There are few times in our lives when we can have an impact on someone else's life, and we have only a short amount of time to do it. But in our pubic speaking class, we can have that chance. Let's all think about how we use our time and energy in our public speaking class. I don't want to waste my time or have any unnecessary stress over [pause] tables. I would like all of us to use our opportunities wisely by choosing topics that are interesting, important, and informative.

Roger provides closure to his message by making a reference to the example he used in his introduction.

A Question of Ethics

Even during times of intense personal crisis—for example, following the death of a family member—the press relentlessly pursues celebrities to try to elicit impromptu statements. Is this an ethical practice? Does the public's right to know justify the invasion of privacy?

Chapter 25

Understanding Principles of Persuasive Speaking

As a persuasive speaker, you will ask your listeners to respond to the information you share. Audience analysis is crucial to achieving your goal. To advocate a particular view or position successfully, you must understand your listeners' attitudes, beliefs, values, and behavior.

Persuasion Defined

Persuasion is the process of changing or reinforcing attitudes, beliefs, values, or behaviors. In a persuasive speech, the speaker explicitly asks the audience to make a choice, rather than just informing them of the options.

Attitudes

Our attitudes represent our likes and dislikes. Stated more technically, an **attitude** is a learned predisposition to respond favorably or unfavorably toward something. Attitudes (likes and dislikes) are easier to change than either beliefs or values.

Beliefs

A **belief** is what you understand to be true or false. If you believe in something, you are convinced that it exists or is true. Beliefs are typically based on past experiences. Beliefs are usually based on evidence, but some beliefs are based on faith—we haven't directly experienced something, but we believe anyway. A belief is more susceptible to change than a value is, but it is still difficult to alter. Beliefs are changed by evidence. Usually it takes a great deal of evidence to change a belief and alter the way your audience structures reality.

Values

A **value** is an enduring conception of right or wrong, good or bad. If you value something, you classify it as good or desirable and you tend to think of its opposite or its lack as bad or wrong. If you do not value something, you are indifferent to it. Values form the basis of your life goals and the motivating force behind your behavior. It is not impossible to change the values of your listeners, but it is much more difficult than changing a belief or an attitude. Speeches that focus on changing or reinforcing audience values emphasize how and why something is better than something else. Understanding what your listeners value can help you refine your analysis of them and adapt the content of your speech to those values.

Behavior

Persuasive messages often attempt to do more than change or reinforce attitudes, beliefs, or values—they attempt to change behavior. Several factors motivate us to respond to persuasive messages with a change in behavior: our actual and perceived needs, our tendency to avoid pain and seek pleasure, our emotional reactions, and our compulsion to seek psychological balance and order in our lives.

How Persuasion Works

The **elaboration likelihood model (ELM) of persuasion** has a long name but is actually a simple idea that explains how you are persuaded to do or think about something.[1] The theory suggests that there are two ways you can be persuaded.

1. You can be persuaded by the logic, reasoning, arguments, and evidence presented to you.
2. You can be persuaded by such peripheral strategies as catchy music used in an advertisement or simply liking the salesperson who is selling you a product. It's not the logic or content of the argument that persuades you; it's the overall feeling you have about the product or salesperson that triggers your purchase.

Aristotle noted that in addition to logical persuasive strategies (*logos*), you can be persuaded by the credibility of the speaker (*ethos*) or by the overall emotional response you have to a message or messenger (*pathos*).

Among the factors that determine whether you are more likely to be persuaded by a direct route (with logic) or a more indirect, peripheral route (with credibility or emotion) is the concept of motivation. Motivation is the underlying internal force that drives people to achieve their goals. Several factors motivate people to respond to persuasive messages; the need to restore balance to their lives so as to avoid stress, the need to avoid pain, and the desire to increase pleasure have been documented as influencing attitudes, beliefs, values, and behavior.

How to Motivate Listeners

Persuasion works because listeners are motivated to respond to a message. An audience is more likely to be persuaded if you help members solve their problems or otherwise meet their needs. They can also be motivated if you convince them good things will happen to them if they follow your advice, or bad things will occur if they don't.

Use Dissonance

According to dissonance theory, when you are presented with information inconsistent with your current attitudes, beliefs, values, or behavior, you become aware that you have a problem; you experience a kind of discomfort called **cognitive dissonance**. The word *cognitive* refers to thoughts; *dissonance* means "lack of harmony or agreement."

Cognitive dissonance means that you are experiencing a way of thinking that is inconsistent and uncomfortable. Most people seek to avoid problems or feelings of dissonance; thus, creating dissonance with a persuasive speech can be an effective way to change attitudes and behavior.

The first tactic in such a speech is to identify an existing problem or need. But effective persuasion requires more than simply creating dissonance and then suggesting a solution to the problem, as there are various things listeners can do to restore balance, only one of which serves your purpose.

- **Listeners may discredit the source.** You need to ensure that your audience will perceive you as competent and trustworthy so that they will accept your message.
- **Listeners may reinterpret the message.** They may choose to focus on the parts of your message that are consistent with what they already believe and ignore the unfamiliar or controversial parts. Your job is to make your message as clear as possible.
- **Listeners may seek new information.** Audience members may look for additional information to negate your position and to refute your well-created arguments.
- **Listeners may stop listening.** Some messages are so much at odds with listeners' attitudes, beliefs, and values that they may decide to stop listening. The principle of selective exposure suggests that we tend to pay attention to messages that are consistent with our points of view and to avoid those that are not.
- **Listeners may change their attitudes, beliefs, values, or behavior.** If listeners change their attitudes, they can reduce the dissonance that they experience.

Use Listener Needs

Need is one of the best motivators. The more you understand what your listeners need, the greater the chances are that you can gain and hold their attention and ultimately get them to do what you want.

Abraham Maslow suggests that there is a hierarchy of needs that motivates everyone's behavior. Basic physiological needs (such as food, water, and air) have to be satisfied before we can be motivated to respond to higher-level needs. Figure 25.1 illustrates Maslow's five levels of needs, with the most basic at the bottom. When attempting to persuade an audience, a public speaker tries to stimulate

Figure 25.1 ■ Maslow's hierarchy of needs.

these needs in order to change or reinforce attitudes, beliefs, values, or behavior.

Physiological Needs   The most basic needs for all humans are physiological: We all need air, water, and food. According to Maslow's theory, unless those needs are met, it will be difficult to motivate a listener to satisfy other needs.

Safety Needs   Once basic physiological needs are met, listeners are concerned about their safety. We have a need to feel safe, secure, and protected, and we need to be able to predict that our own and our loved ones' need for safety will be met.

Social Needs   We all need to feel loved and valued. We need contact with others and reassurance that they care about us. According to Maslow, these social needs translate into our need for a sense of belonging to a group (a fraternity, a religious organization, a circle of friends). Powerful persuasive appeals are based on our need for social contact.

Self-Esteem Needs   The need for self-esteem reflects our desire to think well of ourselves.

Self-Actualization Needs   The need for **self-actualiza-tion** is the need to fully realize one's highest potential. According to Maslow's assumption that our needs are organized into a hierarchy, needs at the other four levels must be satisfied before we can be motivated to satisfy the highest-level need.

Use Positive Motivation

Positive motivational appeals are statements that suggest good things will happen if the speaker's advice is heeded. A key to using positive motivational appeals effectively is to know what your listeners value. Knowing what audience members view as desirable, good, and virtuous can help you select the benefits of your persuasive proposal that will best appeal to them.

Use Negative Motivation

The use of a threat to change someone's attitude or behavior is one of the most effective approaches. The appeal to fear takes the form of an "if–then" statement. If you don't do X, then awful things will happen to you. A persuader builds an argument on the assertion that a need will not be met unless the desired behavior or attitude change occurs.

- A strong threat to a loved one tends to be more successful than a fear appeal directed at the audience members.
- The more competent, trustworthy, or respected the speaker, the greater the likelihood that an appeal to fear will be successful.
- Fear appeals are more successful if you can convince listeners that the threat is real and will probably occur unless they take the action you are advocating.
- Increasing the intensity of a fear appeal increases the chances that the fear appeal will be effective; this is especially true if the listener can take some action (the action the persuader is suggesting) to reduce the threat.[2]

The speaker who uses fear appeals has an ethical responsibility to be truthful and not exaggerate when trying to arouse listeners' fear.

✔ *QuickCheck*
Using Fear Appeals to Persuade

■ Fear appeals involving loved ones are often more effective than those involving audience members themselves.
■ The greater your credibility, the more likely it is that your fear appeal will be effective.
■ You must convince your audience that the threat is real and the feared event could actually happen.
■ Strong fear appeals are more effective than mild fear appeals if there is evidence to support the threat made by the speaker.

Developing Your Persuasive Speech

Don't design a persuasive message using strategies that would be effective only for you or those from your cultural background. The wise persuader consciously thinks about the persuasive strategies that will be effective for his or her listeners.

Consider the Audience

An effective communicator is especially sensitive to cultural differences between himself or herself and the audience, while at the same time being cautious not to make stereotypical assumptions about an audience based only on cultural factors.

Select and Narrow Your Persuasive Topic

You'll present a better speech if you select a topic you can speak about with sincere conviction. In addition to your interests, always reflect on your audience's passions and convictions. The ideal topic speaks to a need, concern, or issue of the audience as well as to your interests and zeal.

Controversial issues make excellent sources for persuasive topics. A controversial issue is a question about which people disagree. In choosing a controversial topic, you need to be audience-centered—to know the local, state, national, or international issues that interest your listeners. The best persuasive-speech topics focus on important rather than frivolous issues.

Determine Your Persuasive Purpose

When your goal is to persuade, you've already decided on your general purpose: You want the members of your audience to change or reinforce their attitudes, beliefs, values, or behavior. But you still must develop your specific purpose.

When you try to persuade others, you don't always have to strive for dramatic changes. People rarely make major life changes after hearing just one persuasive message. Your persuasive-speaking goal may be to move listeners *a bit closer* to your ultimate objective.

Develop Your Central Idea and Main Ideas

When persuading others, most speakers find it useful to state their central idea in the form of a proposition. A **proposition** is a statement with which you want your audience to agree.

There are three categories of propositions: propositions of fact, propositions of value, and propositions of policy. Determining which category your persuasive proposition fits into will not only help you clarify your central idea but also give you an idea of how to select specific persuasive strategies that will help you achieve your specific purpose.

Proposition of Fact   A **proposition of fact** focuses on whether something is true or false, on whether it did or did not happen. To persuade listeners to agree with a proposition of fact, you must focus on changing or reinforcing their beliefs. Most persuasive speeches that focus on a proposition of fact begin by identifying one or more reasons that the proposition is true.

Proposition of Value   A **proposition of value** is a statement that calls for the listener to judge the worth or importance of something. Value propositions are statements that something is either good or bad or that one thing or course of action is better than another thing or action. Value propositions often directly compare two things and suggest that one of the options is better than the other.

Proposition of Policy   The third type of proposition, a **proposition of policy**, advocates a specific action—changing a policy, procedure, or behavior.

Putting Persuasive Principles into Practice

There are three general principles to help you link the theory of persuasion with the practice of persuasion:

1. Express your goal in terms that are consistent, rather than dissonant, with the attitudes, beliefs, values, and behavior of your audience.
2. Make the advantages of your proposition greater than the disadvantages. Your job as a speaker is to convince your listeners that the benefits or advantages of adopting your point of view will outweigh whatever costs or disadvantages are associated with your proposal.
3. Be sure your proposal meets your listeners' needs.

A Question of Ethics

Kristi believes she has a flair for words and, in her speech on ecology, uses many metaphoric and alliterative expressions like "trembling trees" and "lacy leaves." She believes that poetic language will persuade her listeners more than basic facts and statistics. Do you agree? Explain your answer.

Chapter 26

Using Persuasive Strategies

The ancient Greek philosopher Aristotle defined *rhetoric* as the process of discovering the "available means of persuasion." What are these "available means" that can help you persuade an audience?

Establish Credibility

Credibility is the audience's perception of a speaker's competence, trustworthiness, and dynamism. The more believable you are to your listeners, the more effective you will be as a persuasive communicator.

Competence

One factor in credibility is **competence**. To be credible, a speaker should be informed, skilled, or knowledgeable about the subject he or she is talking about. One way to enhance your competence is to cite credible evidence to support your point.

Trustworthiness

Another factor is **trustworthiness**. People trust those they believe to be honest. While delivering your speech, you have to convey honesty and sincerity.

One way to earn the audience's trust is by demonstrating that you have had experience dealing with the issues you talk about. Your trustworthiness may be suspect if you advocate something that will result in a direct benefit to you.

Dynamism

A third factor in credibility is the speaker's **dynamism**, or energy. Dynamism is often projected through delivery. **Charisma** is a form of dynamism. A charismatic person possesses charm, talent, magnetism, and other qualities that make the person attractive and energetic.

Enhance Credibility

Speakers establish their credibility in three phases.

Initial Credibility

Initial credibility is the impression of your credibility your listeners have even before you speak. Give careful thought to your appearance and establish eye contact before you begin your talk. Prepare a brief description of your credentials and accomplishments so that the person who introduces you can use it in his or her introductory remarks.

Derived Credibility

Derived credibility is the perception of your credibility your audience forms as you present yourself and your message. Here are several specific skills for enhancing your credibility:

- Establish common ground with the audience by indicating in your opening remarks that you share the values and concerns of your audience.
- Support arguments with evidence that supports your persuasive conclusions.
- Present a well-organized, well-delivered message to enhance your credibility as a competent and rational advocate. It is crucial to ensure that your message is logically structured and uses appropriate internal summaries, signposts, and enumeration of key ideas.

Terminal Credibility

The last phase of credibility, called **terminal credibility,** is the perception of your credibility listeners have when you finish your speech. Continue to make eye contact. Also, don't leave the lectern or speaking area until you have finished your closing sentence. Even if there is no planned question-and-answer period following your speech, be ready to respond to questions.

Use Logic and Evidence to Persuade

Logic is a formal system of rules for making inferences. Because wise audience members will be listening, persuasive speakers need to give careful attention to the way they use logic to reach a conclusion.

Present evidence and then use appropriate reasoning to lead your listeners to the conclusion you advocate. **Reasoning** is the process of drawing a conclusion from evidence. **Evidence** consists of facts, examples, statistics, and expert opinions that you use to support and prove the points you wish to make. Proof consists of the evidence plus the conclusion you draw from it.

Understand Types of Reasoning

There are three major ways to structure an argument to reach a logical conclusion: inductively, deductively, and causally.

Inductive Reasoning   Reasoning that arrives at a general conclusion from specific instances or examples is known as **inductive reasoning**. Using this approach, you reach a general conclusion based on specific examples, facts, statistics, and opinions. You may not know for a certainty that the specific instances prove that the conclusion is true, but you decide that, in all probability, the specific instances support the general conclusion.

To judge the validity of a **generalization** arrived at inductively, ask these questions:

- Are there enough specific instances to support the conclusion?
- Are the specific instances typical?
- Are the instances recent?

Reasoning by Analogy   Reasoning by analogy is a special type of inductive reasoning. An analogy is a comparison. This form of reasoning compares one thing, person, or process with another, to predict how something will perform and respond.

There are questions that you should ask to check the validity of conclusions reached via analogy:

- Do the ways in which the two things are alike outweigh the ways in which they are different?
- Is the assertion about the original thing, person, or process true?

Deductive Reasoning   Reasoning from a general statement or principle to reach a specific conclusion is called **deductive reasoning.** This is just the opposite of inductive reasoning. When the conclusion is certain rather than probable, you are reasoning deductively. The certainty of your conclusion is based on the validity or truth of the general statement that forms the basis of your argument.

Deductive reasoning can be structured in the form of a syllogism. A **syllogism** is a way of organizing an argument based on three elements:

1. You start with a general statement that serves as the **major premise.** The certainty of your conclusion hinges on the soundness of your major premise.
2. The **minor premise** is a more specific statement about an example that is linked to the major premise.
3. The **conclusion** is based on the major premise and the more specific minor premise.

In reasoning deductively, you need to ensure that both the major and the minor premises are true and can be supported with evidence.

Causal Reasoning   A third type of reasoning is called **causal reasoning**—relating two or more events in such a way as to conclude that one or more of the events caused the others.

There are two ways to structure a causal argument. First, you can reason from cause to effect, moving from a known fact to a predicted result. You move from something that has occurred to something that has not yet occurred. A second way to frame a causal argument is to reason backward, from known effect to unknown cause. You cannot be sure of the cause, but you are certain of the effect.

Adapt to Diverse Audiences

Effective strategies for developing your persuasive objective will vary depending on the background and cultural expectations of your listeners. Speakers from the United States typically identify facts and link them to support a specific proposition or conclusion. North Americans also like debates involving a direct clash of ideas and opinions. Our low-context culture encourages people to be more direct in dealing with issues and disagreement than people in high-context cultures generally are.

People from high-context cultures may expect that speakers will establish a personal relationship before debating issues. Some cultures use a deductive pattern of reasoning, rather than an inductive pattern. They begin with a general premise and then link it to a specific situation when they attempt to persuade listeners.

Middle Eastern cultures are more likely to use narrative methods to persuade an audience. They tell stories that evoke feelings and emotions, and use extended analogies, examples, and illustrations, allowing their listeners to draw their own conclusions by inductive association.[1]

Consider the following general principles to help you construct arguments that a culturally diverse audience will find persuasive.

Evidence   What may be convincing evidence to you may not be such an obvious piece of evidence for others. If you are uncertain about whether your listeners will perceive your evidence as valid and reliable, you could, before you address the entire group, test your evidence on a small group of people who will be in your audience.

Appeals to Action   In some high-context cultures, the conclusion to your message can be stated indirectly. You can imply what you'd like your listeners to do. In a low-context culture such as the United States, listeners may expect you to more directly state the action you'd like your audience members to take.

Message Structure   North Americans often like a well-organized message with a clear, explicit link between the evidence used and the conclusion drawn. North Americans also are comfortable with a structure that focuses on a problem and then offers a solution or a message in which the causes are identified and the effects are specified.

Audiences in the Middle East, however, would expect less formal structure and greater use of a narrative style of message development. Either the audience infers the point or the speaker may conclude by making the point clear. In some situations, it's better to get a message out of someone than to put a message into someone. Being indirect or implicit may sometimes be the best persuasive strategy.

Persuasive Communication Style   Another cultural factor that influences how receptive listeners are to a message is the presentation style of the speech. A speaker's overall style includes the use of emotional appeals, delivery style, language choice, and rhythmic quality of the words and gestures used. Some Latin American listeners, for example, expect speakers to express more emotion and passion when speaking than North American listeners are accustomed to.

If you focus only on analyzing and adapting to the audience's expectations about logic and reasoning, without also considering the overall impression you make on your audience, you may present compelling arguments but still not achieve your goal. The best way to assess the preferred speaking style of an audience with which you're not familiar is to observe other successful speakers addressing the audience you will face. Or talk with audience members before your speech to identify expectations and communication-style preferences.

Support Your Reasoning with Evidence

When attempting to persuade listeners, make sure that your evidence logically supports the inductive, deductive, or causal reasoning you are using to reach your conclusion. Evidence in persuasive speeches consists of facts, examples, expert opinions, and statistics.

- A **fact** is something that has been directly observed to be true or can be proved to be true. An inference is a conclusion based on available evidence or partial information.
- **Examples** are illustrations that are used to dramatize or clarify a fact. Only valid, true examples can be used to help prove a point. A hypothetical example, one that is fabricated to illustrate a point, should not be used to reach a conclusion. It should be used only to clarify.
- **Opinions** can serve as evidence if they are expressed by an expert. Opinions are usually most persuasive if they are combined with other evidence, such as facts or statistics that support the expert's position.
- A **statistic** is a number used to summarize several facts or samples.

If you use inductive reasoning (moving from specific examples to a general conclusion), you need to make sure you have enough facts, examples, statistics, and credible opinions to support your conclusion. If you reason deductively (from a generalization to a specific conclusion), you need evidence to document the truth of your initial generalization. When you are developing an argument using causal reasoning, evidence is also vital, as you attempt to establish that one or more events caused something to happen.

Avoid Faulty Reasoning: Ethical Issues

Many persuaders use inappropriate techniques called fallacies. A **fallacy** is false reasoning that occurs when someone attempts to persuade without adequate evidence or with arguments that are irrelevant or inappropriate. You will be both a better and more ethical speaker and a better listener if you are aware of the following eight fallacies.

Causal Fallacy   The **causal fallacy** involves making a faulty causal connection. Simply because one event follows another does not mean that the two are related. There is not enough evidence to support the cause-effect conclusion.

Bandwagon Fallacy Someone who argues that "everybody thinks it's a good idea, so you should too" is using the **bandwagon fallacy**. Simply because someone says that "everyone" is "jumping on the bandwagon," or supporting a particular point of view, does not make the point of view correct.

Either/Or Fallacy Someone who argues that there are only two approaches to a problem is trying to oversimplify the issue by using the **either/or fallacy**. "It's either vote for higher property taxes or close the library." Such a statement ignores a variety of other solutions to a complex problem.

Hasty Generalization A person who reaches a conclusion from too little evidence or nonexistent evidence is making a **hasty generalization**. For example, simply because one person became ill after eating the meat loaf in the cafeteria does not mean that everyone eating in the cafeteria will develop food poisoning.

Ad Hominem Also known as attacking the person, an **ad hominem** (Latin for "to the man") **argument** involves attacking irrelevant personal characteristics of the person who is proposing an idea rather than attacking the idea itself. Don't dismiss an idea solely because you have been turned against the person who presented it.

Red Herring The **red herring** fallacy is used when someone attacks an issue by using irrelevant facts or arguments as distractions. This fallacy gets its name from an old trick of dragging a red herring across a trail to divert any dogs that may be following.

Appeal to Misplaced Authority When ads use baseball players to endorse automobiles, we are faced with the fallacious **appeal to misplaced authority**. Although we have great respect for these people in their own fields, they are no more expert than we are in the areas they are advertising.

Non Sequitur If you argue that a new parking garage should not be built on campus because the grass has not been mowed on the football field for three weeks, you are guilty of a **non sequitur**. Grass growing on the football field has nothing to do with the parking problem. Your conclusion simply does not follow from your statement.

Use Emotion to Persuade

Aristotle used the term **pathos** to refer to the use of appeals to emotion. An appeal to emotion can be an effective way to achieve a desired response from an audience. Whereas logical arguments appeal to our reason, emotional arguments generally appeal to nonrational sentiments. Often we make decisions based not on logic, but on emotion.

Dimensions of Emotional Responses

Pleasure, arousal, and power are believed to form the bases of all our emotional responses. If listeners feel pleasure and are also aroused by something, such as a political candidate or a product, they will tend to form a favorable view of the candidate or product. Whether a listener feels powerful or powerless has to do with the extent to which he or she has a sense of being in control and having permission to behave as he or she wishes. A listener who feels powerful is more likely to respond to the message.

Tips for Using Emotion to Persuade

Your key concern as a public speaker is "How can I ethically use emotional appeals to achieve my persuasive purpose?"

- Use concrete examples that help your listeners visualize what you describe.
- Use emotion-arousing words.
- Use nonverbal behavior to communicate your emotional response.
- Use visual images to evoke emotions.

> ✓ *QuickCheck*
> *Use Emotion to Persuade*
> ■ Use concrete examples.
> ■ Use emotion-arousing words.
> ■ Use nonverbal behavior to communicate your emotional response.
> ■ Use visual images.
> ■ Use appropriate metaphors and similes.
> ■ Use appropriate fear appeals.
> ■ Use appeals to a variety of emotions, such as hope, pride, courage, or reverence.
> ■ Tap audience members' beliefs in shared myths.

- Use appropriate metaphors and similes.
- Use appropriate fear appeals.
- Consider using appeals to several emotions, including hope, pride, courage, and reverence.
- Tap audience members' beliefs in shared myths.

A **myth** is a belief held in common by a group of people and based on their values, cultural heritage, and faith. Referring to a shared myth is a way for you to identify with your listeners and help them see how your ideas support their ideas; it can help you identify with your audience and develop a common bond with its members.

Avoid Misusing Emotional Appeals: Ethical Issues

Regardless of which emotions you use to motivate your audience, you have an obligation to be ethical and forthright. Making false claims, misusing evidence to arouse emotions, or relying only on emotions without supplying any evidence to support a conclusion violates ethical standards of effective public speaking.

Strategies for Adapting Ideas to People and People to Ideas

Audience members may hold differing views of you and your subject. Your task is to find out if there is a prevailing viewpoint held by a majority of your listeners. If they are generally friendly toward you and your ideas, you need to design your speech differently than you would if your listeners were neutral, apathetic, or hostile.

Persuading the Receptive Audience

In speaking to a receptive group, you can explore your ideas in greater depth. Here are some suggestions that may help you make the most of your speaking opportunity.

■ Identify with your audience. Emphasize the similarities between you and your audience.

■ Clearly state your speaking objective. Provide an overview of your major point or purpose.

■ Tell your audience exactly what you want them to do. Tell them how you expect them to respond to your message. Be explicit in directing your listeners' behavior.

■ Ask listeners for an immediate show of support to help cement the positive response you have developed during your speech.

■ Use emotional appeals effectively. You can usually move a favorable audience to action with strong emotional appeals while also reminding them of the evidence that supports your conclusion.

■ Make it easy for your listeners to act. Make sure that what you're asking them to do is clear and simple.

Persuading the Neutral Audience

Many audiences will simply be neutral or indifferent. Your challenge is to make them interested in your message.

■ Capture your listeners' attention early in your speech.

■ Refer to beliefs that many listeners share.

■ Relate your topic not only to your listeners but also to their families, friends, and loved ones. People are generally interested in matters that may affect their friends, neighbors, and others with whom they identify.

■ Be realistic about what you can accomplish. People who start with an attitude of indifference are probably not going to become enthusiastic after hearing just one speech.

Persuading the Unreceptive Audience

One of the biggest challenges in public speaking is to persuade audience members who are against you or your message. If they are hostile toward you personally, your job is to find ways to enhance your acceptability and persuade them to listen to you. If they are unreceptive to your point of view, there are several approaches that you can use.

- Don't immediately announce that you plan to change their minds.
- Begin your speech by noting areas of agreement before you discuss areas of disagreement.
- Don't expect a major shift in attitude from a hostile audience. Set a realistic limit on what you can achieve.
- Acknowledge the opposing points of view that members of your audience may hold. Your listeners will be more likely to listen to you if they know that you understand their viewpoint.
- Establish your credibility. Let your audience know about the experience, interest, knowledge, and skills that give you special insight into the issues at hand.
- Consider making understanding rather than advocacy your goal.

Sometimes your audience disagrees with you because its members just don't understand your point. Or they may harbor a misconception of you and your message. To change such a misconception and enhance accurate understanding, experienced speakers use a four-part strategy.[2]

1. Summarize the common misconceptions about the issue or idea you are discussing.
2. State why these misconceptions may seem reasonable.
3. Dismiss the misconceptions and provide evidence to support your point. Here you need sound and credible data to be persuasive.
4. State the accurate information that you want your audience to remember. With a clear

summary statement, reinforce the conclusion you want your listeners to draw from the information you presented.

Strategies for Organizing Persuasive Messages

How you organize your speech does have a major effect on your listeners' response to your message.

- If you feel that your audience may be hostile to your point of view, advance your strongest arguments first. If you save your best argument for last, your audience may have already stopped listening.
- Do not bury key arguments and evidence in the middle of your message. Information presented first and last is more likely to be remembered by your listeners.
- If you want your listeners to take some action, it is best to tell them what you want them to do at the end of your speech. Making a call for action in the middle of your speech won't have the same power as including one in your conclusion.
- It is usually better to present both sides of an issue rather than just the advantages of the position you advocate. If you don't acknowledge arguments your listeners have heard, they will probably think about them anyway.
- Make some reference to the counterarguments, and then refute them with evidence and logic. By comparing and contrasting your solution with another recommendation, you can show how your proposal is better.

Problem-Solution

The problem-solution pattern works best when a clearly evident problem can be documented and a solution can be proposed to deal with the well-documented problem.

If you are speaking to an apathetic audience or if listeners are not aware that a problem exists, a problem-solution pattern works nicely. Your challenge will be to provide ample evidence to document that your perception of the problem is accurate. You'll also need to convince your listeners that the solution you advocate is the most appropriate one to resolve the problem.

Refutation

Another way to persuade an audience to support your point of view is to prove that the arguments against your position are false—that is, to refute them. To use refutation as a strategy for persuasion, first identify objections to your position that your listeners might raise and then refute or overcome those objections with arguments and evidence.

Credible evidence, facts, and data will be more effective than emotional arguments alone when you are attempting to persuade an audience that you know is not in favor of your persuasive objective.

Cause and Effect

One way to use the cause-and-effect method is to begin with an effect, or problem, and then identify the causes of the problem in an effort to convince your listeners that the problem is significant.

The goal of using cause-and-effect organization for a persuasive speech is to convince your listeners that one event caused another. You argue that something known caused something else to happen.

The challenge in using a cause-and-effect organization is to prove that one event caused something else to occur. Simply because two events occurred at the same time or in close succession does not prove that there is a cause-and-effect relationship.

The Motivated Sequence

The motivated sequence is a five-step organizational plan. It uses the cognitive dissonance approach: First disturb your listeners, and then point them toward the specific change you want them to adopt.

1. **Attention.** Your first goal is to get your listeners' attention. Use a personal or hypothetical example, a startling statement, an unusual

statistic, a rhetorical question, or a well-worded analogy. The attention step is, in essence, the introduction to your speech.

2. **Need.** After getting the attention of your audience, establish why your topic, problem, or issue should concern your listeners. Arouse dissonance. Convince them there is a need for a change. You must also convince your listeners that this need for a change affects them directly.

3. **Satisfaction.** After you present the problem, briefly identify how your plan will satisfy the need. What is your solution? Present enough information so that your listeners have a general understanding of how the problem may be solved.

4. **Visualization.** Use positive visualization to paint a verbal picture of how wonderful the future will be if your solution is adopted. Or take a negative-visualization approach: Tell your listeners how awful things will be if your solution is not adopted. Or present both a positive and a negative visualization of the future: The problem will be solved if your solution is adopted, and the world will be a much worse place if your solution is not adopted.

5. **Action.** This last step forms the basis of your conclusion. Tell your audience the specific action they can take to implement your solution. Identify exactly what you want your listeners to do. Give them simple, clear, easy-to-follow steps to achieve your goal.

You can modify the motivated sequence to suit the needs of your topic and audience. If you are speaking to a receptive audience, do not spend a great deal of time on the need step. If you are speaking to a hostile audience, spend considerable time on need. If your audience is neutral or indifferent, spend time getting their attention and inviting their interest in the problem.

The motivated sequence is a guide, not an absolute formula. Use it and the other suggestions about speech organization to help you achieve your specific objective. Be audience-centered; adapt your message to your listeners.

A Question of Ethics

The keynote speaker at a college graduation is not a college graduate. Is it ethical for that person to give a college graduation speech? Would the fact that the speaker was not a college graduate affect his or her credibility with you and your classmates? Explain your answer.

Chapter 27

Speaking on Special Occasions

I t is likely that you will at some time be asked to make a business or professional presentation or to speak on some occasion that calls for celebration, commemoration, inspiration, or entertainment.

Public Speaking in the Workplace

Nearly every job requires some public-speaking skills. Workplace audiences may range from a group of three managers to a huge auditorium filled with company employees. Presentations may be a routine aspect of meeting management or may take the form of reports to company executives, training seminars within the company, or public-relations speeches to people outside the company.

Reports

One of the most common types of on-the-job presentation is the **report**. Whatever the specific objective of the report, the general purpose is to communicate information or policy; sometimes reports end with a persuasive appeal to try some new course of action.

Most successful reports include the same structural elements:

- Begin by briefly acknowledging the situation. Keep in mind that your audience is there to hear you address a particular need or problem.
- If you are reporting on a particular project or study, first discuss what your research group did to explore the problem. Then explain how you gathered the information.
- Finally, present the possible solutions. For some reports, the most important part is this outline

of new courses of action or changes in present policy. In addition, tell your audience what's in it for them—what benefits will accrue to them directly as a result of the new proposal.

Public-Relations Speeches

Public-relations speeches are designed to inform the public and improve relations with them—either in general or because a particular program or situation has raised some questions.

Discuss the Need or Problem First discuss the need or problem that has prompted the speech. Then go on to explain how the company or organization is working to meet the need or solve the problem or why it feels there is no problem.

Anticipate Criticism Anticipate criticism, whether it comes from the audience as a whole or from a minority contingent. Suggest and counter potential problems or objections, especially if past presentations have encountered some opposition to the policy or program. Emphasize the positive aspects of the policy or program, and take care not to become unpleasantly defensive. You want to leave the impression that the company or organization has carefully worked through potential pitfalls and drawbacks.

Ceremonial Speaking

Ceremonial speeches make up a broad class of speeches delivered on many kinds of occasions.

Introductions

A **speech of introduction** is much like an informative speech. The speaker provides information about the main speaker to the audience. The ultimate purpose of an introduction, however, is to arouse interest in the speaker and his or her topic.

You need to get the attention of the audience, build the speaker's credibility, and introduce the speaker's general subject. You also need to make the speaker feel welcome while revealing some of his or

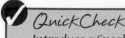

QuickCheck
Introduce a Speaker

■ Relate the speaker's background to the speaking occasion.
■ Correctly identify the speaker's title.
■ Pronounce the speaker's name correctly.
■ Verify the speaker's credentials ahead of time.
■ Be brief.

her personal qualities to the audience so that they can feel they know the speaker more intimately.

There are two cardinal rules of introductory speeches:

■ **Be brief.** The audience has come to hear the main speaker or to honor the guest, not to listen to you.
■ **Be accurate.** Ask the person you are going to introduce to supply you with relevant biographical data beforehand. If someone else provides you with the speaker's background, make sure the information is accurate. Be certain that you know how to pronounce the speaker's name and any other names or terms you will need to use.

Keep the needs of your audience in mind at all times. If the person you are introducing truly needs no introduction, do not give one! Just welcome the speaker and step aside. "Friends [or Ladies and gentlemen], please join me in welcoming our guest speaker for tonight, the former chairman of this club, Mr. Daniel Jones." Note that the President of the United States is always introduced simply: "Ladies and gentlemen, the President of the United States."

Toasts

Most people are asked at some time or another to provide a **toast** for some momentous occasion—a wedding, a celebration, a birth, a reunion, or a successful business venture. A toast is a brief salute to such an occasion, usually accompanied by a round of drinks and immediately followed by the raising or clinking together of glasses or goblets.

The modern toast is usually quite short—only a few sentences at most. Some toasts are very personal, as, for example, one given by a best man who is a close friend of both the bride and the groom. In contrast, a toast made by someone who does not know the primary celebrants as intimately may be more generic in nature.

If you are asked to make an impromptu toast, let your audience and the occasion dictate what you say. Sincerity is more important than wit.

Award Presentations

Presenting an award is somewhat like introducing a speaker or a guest: Remember that the audience did not come to hear you, but to see and hear the winner of the award. Delivering a **presentation speech** is an important responsibility, one that has several distinct components.

Refer to the Occasion   Awards are often given to mark the anniversary of a special event, the completion of a long-range task, the accomplishments of a lifetime, or high achievement in some field.

Talk about the History and Significance of the Award   This section of the speech may be fairly long if the audience knows little about the award; it will be brief if the audience already knows the history and purpose of the award. Whatever the award, a discussion of its significance will add to its meaning for the person who receives it.

Name the Person   The longest part of this segment is the description of the achievements that elicited the award. That description should be given in glowing terms. Hyperbole is appropriate here.

If the name of the person getting the award has already been made public, you may refer to him or her by name throughout your description. If you are going to announce the individual's name for the first time, you will probably want to recite the achievements first and leave the person's name for last. Even though some members of the audience may recognize from your description the person you are talking about, you should still save the drama of the actual announcement until the last moment.

Nominations

Nomination speeches are similar to award presentations. They, too, involve noting the occasion and describing the purpose and significance of, in this case, the office to be filled. The person making the nomination should explain clearly why the nominee's skills, talents, and past achievements serve as qualifications for the position. And the actual nomination should come at the end of the speech.

Acceptances

For every award or nomination, there is usually at least a brief **acceptance speech**. If you ever have to give an acceptance speech, it may be impromptu, because you may not know that you have won until the award is presented. A fairly simple formula should help you compose a good acceptance speech on the spur of the moment.

- First, thank the person making the presentation and the organization that he or she represents. It is also gracious to thank a few people who have contributed greatly to your success—but not a long list of everyone you have ever known, down to the family dog.
- Next, comment on the meaning or significance of the award to you. You may also wish to reflect on the larger significance of the award to the people and ideals it honors.
- Finally, try to find some meaning the award may have for your audience—people who respect your accomplishments and who may themselves aspire to similar achievements.

Keynote Addresses

A **keynote address** is usually presented at or near the beginning of a meeting or conference. The keynote emphasizes the importance of the topic or the purpose of the meeting, motivates the audience to learn more or work harder, and sets the theme and tone for other speakers and events.

The hardest task the keynote speaker faces is being specific enough to arouse interest and inspire the audience. One way in which a keynote speaker can succeed in his or her task is to incorporate examples and illustrations to which the audience can relate.

Commencement Addresses

To be audience-centered, a **commencement address** must fulfill two important functions. First, the commencement speaker should praise the graduating class. Because the audience includes the families and friends of the graduates, the commencement speaker can gain their goodwill (as well as that of the graduates themselves) by pointing out the significance of the graduates' accomplishments.

A second function of an audience-centered commencement speaker is to turn graduates toward the future. Commencement speakers should suggest new goals and try to inspire the graduates to reach for them.

Commemorative Addresses and Tributes

Commemorative addresses—those delivered during special ceremonies held to celebrate some past event—are often combined with tributes to the person or persons involved.

The speaker who commemorates or pays tribute is, in part, an informative speaker. He or she needs to present some facts about the event and/or people being celebrated. Then the speaker builds on those facts, urging the audience to let past accomplishments inspire them to achieve new goals.

Eulogies

Speeches of tribute delivered when someone has died are an especially difficult form of commemorative address. When you deliver a **eulogy**, you should mention—indeed, linger on—the unique achievements of the person to whom you are paying tribute and, of course, express a sense of loss.

It is also proper in a eulogy to include personal and even tasteful humorous recollections of the person who has died.

Finally, turn to the living, and encourage them to transcend their sorrow and sense of loss and feel instead gratitude that the dead person had once been alive among them.

After-Dinner Speaking: Using Humor Effectively

After-dinner speeches may present information or persuade, but their primary purpose is to entertain. To entertain is to make people laugh. Speakers, actors, and comedians frequently employ the following strategies to make audiences laugh.

Humorous Stories

Chances are that if you have found an experience or event funny, an audience will, too. One of the best ways to create humor is to start with what speakers know—"themselves, their lives, what makes them laugh."[1]

Humorous stories should be simple. Complicated stories and jokes are rarely perceived by audiences as funny. Successful humorous speakers also need a broad repertoire. And, it is important to know one's anecdotes very well. Only if you know the material can you hope to deliver it with the intonation and timing that will make it funny.

Humorous Verbal Strategies

Either a humorous anecdote or a shorter "one-liner" may rely on one of the following verbal strategies for humorous effect.

Play on Words   **Puns** rely on double meanings to create humor. **Spoonerisms** occur when someone switches the initial sounds of words in a single phrase—for example, "sublic peaking" instead of "public speaking." **Malapropism** is the mistaken use of a word that sounds much like the intended word—"destruction" for "instruction," for example.

Hyperbole Hyperbole, or exaggeration, is often funny. In an after-dinner speech on "The Alphabet and Simplified Spelling," Mark Twain claimed,

> Simplified spelling brought about sun-spots, the San Francisco earthquake, and the recent business depression, which we would never have had if spelling had been left all alone.[2]

Of course, spelling could not have caused such catastrophes, but by using hyperbole, Twain makes his point in a humorous way.

Understatement The opposite of hyperbole, **understatement** involves downplaying a fact or event.

Verbal Irony A speaker who employs **verbal irony** says just the opposite of what he or she really means. Student Chris O'Keefe opens his speech on reading Shakespeare with the following statement:

> At a certain point in my life, I came to the realization that I wanted to spend my life's effort to become a great playwright.[3]

Chris reveals the irony of the statement when he continues:

> It has been about an hour and a half now and the feeling is still going strong.

Wit One of the most frequently used verbal strategies for achieving humor is the use of **wit**: relating an incident that takes an unexpected turn at the end. In an after-dinner speech on the weather, Twain related this brief incident:

> You make up your mind that the earthquake is due; you . . . take hold of something to steady yourself, and the first thing you know you get struck by lightning.[4]

The wit occurs in the final phrase, "you get struck by lightning," which catches off guard the listeners, who are anticipating some detail related to earthquakes.

Humorous Nonverbal Strategies

After-dinner speakers often create humor through such nonverbal cues as posture, gesture, and voice.

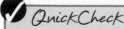

QuickCheck

Strategies for Achieving Humor in After-Dinner Speeches

Humorous stories	Anecdotes
Humorous verbal strategies	
Plays on words	Intentional errors such as puns, spoonerisms, and malapropisms
Hyperbole	Exaggeration
Understatement	Downplaying a fact or event
Verbal irony	Saying just the opposite of what one means
Wit	An unexpected turn at the end of a fact or incident
Humorous nonverbal strategies	Physical or vocal elements such as posture, gestures, pauses, and intonation

Well-timed pauses are especially crucial delivery cues for after-dinner speakers to master.

Even if you are person who is not naturally funny, you can use the strategies outlined above to prepare and deliver an after-dinner speech that is lighthearted and clever. Such a speech can still be a success.

Question of Ethics

You have been a member of the jury for a highly publicized and controversial murder trial in your community. After the verdict is delivered, you find yourself in great demand as a keynote speaker for meetings of local organizations. Several offer to pay you well. Is it ethical to "cash in" on your experience in this way?

Chapter 28

Speaking in Small Groups

Small group communication is interaction among three to around a dozen people who share a common purpose, feel a sense of belonging to the group, and influence one another.

Solving Problems: Reflective Thinking

A central purpose of many groups is solving problems. Problem solving is a means of finding ways of overcoming obstacles to achieve a desired goal.

John Dewey, a philosopher and educator, called his method of problem solving **reflective thinking**. Here are his problem-solving suggestions:

1. Identify and define the problem.
2. Analyze the problem.
3. Generate possible solutions.
4. Select the best solution.
5. Test and implement the solution.

Not every problem-solving discussion has to follow these steps. Use them as a blueprint to relieve some of the uncertainty that exists when groups try to solve problems.

Identify and Define the Problem

Groups work best when they define their problem clearly and early in their problem-solving process. To reach a clear definition, the group should consider the following questions:

- What is the specific problem that concerns us?
- What terms, concepts, or ideas do we need to understand in order to solve the problem?
- Who is harmed by the problem?
- When do the harmful effects occur?

Policy questions can help define a problem and also identify the course of action that should be taken to solve it. Policy questions begin with phrases such as "What should be done about ..." or "What could be done to improve...." Here are some examples:

■ What could be done to improve security at U.S. airports?
■ What should be done about the tax base in our state?
■ What steps can be taken to improve the U.S. trade balance with other countries?

Analyze the Problem

Once the group understands the problem and has a well-worded question, the next step is to analyze the problem. **Analysis** is a process of examining the causes, effects, symptoms, history, and other background information that will help a group eventually reach a solution. When analyzing a problem, a group should consider the following questions:

■ What is the history of the problem?
■ How extensive is the problem?
■ What are the causes, effects, and symptoms of the problem?
■ Can the problem be subdivided for further definition and analysis?
■ What methods do we already have for solving the problem, and what are their limitations?
■ What new methods can we devise to solve the problem?
■ What obstacles might keep us from reaching a solution?

Included in the process of analyzing the problem is identifying criteria. **Criteria** are standards for identifying an acceptable solution. They help you recognize a good solution when you discover one; criteria also help the group stay focused on its goal. Typical criteria for an acceptable solution specify that the solution should be implemented on schedule, should be agreed to by all group members, should be achieved within a given budget, and should remove the obstacles causing the problem.

Generate Possible Solutions

When your group has identified, defined, and analyzed the problem, you will be ready to generate possible solutions using group brainstorming. Observe the following guidelines:

■ Set aside judgment and criticism. Criticism and faultfinding stifle creativity. If group members find withholding judgment difficult, have the individual members write suggestions on paper first and then share the ideas with the group.

■ Think of as many possible solutions to the problem as you can. All ideas are acceptable, even wild and crazy ones. Piggyback off one another's ideas. All members must come up with at least one idea.

■ Have a member of the group record all the ideas that are mentioned. Use a flipchart or chalkboard, if possible, so that all group members can see and respond to all the ideas.

■ After a set time has elapsed, evaluate the ideas, using criteria the group has established. Approach the solutions positively. Do not be quick to dismiss an idea, but do voice any concerns or questions you might have. The group can brainstorm again later if it needs more creative ideas.

Select the Best Solution

Next, the group needs to select the solution that best meets the criteria and solves the problem. At this point, the group may need to modify its criteria or even its definition of the problem.

In evaluating the solution, consider the following questions:

■ Which of the suggested solutions deals best with the obstacles?
■ Does the suggestion solve the problem in both the short and the long term?
■ What are the advantages and disadvantages of the suggested solution?
■ Does the solution meet the established criteria?
■ Should the group revise its criteria?
■ What is required to implement the solution?

- When can the group implement the solution?
- What result will indicate success?

To achieve **consensus**—all members supporting the final decision—it helps to summarize frequently and keep the group oriented toward its goal. Emphasizing where group members agree, clarifying misunderstandings, writing down known facts for all members to see, and keeping the discussion focused on issues rather than on emotions are also strategies that facilitate group consensus.[1]

Test and Implement the Solution

The group may want to develop a step-by-step plan that describes the process for implementing the solution, a time frame for implementation, and a list of individuals who will be responsible for carrying out specific tasks.

Tips for Participating in Small Groups

To be an effective group participant, you have to understand how to manage the problem-solving process. You also need to prepare for meetings, evaluate evidence, effectively summarize the group's progress, listen courteously, and be sensitive to conflict.

Come Prepared for Group Discussions

Prepare for group discussions by researching the issues. Use the library and the Internet to gather information. Bring your research notes to the group. Without research, you will not be able to analyze the problem adequately.

Do Not Suggest Solutions before Analyzing the Problem

Resist the temptation to settle quickly on one solution before your group has systematically examined the causes, effects, history, and symptoms of a problem.

Evaluate Evidence

To make a successful decision, examine and evaluate evidence. Ineffective groups are more likely to reach decisions quickly without considering the validity of evidence (or sometimes without any evidence at all). Such groups usually reach flawed conclusions.

Help Summarize the Group's Progress

Because it is easy for groups to get off the subject, group members need to summarize frequently what has been achieved and to point the group toward the goal or task at hand. Ask questions about the discussion process rather than about the topic: "Where are we now?" "Could someone summarize what we have accomplished?" and "Aren't we getting off the subject?"

Listen and Respond Courteously to Others

Understanding what others say is not enough. You also need to respect their points of view. Even if you disagree with someone's ideas, keep your emotions in check and respond courteously. Being closed-minded and defensive usually breeds group conflict.

Help Manage Conflict

In the course of exchanging ideas and opinions about controversial issues, disagreements are bound to occur.[2] You can help prevent conflicts from de-railing the problem-solving process by doing the following:

■ Keep the discussion focused on issues, not on personalities.
■ Rely on facts rather than on personal opinions for evidence.
■ Seek ways to compromise; don't assume that there must be a winner and a loser.
■ Try to clarify misunderstandings in meaning.
■ Be descriptive rather than evaluative and judgmental.
■ Keep emotions in check.

Leadership in Small Groups

To lead is to influence others. Some think of a leader as one individual empowered to delegate work and direct the group. In reality, however, group leadership is often shared.

Leadership Responsibilities

Leaders help get tasks accomplished and maintain a healthy social climate for the group. Rarely does one person perform all these leadership responsibilities, even if a leader is formally appointed or elected. Most often a number of individual group members assume some specific leadership task, based on their personalities, skills, sensitivity, and the group's needs.

If you determine that the group needs a clearer focus on the task or that maintenance roles are needed, be ready to influence the group appropriately to help get the job done in a positive, productive way.

Leadership Styles

Leaders can be described by the types of behavior, or leadership styles, that they exhibit as they influence the group to help achieve its goal. The following describe general leadership styles.

- **Authoritarian leaders** assume positions of superiority, giving orders and assuming control of the group's activity. Although authoritarian leaders can usually organize group activities with a high degree of efficiency and virtually eliminate uncertainty about who should do what, most problem-solving groups prefer democratic leaders.
- **Democratic leaders** involve group members in the decision-making process rather than dictating what should be done. Democratic leaders focus more on guiding discussion than on issuing commands.
- **Laissez-faire leaders** allow group members complete freedom in all aspects of the decision-making process. They do little to help the group achieve its goal. This style of "nonleadership" often leaves a group frustrated because it lacks guidance and has to struggle with organizing the work.
- **Transformational leaders** influence others by building a shared vision of the future, inspiring

others to achieve, developing high-quality individual relationships with others, and helping people see how what they do is related to a larger framework or system. Transformational leaders are good communicators who support and encourage rather than demean or demand.

What is the most effective leadership style? No single style is effective in every group situation. The best leadership style depends on the nature of the group task, the power of the leader, and the relationship between the leader and his or her followers.

Managing Meetings

To be effective, a meeting should have two characteristics: structure and interaction. *Structure* involves such attributes as an organized agenda and a logical, rational approach to discussing the issues. A meeting with too much structure resembles a speech. *Interaction* includes the dynamic process of group discussion. A meeting with too much interaction and not enough structure rambles and digresses and has no clear purpose. The key to managing a meeting is to strike a proper balance between structure and interaction.

Give Meetings Structure

As a leader, use an **agenda,** a brief list or description of what you will discuss, arranged in chronological order, to give a meeting structure. Develop an agenda by determining your overall goal. Most meetings have one or more of the following goals: to share information, to discuss issues, to make decisions, and to solve problems.

Often groups spend too much time on early agenda items and give less attention to those scheduled for late in the meeting (when most people want to leave). Therefore, cover vital issues early and use the end of the meeting to determine what needs to happen at the next meeting, to summarize the action that needs to be taken, and to determine who will do what.

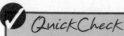

QuickCheck
Manage Meetings

- Develop an agenda (a brief list or description of what you will discuss, arranged in chronological order) by determining your overall goal.
- Keep your eye on the clock and the agenda.
- Ensure that the meeting is interactive.
- Organize your contributions, and make one point at a time.
- Support your ideas with evidence.
- Check your understanding of group-member comments by summarizing or paraphrasing.
- Watch your body language.

Foster Group Interaction

Leaders should ensure that a meeting is interactive. Draw out quiet members by calling on them by name and asking for their opinions. Ask more talkative members to hold their comments until all have contributed to the discussion. Periodically summarize group members' contributions.

Even if you are not the designated leader or meeting facilitator, you can use strategies to enhance the quality of discussion. One research team made the following recommendations for meeting participants:[3]

- Organize your contributions, and make one point at a time. Rambling and disorganized comments increase the likelihood that the meeting will stray from the agenda.
- Support your ideas with evidence. Facts, statistics, and well-selected examples help keep the group focused on the task.
- Listen actively and monitor your nonverbal messages. Check your understanding of group-member comments by summarizing or paraphrasing, and watch your own body language.

Presenting Group Recommendations

When it comes time to present the group's recommendations, the first and most important step is to analyze the audience. Who are the listeners? What do they need to know? What are their interests and backgrounds?

You need not summarize every action and method the group used to reach its conclusion. Tell the listeners the essential information. Often the group can summarize the details in writing rather than verbalize them in an oral presentation.

Purpose

Make sure that you have a clear purpose with a developed central idea and that you have clear major ideas to present. This is a group effort, so you need to make sure each group member can articulate the purpose of the oral presentation.

Support

Share with the audience the key forms of support. And don't forget to use examples, analogies, illustrations, and other forms of supporting material that will help maintain interest.

Organization

In organizing your group's oral presentation, review the methods of organizing a speech. If your group is presenting recommendations to solve a problem, you could use the steps in the reflective-thinking problem-solving process to organize the key pieces of your report.

Rehearsal

Make sure your group has rehearsed the presentation. The first time you hear what your fellow group members are going to say should *not* be when your group is delivering the presentation to an audience.

Format

Unless a format for your group presentation has been specified, your group will need to determine what type of presentation you will deliver. Three primary oral formats exist for sharing recommendations: symposium, forum presentation, and panel discussion. Finally, you will need to decide whether your group will prepare a written report.

- A **symposium** is a public discussion in which an audience is presented with a series of short speeches. The members of the group share the responsibility of presenting information to a larger group. Usually a moderator and the group members are seated in front of the audience, each prepared to deliver a brief report. Each speaker should know what the others will present so that the same ground is not covered twice.

- In a **forum presentation**, an audience directs questions and comments to a group, and group members respond with short impromptu speeches. Forum presentations work best when all group members know the issues and are prepared to respond unhesitatingly to questioners.

- A **panel discussion** is an informative group presentation. Individuals on the panel may use notes containing key facts or statistics, but they do not present formal speeches. Usually a panel discussion is organized and led by an appointed chairperson or moderator.

- Written reports summarize a group's key deliberations and final recommendations. Begin by describing the group members; then present the definition of the problem. Next, include the problem analysis, criteria that were established, possible solutions, the best solution, and suggestions for implementing the solution. For the sake of clarity, use headings and subheadings liberally throughout the report. Include a bibliography of the sources used to reach the group's conclusion.

Tips for Planning a Group Presentation

Working in groups takes a coordinated team effort. Consider these suggestions to enhance teamwork:

- Make sure each group member understands the task or assignment, and work together to identify a topic. Take a few moments to verbalize the goals and objectives of the assignment.

- If your group assignment is to solve a problem or to inform the audience about a specific issue, try brainstorming to develop a topic or problem question. Then assess your audience's interests as well as group members' interests and talents to help you choose among your ideas.

■ Give group members individual assignments. After you decide on your group's presentation topic, divide up the tasks involved in investigating the issues. Also, devise a plan for keeping in touch with one another frequently to share information and ideas.

■ Develop a group outline and decide on an approach. After group members have researched key issues, begin drafting an outline of your group presentation, following the steps of the reflective-thinking process.

■ Decide on your presentation approach: symposium, forum presentation, panel discussion, or some combination of these. Decide who will present which portions of your outline and how to integrate them. Your presentation should have an introduction and a definite ending that reflect your group's work as an integrated problem-solving team.

■ Rehearse the presentation. If you are using visual aids, be sure to incorporate them in your rehearsal. Also, be sure to time your presentation when you rehearse.

■ Incorporate principles and skills of effective audience-centered public speaking when giving the group presentation.

QuickCheck
Plan a Group Presentation

■ Make sure each group member understands the task or assignment, and work together to identify a topic.

■ If your group assignment is to solve a problem or to inform the audience about a specific issue, try brainstorming to develop a topic or problem question.

■ Give group members individual assignments.

■ Develop a group outline, and decide on an approach.

■ Decide on your presentation approach.

■ Rehearse the presentation.

■ Armed with a well-planned outline, present your findings to your audience, incorporating the skills and principles of effective public speaking. Your delivery and comments should be well organized, and your visual aids should enhance your presentation by being clear and attractive.

Tips for Making a Group Presentation

Keep the following tips in mind as you offer your conclusions or recommendations.

■ Clarify your purpose. It's important to let listeners know what your speaking goal is and to explain why you are presenting the information to them; it's also important for each group member to be reminded of what the overarching goal of the presentation is. If your group is responding to a specific question, it may be helpful to visually display the question or purpose of the presentation.

■ Use presentation aids effectively. Visual aids can serve the important function of unifying your group presentation. Consider having each group member use the same template and font style to add to the coordinated look and feel of your presentation.

■ Assign someone to serve as coordinator or moderator. A moderator can provide needed structure to a group presentation by introducing both the topic and the group members, keeping track of time, and ensuring that one or more people don't dominate the discussion or speak too little.

■ Be ready to answer questions. Besides being informed about your topic, it's a wise idea to have thoroughly read any written report the group has distributed.

■ Be prepared for pointed or hostile questions. First, keep your composure. Second, try to rephrase a negative question to defuse the sting embedded in it. For example, if someone asks "Why did you make such a mess of things by recommending a budget increase?" you could

✔ *QuickCheck*
Make a Group Presentation

■ Clarify your purpose.
■ Use presentation aids effectively.
■ Assign someone to serve as coordinator or moderator.
■ Be ready to answer questions.
■ Be prepared for pointed or hostile questions.
■ If someone asks a question that has just been asked and answered or asks an irrelevant or poorly worded question, don't criticize the questioner.

rephrase by saying "Why did we recommend a controversial budget increase?"

■ If someone asks a question that has just been asked and answered or asks an irrelevant or poorly worded question, don't criticize the questioner. Be polite, tactful, and gracious. Calmly provide an answer and move on. If you don't understand a question, ask for more clarification. Also, don't let a questioner start making a speech. If it looks as if a questioner is using the question-and-answer period to give an oration, gently ask: "And what is your question?" or "How can we help you?" Such questions should result in a question that you can address and then return the communication process back to the control of the group.

A Question of Ethics

During a speech, you hear the speaker say, "Consistency is the hobgoblin of little minds." The speaker does not attribute the quote to any source and continues on with the speech. You know that the correct quotation is "A foolish consistency is the hobgoblin of little minds" and the source is Ralph Waldo Emerson. What should you do? Explain your answer.

Notes

Chapter 1 Speaking in Public

1. Dee-Ann Durbin, "Study: Plenty of Jobs for Graduates in 2000," *Austin American-Statesman* 5 Dec. 1999: A28.
2. Dan B. Curtis, Jerry L. Winsor, and Ronald D. Stephens, "National Preferences in Business and Communication Education," *Communication Education* 38 (Jan. 1989): 6–14. See also Iain Hay, "Justifying and Applying Oral Presentations in Geographical Education," *Journal of Geography in Higher Education* 18.1 (1994): 44–45.

Chapter 3 Ethics and Free Speech

1. National Communication Association, "NCA Credo for Communication Ethics," 1999, 27 June 2001 <http://www.natcom.org/conferences/Ethics/ethicsconfcredo99.htm>.
2. Samuel Walker, *Hate Speech* (Lincoln: University of Nebraska Press, 1994) 162.
3. "Libel and Slander," *The Ethical Spectacle*, 1 June 1997, 1 June 1998 <http://www.spectacle.org/freespch/musm/libel.html>.
4. "Supreme Court Rules: Cyberspace Will Be Free! ACLU Hails Victory in Internet Censorship Challenge," American Civil Liberties Union Freedom Network, 26 June 1997, 1 June 1998 <http://www.aclu.org/news/no62697a.html>.
5. Bill Carter and Felicity Barringer, "Patriotic Time, Dissent Is Muted," *New York Times* 28 Sept. 2001: B8.
6. New York City Department of Health, "Facts about Mold," March 2001, 27 June 2001 <http://www.ci.nyc.ny.us/html/doh/html/ei/eimold.html>.

Chapter 5 Listening

1. M. Fitch-Hauser, D. A. Barker, and A. Hughes, "Receiver Apprehension and Listening Comprehension: A Linear or Curvilinear Relationship?" *Southern Communication Journal*, 1988: 62–71.
2. S. L. Sargent and James B. Weaver, "Correlates Between Communication Apprehension and Listening Style Preferences," *Communication Research Reports* 14 (1997): 74–78.
3. Harold Barrett, *Rhetoric and Civility: Human Development, Narcissism, and the Good Audience* (Albany: SUNY, 1991) 154.
4. John T. Masterson, Steven A. Beebe, and Norman H. Watson, *Invitation to Effective Speech Communication* (Glenview, IL: Scott, Foresman, 1989) 4.
5. Robert Rowland, *Analyzing Rhetoric: A Handbook for the Informed Citizen in a New Millennium* (Dubuque, IA: Kendall/Hunt Publishing Company, 2002) 17–28.

Chapter 6 Analyzing Your Audience

1. Devorah Lieberman, *Public Speaking in the Multicultural Environment* (Boston: Allyn and Bacon, 2000). Also see Edward T. Hall, *The*

Silent Language (Greenwich, CT: Fawcett, 1959); and Edward T. Hall, *The Hidden Dimension* (Garden City, NY: Doubleday, 1966).

Chapter 9   Gathering Supporting Material

1. The authors are indebted to Terrence A. Doyle's *Quick Guide to the Internet for Speech Communication* (Boston: Allyn and Bacon, 1998), from which much of the information in this section, including the advanced search activity and the Web site annotations, is taken or adapted.
2. Elizabeth Kirk, "Practical Steps in Evaluating Internet Resources," 7 May 2001, 22 May 2001 <http://milton.mse.jhu.edu:8001/research/education/practical.html>.
3. James A. W. Heffernan et al., *Writing: A College Handbook*, 5th ed. (New York: Norton, 2001) 53–54.
4. Paul Gorski, "A Multicultural Model for Evaluating Educational Web Sites," Dec. 1999, 22 May 2001 <http://curry.edschool.virginia.edu/go/multicultural/net/comps/model.html>.

Chapter 11   Organizing Your Speech

1. The following information is adapted from Devorah A. Lieberman, *Public Speaking in the Multicultural Environment* (Englewood Cliffs, NJ: Prentice Hall, 1994).
2. Ben Sutherland, "Terminator 101: Media Literacy in the Information Age," *Winning Orations 1995* (Mankato, MN: Interstate Oratorical Association, 1995) 33.
3. Molly A. Lovell, "Hotel Security: The Hidden Crisis," *Winning Orations 1994* (Mankato, MN: Interstate Oratorical Association, 1994) 18.
4. Heather Green, "Radon in Our Homes," *Winning Orations 1986* (Mankato, MN: Interstate Oratorical Association, 1986) 5.
5. Ben Crosby, "The New College Disease," *Winning Orations 2000* (Mankato, MN: Interstate Oratorical Association, 2000) 133.
6. Lori Van Overbeke, "NutraSweet," *Winning Orations 1986* (Mankato, MN: Interstate Oratorical Association, 1986) 58.

Chapter 15   Using Words Well

1. Michiko Kakutani, "Struggling to Find Words for a Horror Beyond Words," *New York Times* 13 Sept. 2001: E1.
2. John F. Kennedy, Inaugural Address (20 Jan. 1961), *Speeches in English*, ed. Bower Aly and Lucille F. Aly (New York: Random House, 1968) 272.
3. Ralph Waldo Emerson, "The American Scholar," *Famous Speeches in American History*, ed. Glenn R. Capp (Indianapolis: Bobbs-Merrill, 1963) 84.
4. Franklin Roosevelt, Inaugural Address of 1933 (Washington, DC: National Archives and Records Administration, 1988) 13–14.
5. Rudy de Leon, "The Tuskegee Airmen," *Vital Speeches of the Day*, 1 Nov. 2000: 43.

Chapter 16   Methods of Delivery

1. Roger Ailes, *You Are the Message* (New York: Doubleday, 1989) 37–38.

Chapter 17   Nonverbal Communication

1. Paul Ekman, Wallace V. Friesen, and S. S. Tomkins, "Facial Affect Scoring Technique: A First Validity Study," *Semiotica* 3 (1971).

Chapter 18   Verbal Communication

1. Adapted from Lester Schilling, *Voice and Diction for the Speech Arts* (San Marcos: Southwest Texas State UP, 1979).

2. Mary M. Gill, "Accent and Stereotypes: Their Effect on Perceptions of Teachers and Lecture Comprehension," *Journal of Applied Communication* 22 (1994): 348–61.

3. These suggestions were made by Jo Sprague and Douglas Stuart, *The Speaker's Handbook* (Fort Worth, TX: Harcourt Brace Jovanovich, 1992) 331, and were based on research by Patricia A. Porter, Margaret Grant, and Mary Draper, *Communicating Effectively in English: Oral Communication for Non-Native Speakers* (Belmont, CA: Wadsworth, 1985).

4. James W. Neuliep, *Intercultural Communication: A Contextual Approach* (Boston: Houghton Mifflin, 2000) 247.

5. Research cited by Leo Fletcher, *How to Design and Deliver Speeches* (New York: Addison Wesley Longman, 2001) 73.

Chapter 19   Delivering Your Speech

1. For an excellent review of the effects of immediacy in the classroom, see Albert Mehrabian, *Silent Messages* (Belmont, CA: Wadsworth, 1981).

2. James C. McCroskey, Aino Sallinen, Joan M. Fayer, Virginia P. Richmond, and Robert A. Barraclough, "Non-verbal Immediacy and Cognitive Learning: A Cross-Cultural Investigation," *Communication Education* 45 (1996): 200–11.

3. Larry A. Samovar and Richard E. Porter, *Communication between Cultures* (Belmont, CA: Wadsworth, 2001) 166.

4. William B. Gudykunst, *Bridging Differences: Effective Intergroup Communication* (Thousand Oaks, CA: Sage, 1998) 12.

Chapter 20   Selecting Presentation Aids

1. Emil Bohn and David Jabusch, "The Effect of Four Methods of Instruction on the Use of Visual Aids in Speeches," *The Western Journal of Speech Communication* 46 (Summer 1982): 253–65.

2. Michael E. Patterson, Donald F. Dansereau, and Dianna Newbern, "Effects of Communication Aids and Strategies on Cooperative Teaching," *Journal of Educational Psychology* 84 (1992): 453–61.

3. Richard E. Mayer and Valerie K. Sims, "For Whom Is a Picture Worth a Thousand Words? Extensions of a Dual-Coding Theory of Multimedia Learning," *Journal of Educational Psychology* 86 (1994): 389–401.

Chapter 23   Using Presentation Software

1. We acknowledge Dan Cavanaugh's excellent supplement *Preparing Visual Aids for Presentation* (Boston: Allyn and Bacon, 2001) as a source for many of our tips and suggestions.

Chapter 24   Informative Speaking

1. Joseph L. Chesebro, "Effects of Teacher Clarity and Nonverbal Immediacy on Student Learning, Receiver Apprehension, and Affect," *Communication Education* 52 (April 2003): 135–47.

2. Katherine E. Rowan, "A New Pedagogy for Explanatory Public Speaking: Why Arrangement Should Not Substitute for Invention," *Communication Education* 44 (1995): 236–50.

3. Rowan, "A New Pedagogy."

4. Michael A. Boerger and Tracy B. Henley, "The Use of Analogy in Giving Instructions," *Psychological Record* 49 (1999): 193–209.

5. Marcie Groover, "Learning to Communicate: The Importance of Speech Education in Public Schools," *Winning Orations 1984* (Mankato, MN: Interstate Oratorical Association, 1984) 7.

6. Roger Fringer, "Choosing a Speech Topic," in *Allyn & Bacon Video II User's Guide*, ed. Tasha Van Horn, Lori Charron, and Michael Charron (Boston: Allyn and Bacon, 2002).

Chapter 25   Understanding Principles of Persuasive Speaking

1. For a discussion of the elaboration likelihood model, see R. Petty and D. Wegener, "The Elaboration Likelihood Model: Current Status and Controversies," in *Dual Process Theories in Social Psychology* ed. S. Chaiken and Y. Trope (New York: Guilford, 1999) 41–72; also see R. Petty and J. T. Cacioppo, *Communication and Persuasion: Central and Peripheral Routes to Attitude Change* (New York: Springer-Verlag, 1986).
2. Paul A. Mongeau, "Another Look at Fear-Arousing Persuasive Appeals," *Persuasion: Advances through Meta-Analysis*, ed. Mike Allen and Raymond W. Preiss (Cresskill, NJ: Hampton Press, 1998) 65.

Chapter 26   Using Persuasive Strategies

1. Devorah Lieberman and G. Fisher, "International Negotiation," *Intercultural Communication: A Reader*, ed. Larry A. Samovar and Richard E. Porter (Belmont, CA: Wadsworth, 1991) 193–200.
2. K. Rowan, "A New Pedagogy for Explanatory Public Speaking: Why Arrangement Should Not Substitute for Invention," *Communication Education* 44 (1995): 236–50.

Chapter 27   Speaking on Special Occasions

1. Debi Martin, "Laugh Lines," *Austin American-Statesman* 20 May 1988: D1.
2. Mark Twain, "The Alphabet and Simplified Spelling," address at the dedication of the New York Engineers' Club, December 9, 1907, *Mark Twain's Speeches; with an Introduction by William Dean Howells*, Electronic Text Center, University of Virginia Library, 4 June 2004 <etext.lib.Virginia.edu>.
3. Chris O'Keefe, untitled speech, in *Championship Debates and Speeches*, ed. John K. Boaz and James Brey (Speech Communication Association and American Forensic Association, 1987) 99.
4. Mark Twain, "The Weather," address at the New England Society's seventy-first Annual Dinner, New York City, *Mark Twain's Speeches; with an Introduction by William Dean Howells*, Electronic Text Center, University of Virginia Library, 4 June 2004 <etext.lib .Virginia.edu>.

Chapter 28   Speaking in Small Groups

1. C. A. VanLear and E. A. Mabry, "Testing Contrasting Interaction Models for Discriminating between Consensual and Dissentient Decision-Making Groups," *Small Group Research* 30 (1999): 29–58; also see T. J. Saine and D. G. Bock, "A Comparison of the Distributional and Sequential Structures of Interaction in High and Low Consensus Groups," *Central States Speech Journal* 24 (1973): 125–39.
2. For a summary of research about conflict management in small groups, see S. M. Farmer and J. Roth, "Conflict-Handling Behavior in Work Groups: Effects of Group Structure, Decision Processes, and Time," *Small Group Research* 29 (1998): 669–713; also see Steven A. Beebe and John T. Masterson, *Communicating in Small Groups: Principles and Practices*, 7th ed. (Boston: Allyn and Bacon, 2003).
3. Roger K. Mosvick and Robert B. Nelson, *We've Got to Start Meeting Like This! A Guide to Successful Business Meeting Management* (Glenview, IL: Scott, Foresman, 1987) 3.

Glossary

acceptance speech: A speech of thanks for an award, nomination, or other honor

accommodation: Sensitivity to the feelings, needs, interests, and backgrounds of other people

ad hominem argument: An attack on irrelevant personal characteristics of the person who is proposing an idea, rather than on the idea itself

after-dinner speech: An entertaining speech, usually delivered in conjunction with a mealtime meeting or banquet

agenda: A written description of the items and issues that a group will discuss during a meeting

alignment: Placement of text and images on a presentation aid

alliteration: The repetition of a consonant sound (usually the first consonant) several times in a phrase, clause, or sentence

analogy: A comparison between two things; also, a special type of inductive reasoning that compares one thing, person, or process with another to predict how something will perform and respond

analysis: Examination of the causes, effects, and history of a problem to understand it better

andragogy: The art and science of teaching adults

anecdote: An illustration or brief story

animations: In PowerPoint, a function that allows a user to animate text, graphics, and other objects

antithesis: Opposition, such as that used in two-part sentences in which the second part contrasts in meaning with the first

appeal to misplaced authority: Use of the testimony of an expert in a given field to endorse an idea or product for which the expert does not have the appropriate credentials or expertise

articulation: The production of clear and distinct speech sounds

attend: To focus on incoming information

attitude: A learned predisposition to respond favorably or unfavorably toward something; a like or dislike

audience analysis: The process of examining information about those who are expected to listen to a speech

authoritarian leader: A leader who assumes a position of superiority, giving orders and assuming control of the group's activity

AutoContent Wizard: In PowerPoint, a feature that provides suggestions and ideas for the new presentation being created

bandwagon fallacy: Reasoning that suggests that because everyone else believes something or is doing something, then it must be valid or correct

bar graph: A graph in which bars of various lengths represent information

behavioral objective: Statement of the specific purpose of a speech, expressed in terms of desired audience behavior at the end of the speech

belief: An individual's perception of what is true or false

black-and-white view: In PowerPoint, a function that allows a user to view and print items in a presentation in black and white

Blank Presentation: In PowerPoint, a feature that enables a user to create a slide design by choosing layout, colors, graphics, fonts, and organization of content

blueprint: The central idea of a speech plus a preview of main ideas

bookmark: A browser feature that allows a user to save a URL for future reference

Boolean search: An advanced Web-searching technique that allows a user to narrow a subject or keyword search by adding various requirements

boom microphone: A microphone that is suspended from a bar and moved to follow the speaker; often used in movies and TV

brainstorming: A problem-solving technique used to generate many ideas

brief illustration: An unelaborated example, often only a sentence or two long

card catalog: A file of information about the books in a library, on index cards or in a computer system

causal fallacy: A faulty cause-and-effect connection between two things or events

causal reasoning: Reasoning in which the relationship between two or more events leads you to conclude that one or more of the events caused the others

cause-and-effect organization: Organization that focuses on a situation and its causes or a situation and its effects

CD: A compact disk that can hold electronic files of images, words, and sounds

central idea: A one-sentence summary of a speech

channels: The visual and auditory means by which a message is transmitted from sender to receiver

charisma: Characteristic of a talented, charming, attractive speaker

chart: A display that summarizes information by using words, numbers, or images

chronological organization: Organization by time or sequence

clip art: Images or pictures, in printed form or stored in a computer file, that can be used in a presentation aid

Clip Gallery: In PowerPoint, clip art that can be used in presentations

closed-ended questions: Questions that offer alternatives from which to choose, such as true/false, agree/disagree, or multiple-choice questions

closure: The quality of a conclusion that makes a speech "sound finished"

code: A verbal or nonverbal symbol for an idea or image

cognitive dissonance: The sense of mental discomfort that prompts a person to change when new information conflicts with previously organized thought patterns

color schemes: In PowerPoint, sets of balanced colors that can be applied to presentations

commemorative address: A speech delivered during ceremonies held in memory of some past event and often the person or persons involved

commencement address: A speech delivered at a graduation or commencement ceremony

competence: An aspect of a speaker's credibility that reflects whether the speaker is perceived as informed, skilled, or knowledgeable

complexity, organization by: Arrangement of the ideas in a speech from the simplest to the more complex

conclusion: The logical outcome of a deductive argument, which stems from the major premise and the minor premise

connotation: The meaning listeners associate with a word, based on past experience

consensus: The support and commitment of all group members to the decision of the group

context: The environment or situation in which a speech occurs

cool colors: Colors (such as greens and blues) that have a calming effect and recede into the background

credibility: An audience's perception of a speaker as competent, trustworthy, knowledgeable, and dynamic

criteria: Standards for identifying an acceptable solution to a problem

critical listening: Evaluating the quality, appropriateness, value, and importance of the information put forth by a speaker

critical thinking: Making judgments about the conclusions presented in what you see, hear, and read

culture: A learned system of knowledge, behavior, attitudes, beliefs, values, and norms that is shared by a group of people

declamation: The delivery of an already famous speech

decode: To translate verbal or nonverbal symbols into ideas and images that constitute a message

decorative fonts: Typefaces in which the letters are stylized and convey a feeling or tone

deductive reasoning: Reasoning that moves from a general statement or principle to a specific, certain conclusion

definition: A statement of what a term means or how it is applied in a specific instance

delivery outline: A condensed and abbreviated outline from which speaking notes are developed

democratic leader: A leader who involves group members in the decision-making process rather than dictating what should be done

demographics: Statistics on population characteristics such as age, sexual orientation, race, gender, educational level, and religious views

denotation: The literal meaning of a word

derived credibility: The perception of a speaker's credibility that is formed during a speech

description: A word picture of something

dialect: A consistent style of pronouncing words that is common to an ethnic group or geographic region

DVD: Digital video disk; an electronic storage mode similar to a CD, except that it can store much more information and display it with exceptional clarity and fidelity

dynamism: An aspect of a speaker's credibility that reflects whether the speaker is perceived as energetic

either/or fallacy: The oversimplification of an issue into a choice between only two outcomes or possibilities

elaboration likelihood model (ELM) of persuasion: The theory that listeners can be persuaded directly, by logic, reasoning, and evidence, or indirectly, by the overall emotional impact of the message

elocution: The expression of emotion through posture, movement, gestures, facial expression, and voice

embedding: In PowerPoint, the insertion of charts, pictures, equations, or other objects into a presentation

empowerment: Influence and potential leadership, gained in part by speaking with competence and confidence

encode: To translate ideas and images into verbal or nonverbal symbols

ethical speech: Speech that is responsible, honest, and tolerant

ethics: The beliefs, values, and moral principles by which people determine what is right or wrong

ethnic vernacular: A variety of English that includes words and phrases used by a specific ethnic group

ethnicity: That portion of a person's cultural background that relates to a national or religious heritage

ethnocentrism: The attitude that one's own culture and cultural perspectives and methods are superior to those of others

eulogy: A speech of tribute to someone who has died

evidence: The facts, examples, opinions, and statistics that a speaker uses to support a conclusion

example: An illustration used to dramatize or clarify a fact

expert testimony: An opinion offered by someone who is an authority on the subject under discussion

explanation: A statement of how something is done or why it exists in its present form or existed in its past form

extemporaneous speaking: Speaking from a written or memorized speech outline without having memorized the exact wording of the speech

extended illustration: A detailed example that resembles a story

external noise: Physical sounds that interfere with communication

fact: Information that direct observation has proven to be true or that can be proved to be true

fallacy: False reasoning that occurs when someone attempts to persuade without adequate evidence or with arguments that are irrelevant or inappropriate

feedback: Verbal and nonverbal responses provided by an audience to a speaker

figurative analogy: A comparison between two essentially dissimilar things that share some common feature on which the comparison depends

figure of speech: Language that deviates from the ordinary, expected meaning of words to make a description or comparison unique, vivid, and memorable

First Amendment: The amendment to the U.S. Constitution that guarantees free speech; the first of the ten amendments to the U.S. Constitution known collectively as the Bill of Rights

font: A typeface of a particular style and design

font size: The size of a typeface

forum presentation: A question-and-answer session, such as those that usually follow a public discussion or symposium

free speech: Legally protected speech or speech acts

full-text database: An indexing system, available on the World Wide Web or on CD-ROM, that provides not only bibliographic data but also full texts of entries

gender: The culturally constructed and psychologically based perception of one's self as feminine or masculine

general purpose: The overarching goal of a speech—to inform, persuade, or entertain

generalization: An all-encompassing statement

graph: A pictorial representation of statistical data

hard evidence: Factual examples and statistics

hasty generalization: A conclusion reached without adequate evidence

hyperbole: Exaggeration

hyperlink: An image, icon, or colored and underlined text on a Web page that connects the user with another Web page or Web site

hypothetical illustration: An example that might happen but that has not actually occurred

illustration: A story or anecdote that provides an example of an idea, issue, or problem the speaker is discussing

immediacy: Nonverbal expressions of closeness to and liking for an audience, made through such means as physical approach or eye contact

impromptu speaking: Delivering a speech without advance preparation

inductive reasoning: Reasoning that uses specific instances or examples to reach a general, probable conclusion

inference: A conclusion based on available evidence or partial information; an evaluation that has not been directly observed

inflection: The variation of the pitch of the voice

initial credibility: The impression of a speaker's credibility that listeners have before the speaker starts a speech

internal noise: Anything physiological or psychological that interferes with communication

invention: The development or discovery of new ideas and insights

inversion: Reversal of the normal word order of a phrase or sentence

jargon: The specialized language of a profession

keynote address: A speech that sets the theme and tone for a meeting or conference

laissez-faire leader: A leader who allows group members complete freedom in all aspects of the decision-making process

lavaliere microphone: A microphone that can be clipped to an article of clothing or worn on a cord around the neck

lay testimony: An opinion or description offered by a nonexpert who has firsthand experience

line graph: A graph that uses lines or curves to show relationships between two or more variables

literal analogy: A comparison between two similar things

literary quotation: An opinion or description by a writer, expressed in a memorable and often poetic way

logic: A formal system of rules used to reach a conclusion

main ideas: The key points of a speech; subdivisions of the central idea

major premise: A general statement that is the first element of a syllogism

malapropism: The mistaken use of a word that sounds like the intended word

manuscript speaking: Reading a speech from a written text

mapping: Use of geometric shapes to sketch how all the main ideas, subpoints, and supporting material of a speech relate to the central idea and to one another

master view: In PowerPoint, a function that allows a user to view text or images that are to appear on every slide, notes page, or handout

memorized speaking: Delivering a speech word for word from memory without using notes

message: The content of a speech plus the way it is said

metaphor: An implied comparison between two things or concepts

minor premise: A specific statement about an example that is linked to the major premise; the second element of a syllogism

model: A small object that represents a larger object

myth: A shared belief based on the underlying values, cultural heritage, and faith of a group of people

newspaper index: A listing of bibliographical data for articles published in a newspaper or group of newspapers during a given time period

nomination speech: A speech that officially recommends someone as a candidate for an office or position

non sequitur: Latin for "it does not follow"; an idea or conclusion that does not logically relate to or follow from the previous idea or conclusion

notes page view: In PowerPoint, a function that allows a user to view and work on speaker notes for a presentation

omission: Leaving out a word or phrase the listener expects to hear

open-ended questions: Questions that allow for unrestricted answers by not limiting answers to choices or alternatives

opinion: Testimony or a quotation that expresses someone's attitudes, beliefs, or values

oral citation: The oral presentation of such information about a source as the author, title, and year of publication

outline view: In PowerPoint, a function that allows a user to view text in outline form while organizing and developing content

panel discussion: A group discussion designed to inform an audience about issues or a problem or to make recommendations

parallelism: Use of the same grammatical pattern for two or more clauses or sentences

patchwork plagiarism: Failure to give credit for compelling phrases taken from another source

pathos: Term used by Aristotle to refer to appeals to emotion

periodical index: A listing of bibliographical data for articles published in a group of magazines and/or journals during a given time period

personification: The attribution of human qualities to inanimate things or ideas

persuasion: The process of changing or reinforcing a listener's attitudes, beliefs, values, or behavior

picture graph: A graph that uses images or pictures to symbolize data

pie graph: A circular graph divided into wedges that show the distribution of data

pitch: The highness or lowness of voice sounds

plagiarism: Presenting someone else's words or ideas as though they were one's own

points: Units of measure for typefaces

prejudice: Preconceived opinions, attitudes, and beliefs about a person, place, or thing

preliminary bibliography: A list of potential resources to be used in the preparation of a speech

preparation outline: A detailed outline that includes main ideas, subpoints, and supporting material and that may also include a speech's specific purpose, introduction, blueprint, internal previews and summaries, transitions, and conclusion

presentation aid: Anything tangible (drawings, charts, graphs, video images, photographs, music) that helps communicate an idea to an audience

presentation speech: A speech that accompanies the presentation of an award

primacy, organization by: Arrangement of the ideas in a speech from the most to the least important

problem-and-solution pattern: Organization that focuses on a problem and various solutions or a solution and the problems it would solve

pronunciation: The proper use of sounds to form words clearly and accurately

proposition: A statement with which a speaker wants an audience to agree

proposition of fact: A proposition that focuses on whether something is true or false or whether it did or did not happen

proposition of policy: A proposition that advocates a change in a policy, procedure, or behavior

proposition of value: A proposition that calls for a listener to judge the worth or importance of something

psychological audience analysis: Analyzing the attitudes, beliefs, values, and other psychological information about an audience in order to develop a clear and effective message

public-relations speech: A speech designed to inform the public, to strengthen alliances with them, and in some cases to recommend policy

pun: A verbal device that uses double meanings to create humor

race: A person's biological heritage

reasoning: The process of drawing a conclusion from evidence

receiver: A listener or an audience member

receiver apprehension: The fear of misunderstanding or misinterpreting the spoken messages of others

recency, organization by: Arrangement of the ideas in a speech from the least to the most important

red herring: Irrelevant facts or information used to distract someone from the issue under discussion

reflective thinking: A method of structuring a problem-solving discussion that involves (1) identifying and defining the problem, (2) analyzing the problem, (3) generating possible solutions, (4) selecting the best solution, and (5) testing and implementing the solution

regionalism: A word or phrase used uniquely by speakers in one part of a country

remember: To recall ideas and information

repetition: Use of a key word or phrase more than once for emphasis

report: An oral presentation of information or policy related to the workplace

rhetorical criticism: The process of using a method or standards to evaluate the effectiveness and appropriateness of messages

rhetorical question: A question intended to provoke thought, rather than elicit an answer

rhetorical strategies: Methods and techniques used by speakers to achieve their goals

sans serif fonts: Typefaces in which the letters do not have serifs (small lines at the tops and bottoms)

script fonts: Typefaces that imitate handwriting

search engine: A Web site that works much like a traditional card catalog, allowing access to the World Wide Web through a subject or keyword search

select: To single out a message from several competing ones

self-actualization needs: The need to realize one's highest potential

serif fonts: Typefaces in which the letters have small lines (serifs) at the tops and bottoms

signpost: A verbal or nonverbal signal that a speaker is moving from one idea to another

simile: A comparison between two things that uses the word *like* or *as*

situational audience analysis: Examining the time and place of a speech, the audience size, and the speaking occasion in order to develop a clear and effective message

slide master: In PowerPoint, the function that controls the format and placement of titles and text on slides

slide sorter view: In PowerPoint, a function that allows a user to view miniature versions of all slides in a presentation so that slides can be added, deleted, or reordered

slide view: In PowerPoint, a function that allows a user to view an entire slide or a portion of a slide while working on it

small group communication: Interaction among from three to twelve people who share a common purpose, feel a sense of belonging to the group, and influence one another

socioeconomic status: A person's perceived importance and influence based on factors such as income, occupation, and educational level

soft evidence: Supporting material based mainly on opinion or inference, including hypothetical illustrations, descriptions, explanations, definitions, analogies, and opinions

source: The public speaker

spatial organization: Arrangement of the ideas in a speech according to location or position

specific purpose: A concise statement indicating what you want your listeners to know, feel, or be able to do when you finish speaking

speech act: A behavior, such as flag burning, that is viewed by law as nonverbal communication and is subject to the same protections and limitations as verbal speech

speech of introduction: A speech that provides information about another speaker

speech to inform: A speech that teaches others new information, ideas, concepts, principles, or processes in order to enhance their knowledge or understanding about something

spoonerism: A play on words involving the switching of the initial sounds of the words in a phrase

stacks: The collection of books in a library

standard outline form: Numbered and lettered headings and subheadings arranged hierarchically to indicate the relationships among parts of a speech

standard U.S. English: The English taught by schools and used in the media, business, and government in the United States

stationary microphone: A microphone attached to a podium, sitting on a desk, or standing on the floor

statistics: Numerical data that summarize facts or samples

storyboarding: A presentation planning technique in which individual points are described in words as well as sketched

suspension: Withholding a key word or phrase until the end of a sentence

syllogism: A three-part way of developing an argument, using a major premise, a minor premise, and a conclusion

symbols: Words, images, and behaviors that create meaning for someone

symposium: A public discussion in which a series of short speeches is presented to an audience

target audience: A specific segment of an audience that you most want to influence

template: In PowerPoint, a model containing color schemes, slide and title masters with custom formatting, and fonts, all of which can be customized for a particular type of presentation

terminal credibility: The final impression listeners have of a speaker's credibility, after a speech concludes

theme: A basic design and color scheme used in a series of presentation aids

thesaurus: A list of words and their synonyms

title master: In PowerPoint, the function that controls the format and placement of the title slides

toast: A brief salute to a momentous occasion, usually accompanied by a round of drinks and immediately followed by the raising or clinking together of glasses or goblets

topical organization: Organization of the natural divisions in a central idea on the basis of recency, primacy, complexity, or the speaker's preference

transformational leader: A leader who influences others by building a shared vision of the future, inspiring others to achieve, developing high-quality individual relationships with others, and helping people see how what they do is related to a larger framework or system

transitions: In PowerPoint, a function that allows a user to control the flow of information through music, sounds, and videos

trustworthiness: An aspect of a speaker's credibility that reflects whether the speaker is perceived as believable and honest

understand: To assign meaning to the stimuli to which you attend

understatement: Downplaying a fact or event

URL: Uniform resource locator; the address of a Web site or Web page

value: An enduring conception of right and wrong, good and bad

verbal irony: A statement that expresses the exact opposite of the intended meaning

volume: The softness or loudness of a speaker's voice

warm colors: Colors (such as oranges and reds) that communicate excitement and interest

Web directory: A Web site that allows access to the World Wide Web by offering the user ever-more-specific categories of information from which to select

Web page: An individual file or screen that is part of a Web site

Web site: A location on the World Wide Web that includes a number of related Web pages

wit: Relating an incident or a statement so that it concludes in an unexpected way

World Wide Web: The most popular information-delivery system of the Internet

written citation: The written presentation of such information about a source as the author, title, and year of publication, usually formatted according to a conventional style guide

Index